The
Corn-Free Cookbook
& Survival Guide

The
Corn-Free Cookbook
& Survival Guide

*For the Corn-Intolerant
and Corn-Allergic*

Laurel Lee Steele, PA-C
and Merelee Knott

CUMBERLAND HOUSE
NASHVILLE, TN

THE CORN-FREE COOKBOOK & SURVIVAL GUIDE
Published by Cumberland House Publishing, Inc.
431 Harding Industrial Drive
Nashville, TN 37211

Cover design: JulesRules Design
Text design: Lisa Taylor

Library of Congress Cataloging-in-Publication Data

Steele, Laurel Lee, 1969–
   The corn-free cookbook & survival guide : for the corn-intolerant and corn-allergic / Laurel Lee Steele, and Merelee Knott.
      p. cm.
   Includes bibliographical references and index.
   ISBN-13: 978-1-58182-482-7 (pbk.)
   ISBN-10: 1-58182-482-3 (pbk.)
   1. Corn-free diet--Recipes. 2. Food allergy—Diet therapy—Recipes. I. Title: Corn-free cookbook and survival guide. II. Knott, Merelee, 1941- III. Title.
   RM231.5.S74 2006
   641.5'631—dc22

                                                                    2006004922

Printed in the United States of America
1 2 3 4 5 6 7 — 11 10 09 08 07 06

To Natalie and Wendy for your endless encouragement.
Thank you from Subc, Merelee, and Laurel Lee.

CONTENTS

FOREWORD

The combined talents of Laurel Lee Steele and Merelee Knott have produced an easy-to-read, entertaining, and information-packed reference detailing how to produce delicious meals without triggering corn-induced reactions. I am confident that this book will be an invaluable resource for anyone with suspected adverse reactions to corn.

As a basic food staple, corn is a significant source of calories in almost every culture worldwide. Corn is also the dominant component of livestock feed, and in processed form, corn is an ingredient in hundreds of prepared foods. Unfortunately, although most people enjoy eating corn or the foods prepared using corn, it also has the potential to cause a variety of ill effects.

There are a variety of ways to categorize adverse food reactions. In the case of peanut anaphylaxis, ingestion of a tiny amount of peanut results in an immediate, explosive reaction such that peanut avoidance becomes a life-or-death priority. Similarly, allergy to corn may result in this same immediate life-or-death risk. However, anaphylaxis to corn is much less common than other adverse reactions to corn. Modern science tends to group adverse food reactions into those that involve the immune system (e.g., food allergy) and those that do not (e.g., food intolerance). In general, immune reactions are easier for doctors and patients to sort out. They tend to follow basic rules that we have learned from years of controlled scientific experiments describing how immune reactions happen. For example, a person who develops sudden hives, wheezing, and nausea while eating at a restaurant can be pretty certain that something he or she was eating caused the reaction. Physicians understand that hives, wheezing, and gastroenterological symptoms may all be the result of a single immune reaction to that food, typically involving allergic antibodies that can be demonstrated by appropriate testing. In contrast, many food intolerances are much more difficult to sort out. For example, there may be a delay in the onset of symptoms, and the symptoms may only occur when the food is eaten in a large quantity or in combination with another food. In addition, food intolerance symptoms themselves may be somewhat nonspecific, such as fatigue, headache, or difficulty concentrating.

In general terms, diagnostic testing available for intolerances is much less reliable than for food allergies. This would appear to be bad news for those who do not tolerate corn, but fortunately it is not always necessary to "prove" particular food intolerance with testing. In many cases of food intolerance, empiric food elimination is very helpful.

In fact, regardless of the cause of an adverse food reaction, the best treatment is to avoid the offending food. In the case of dietary staples such as milk, eggs, wheat, soy, or corn, strict avoidance diets can have a devastating impact on nutrition and the pleasure associated with eating. For those whose symptoms are suspected to be due to corn, *The Corn-Free Cookbook and Survival Guide* can help restore a healthy and pleasurable eating experience.

—Stephen A. Tilles, M.D.

ACKNOWLEDGMENTS

We would like to thank the many people who shared personal and family recipes and cooking skills, especially: Ros Bernard, Clarissa Blair, Buff Brigham, Dr. James Carpenter, Natalie Dehn, Dr. David Goodman, Peg Hartlaub, Jim Oliver, Wendy Oliver, Catherine Peterson, Kathy Spink, Bernie Steele, Bonnie Steele, Lara Steele, Shawn Steele, J. Stover and Marilyn Stover. Amazingly, most of these great cooks also helped with editing, computer technology, and medical information. Without their multiple skills, this book would not have been possible.

Special thanks go to Dr. Stephen Tilles, Ron Pitkin, Lisa Taylor, and the staff at Cumberland House Publishing. Thank you also to the many other people who have helped with this project. We cannot begin to name all of you who provided encouragement, recipe testing, cooking tips, editing tips, marketing ideas, and more.

The
Corn-Free Cookbook
& Survival Guide

PART II

INTRODUCTION

If you can't have corn, this book is for you. It contains a tear-out, take-to-the-grocery list of food additives you'll need to avoid. More important, it outlines the foods you *can* eat.

You don't have to risk a reaction to enjoy a snack or a happy holiday meal. You don't have to make difficult changes either, like shopping at inconvenient health food stores, eating weird dishes, or taking the time to become a gourmet cook. In this book you will find information about:

- ↪ safe foods from ordinary grocery stores
- ↪ quick, easy-to-fix meals
- ↪ comfortable, familiar American dishes
- ↪ seasoning variations for any preference
- ↪ cooking with few kitchen gadgets and little clean-up time
- ↪ balanced, healthy meals
- ↪ corn-syrup-free dieting for weight loss

In this cookbook, you will *not* find:

- ↪ recipes for goat's rib soup or other esoteric "health foods"
- ↪ recipes that try to fake the flavor of corn bread or corn on the cob

This is *your* book. Feel free mark it up. Put notes on the recipe pages about the variations you prefer. Write in your own additions. Use sticky-note bookmarks to find your favorites quickly.

Is there life beyond the kitchen for the corn-allergic and corn-intolerant? Yes! See the chapters on eating out, social events, and food for travel.

Do you want more information? What is a food intolerance or a food allergy? What's the difference between the two? What do corn syrup additives have to do with recent trends toward obesity and diabetes? The information in this book comes from state-of-the-art medical research in the U.S., England, and around the world. You can learn more about . . .

Wait, what was that? You say you're hungry right *now*? Turn the page.

Part I
Recipes

CHAPTER 1: HUNGRY NOW? QUICK MEALS TO FIX

Hungry now? Munch on an apple! If your cupboard is bare, make a quick stop at the grocery store. From the produce section, just rinse and eat a variety of healthy, whole foods: carrots, cherry tomatoes, grapes, snap peas, snow peas, etc. Protein staves off those hunger pangs a bit longer. Does the delicatessen offer hard-boiled eggs? When selecting cold cuts and other packaged foods, be sure to read ingredients. Start with items that have a short lists of ingredients as they are much more likely to be corn-free.

While you're at the grocery, pick up some food to cook at home. For fast meals, take a look at the Quick-to-Fix recipes (see list below). You'll need corn-free basics like flour, meat, fish, eggs, fruits, and vegetables, plus cooking oil and a few seasonings. (Make sure that your salt and baking powder contain no corn derivatives.) You have a stove, right? If not, grab an electric skillet and a spatula at the store, too. All of these Quick-to-Fix meals can be made in a skillet or frying pan:

Can't find bread without corn derivatives? Try pasta (noodles) or couscous instead. Both are fast to cook in a saucepan or kettle and both replace the grains in bread.

For the Novice Cook

If you don't have much cooking experience, you may want to try some basic recipes first to learn the fundamentals. For example:

The easiest recipes usually come first in the chapter or section. You'll need measuring cups and spoons, and at least one mixing bowl. A saucepan, a skillet, and an ovensafe baking dish will do for the least complicated recipes. An electric mixer is not needed for most of these recipes. (A small, battery-powered latte mixer can froth eggs, if you like fluffy baked goods.) A blender comes in handy for smoothies and sauces, and if you like fresh fruit juice you'll want a juicer.

A crock pot can be very handy for cooking meals or soups, untended, while you are away for hours. A stove-top kettle with a lid that seals well can do the same job, but it needs more supervision. Bread machines can be pricey, but they can also bake a loaf of yeast bread in 10 minutes instead of hours.

For the Experienced Cook

After you have more cooking experience, you may want to try more complicated recipes, such as yeast breads (very simple with a bread machine!), cooked salsa, roasts, pies, and recipes with egg whites beaten to stiff peaks. For example:

Some of these recipes may need special equipment, such as a blender or a roasting pan or dish. For beating egg whites to stiff peaks, an electric mixer and metal or glass bowls will be needed. (Yes, you can do it with a wire whisk—and a very, very, very strong arm.) Nice pie crusts need a rolling pin and rolling surface. Angel food cake requires a special pan—one that has never been oiled. If you enjoy cooking or simply want a new way to fix that old favorite, check out Chapter 13, "Customizing Recipes," page 221.

Maybe you'd rather get the meals made quickly. Fortunately, you don't need fancy gadgets, a gourmet kitchen, or a lot of time to prepare safe, nutritious meals. Be sure to check out the variations shown with most of the recipes—you have endless choices.

Bon appétit!

CHAPTER 2: BREADS / GRAINS

Quick Breads (Wheat)

Yeast Breads (Wheat)

Non-Wheat Grains

Mixed Grains

The symbol ▼ marks healthier recipe choices.

CORN-FREE BAKING POWDER

1   Tablespoon baking soda
3   Tablespoons arrowroot powder (or cream of tartar)

Use the back of a spoon to press out any lumps in the ingredients. Measure the baking soda and arrowroot powder into a container and close the lid tightly.

Mix the ingredients thoroughly by shaking and turning the container.

Use corn-free baking powder in place of commercial baking powder.*
After mixing corn-free baking powder with wet ingredients, bake the batter immediately.

*Note: Use the same amount called for by the recipe.

Yield: 4 tablespoons (12 teaspoons) of corn-free baking powder

---

Mix by sifting the ingredients four or five times for an even smoother consistency.

Store the corn-free baking powder in a glass jar with a glass or metal lid, tightly closed, and use it within a few months. This preservative-free baking powder will not keep as long as commercial mixes.

FLUFFY POWDER

1   Tablespoon baking soda
2   Tablespoons cream of tartar
2   Tablespoons arrowroot powder (or potato flour or tapioca flour)

See directions above for mixing.

Yield: 5 tablespoons (15 teaspoons) of corn-free baking powder

---

Arrowroot powder may add a faint, creamy flavor. It is found with the spices in grocery stores. Health food stores carry arrowroot powder in bulk, which is less expensive. You may prefer other flavors, such as potato or tapioca flour or cream of tartar.

PANCAKES

1¼	cups flour (unbleached, whole wheat, or a mix)
1	Tablespoon sugar
½	teaspoon corn-free salt
½	teaspoon corn-free baking powder
1	egg
1¼	cups cold water (or milk)
2	Tablespoons cooking oil (or melted butter)

In a medium bowl combine the flour, sugar, salt, and baking powder. Stir.

Break the egg into one side of the mixture, and beat the egg by itself, without stirring it into the flour mixture. Add the water and oil.

Mix well, until all the flour is moistened. The batter will be slightly lumpy.

Heat a large skillet until a few droplets of water sprinkled from the fingertips sizzle, not dance, in the pan. Coat or spray the skillet lightly with oil and pour the batter into any size pancake desired. Bubbles will form as the batter cooks. When the bubbles break, turn the pancake to cook it on the other side.

If the pancake is too dark or not done on the inside, adjust the heat for the next pancake.

Keep the finished pancakes warm in a low oven (about 200°) while the rest are cooking.

Toppings: 100 percent natural maple syrup has no corn derivatives. Also try brown sugar or fruit syrups (see recipes, page 94).

Yield: 1–2 servings

Maple-flavored syrups may be made with corn syrup. Read ingredients.

If you are out of corn-free baking powder, use ¼ teaspoon baking soda instead, dissolved in 2 tablespoons of warm water. Add this after stirring in the cold water.

WAFFLES

1¼	cups flour (unbleached or mix with oat flour)
2	teaspoons corn-free baking powder (see page 11)
¼	teaspoon corn-free salt (optional, to taste)
1–3	teaspoons sugar (optional—sugar browns the waffles more and makes them more crisp)
1	cup cold water
¼–⅓	cup cooking oil, to taste
1	egg

Preheat the waffle iron according to the manufacturer's instructions.
If you do not have a waffle iron, see the stove-top directions below.

In a medium bowl combine the flour, baking powder, salt, and sugar and stir. Add cold water and stir until smooth. Stir in the oil. Break and stir the egg in a measuring cup; then stir the egg into the mixture and beat until smooth.

Spoon the batter into the center of the preheated waffle iron. Do not fill the spaces in all corners, as this may cause the batter to overflow. Close the waffle iron.

Cook until the waffle iron stops steaming (about 5–7 minutes) or the indicator light shows that the waffle is done. Remove the waffle. Close and reheat the waffle iron before adding the next batch.

Stove-top method: Use a nonstick frying pan and do not oil. Spoon a small amount of the batter into the center of the pan, as you would with a waffle iron. Spread the batter thin with the spoon or a spatula. Do not fill the pan all the way to the sides, as this will make the batter curl when cooking and the second side will not cook evenly.

Cook, covered, on medium heat. When the underside of the batter is golden brown, turn and cook the other side, about 4–5 minutes per side.

For a more crisp waffle, spread the batter more thinly or cook the waffle at lower heat for a longer time.

Variation: For lighter, fluffier waffles, separate the egg. Stir the yolk into the batter. Beat the egg whites to stiff peaks and then fold them gently into the batter. Egg whites will not stiffen easily in a plastic bowl; use a glass or metal container.

Toppings: 100 percent natural maple syrup has no corn derivatives. Also try brown sugar or fruit syrups (see recipes, page 94). Or skip the sugar and use eggs, veggies, or meat toppings.

Yield: 1–2 servings

BAKING SODA BISCUITS

Preheat oven to 425° • Baking time: 12–16 minutes

2	cups flour (unbleached, whole wheat, or mixed)
½	teaspoon corn-free salt
3	teaspoons corn-free baking powder (see page 11 or see box below to use plain baking soda)
3	Tablespoons cooking oil
⅔	cup cool water (or milk)

Preheat the oven to 425°.

In a medium bowl combine the flour, salt, and baking powder and stir. Add the oil and stir. At this point, the mixture will form uneven crumbles of flour and oil. Add the water or milk. Stir until the dough forms a ball and cleans the sides of the mixing bowl. (If the dough does not clean the bowl, see the note below.)

Form the dough into 6 balls and drop them onto an ungreased cookie sheet.

Bake at 425° for 12–16 minutes, until lightly golden-brown.

> Note: If the dough is too sticky to clean the bowl, add a little flour, about 1 teaspoon at a time. If the dough breaks or is hard to stir, add a little water, about 1 teaspoon at a time. For fluffier biscuits, knead the dough a few times.

Variations:

Plain Biscuits: Serve hot with butter, margarine, oil, and/or jelly for toppings. If corn-free bread is not available, plain baking powder biscuits can substitute.

Biscuits with Cream Sauces: For a full meal, serve the biscuits with creamed chicken, creamed tuna, or creamed beef, plus vegetables and fruit. (See Creamed Tuna, page 114.)

> If baking powder is not available, you can substitute ¾ teaspoon baking soda, dissolved in ½ teaspoon hot water.
> Stir this mixture into the cold water. Bake the dough immediately after moistening it, or knead briefly and then bake.

Biscuit Desserts: For strawberry (or other fruit) shortcake, add 2 table-spoons sugar to the dry ingredients in the full recipe. Top with sweetened fruit, such as strawberries, peaches, or blueberries. (See Strawberry Short-cake, page 89.)

Dumpling Stew: For dumplings, do not bake the batter. Instead, drop the batter by small spoonfuls into a very moist chicken or beef stew. Simmer until the dumplings are cooked through, about a half hour. (See Chicken Dumplings, page 105.)

Yield: 6 servings

MUFFINS

Preheat oven to 400° • Baking time: 22–25 minutes

1¾	cups flour
2½	teaspoons corn-free baking powder (see page 11)
¾	teaspoon corn-free salt
¼–½	cup sugar, to taste
¾	cup cold milk (or water)
⅓	cup cooking oil (or melted butter or corn-free margarine)
2	eggs, well-beaten

Preheat the oven to 400°.

In a medium bowl mix the flour, baking powder, salt, and sugar. Add the cold milk. Mix completely. Stir in the oil and beat for about 1 minute.

For lighter muffins, use a separate cup or bowl to beat the eggs to a fine foam. Fold in the eggs. Fold in fruit, if desired.

Line or oil the muffin-tin cups. Fill them two-thirds full with the muffin batter. Bake at 400° for 22–25 minutes. Muffins will turn golden-brown long before they are done. When the muffins are done, the centers will be cooked through.

Variations:

Blueberry Muffins: Make the recipe above. Fold in about 1 cup fresh blueberries. Add 5–10 minutes to the baking time.

Strawberry Muffins: Make the recipe above. Fold in about 1 cup strawberry slices. Add 5–10 minutes to the baking time.

Yield: 12–14 muffins or 16–18 muffins with fruit

CHERRY MUFFINS

Preheat oven to 400° • Baking time: 15–20 minutes

1	14½-ounce can tart pie cherries
⅓	cup sugar for sweetening cherries (optional, to taste)
1½	cups flour
⅓	cup sugar (or more, to taste)
1	teaspoon corn-free salt
1	teaspoon corn-free baking powder (see page 11)
½	cup milk (or water)
¼	cup cooking oil
1	egg

Preheat the oven to 400°.

Drain the canned cherries and save the juice for cherry syrup or cobbler liquid. Put the cherries in a small bowl and add sugar, if desired, to taste.

In a medium bowl mix the flour, ⅓ cup sugar, salt, and baking powder. Stir in the milk and then the oil. Beat an egg slightly and add it. Stir until the mixture is fairly smooth.

Coat or spray muffin tins with oil. Fill the cups half to two-thirds full with the batter. Bake at 400° for 15–20 minutes, until golden brown. When the muffins are done, a fork pricked into the center should come out clean.

Variations:

↪ Use fresh sour cherries instead of canned. Rinse the cherries and discard any with mold or brown spots. Discard the stems. Pit cherries from the stem end with the tip of a vegetable peeler. Continue with instructions above.

↪ Use blueberries instead of red sour cherries. For fresh berries, rinse and discard any that are moldy or shriveled. Pick off any stems. Continue with instructions above.

Yield: 10 muffins

Sour cherries are red and round instead of dark and heart-shaped (like sweet cherries). Sweet cherries, such as Bing cherries, can be used for a variation.

BANANA BREAD

Preheat oven to 350° • Baking time: 45–55 minutes

3	large bananas (or 4 small bananas)
1	cup sugar (or brown sugar or a mixture of both)
½	cup butter (or corn-free margarine or cooking oil)
1	egg
2	cups flour
1	teaspoon baking soda
¼	teaspoon corn-free salt
½	teaspoon nutmeg (optional)
½	teaspoon allspice (optional)
½	teaspoon cinnamon (optional)

Preheat the oven to 350°.

In a large bowl mash the bananas with a fork or potato masher. Add the sugar and stir well. Add the butter and egg; stir. Add the flour, baking soda, and salt and stir well. If desired, add the nutmeg, allspice, and cinnamon. Stir.

Coat or spray a bread pan with cooking oil. Pour the mixture into the bread pan. You can use muffin tins, if you prefer.

Bake the bread at 350° for 45–55 minutes. In muffin tins, the batter will bake in less time, about 35–45 minutes. The bread is done when a fork inserted into the center comes out clean.

Remove the bread from the pan and cool before serving.

Variations:
↪ Add ½ cup walnut pieces.
↪ Add 1 teaspoon vanilla (or to taste).

Yield: 6–8 servings

SCONES
Preheat oven to 375° • Baking time: 12 minutes

2	cups unbleached flour
6	Tablespoons sugar
3	teaspoons corn-free baking powder (see page 11)
½	teaspoon corn-free salt
6	Tablespoons cold butter
1	egg
1	cup corn-free buttermilk (or heavy cream or whole milk)

Preheat the oven to 375°. In a large bowl mix the flour, sugar, baking powder, and salt. Cut the butter into small, pea-sized pieces and scatter them into the dry mixture.

In a separate bowl beat the egg with a whisk. Add the buttermilk. Set aside 2 tablespoons of this mixture for later to be brushed on top of finished scones.

Using a wooden or plastic spoon, stir the liquid into the flour mixture a little at a time until the dough is soft and slightly sticky.

Coat or spray a baking sheet with cooking oil. Drop the batter by heaping tablespoonfuls onto the baking sheet, about 1 inch apart. Brush the scones with reserved egg and milk mixture. If desired, sprinkle with some extra sugar.

Bake at 375° for about 12 minutes, until the tops of the scones are lightly brown and a fork or cake tester comes out clean when inserted into the thickest part of a scone.

Serve with butter, jam, marmalade, or other toppings, as desired.

Variations:

⋟ Instead of dropping batter, knead the batter and place the dough ball on a floured surface. Separate it into about 8 balls. Pat each ball flat, and pat it into a wedge (triangle) shape. Place the wedges on the baking sheet and bake, as above.

⋟ For a classic scone shape, roll the dough into a ball and place it on the baking sheet. Pat it into a circle about 8 inches across. Use a serrated knife to score the dough crosswise into 8 wedges. Do not cut all the way through the dough. Bake this larger scone longer, about 15–18 minutes.

⋟ Add ⅓ cup berries, nuts, or chocolate chips.

Yield: 6–8 servings

If you cannot find corn-free buttermilk in a corn-free container, substitute corn-free heavy sweet cream (whipping cream). If you prefer the tangy flavor of buttermilk, stir a tiny amount (¼ teaspoon) of lemon juice or vinegar into the cream and allow it to stand for a few minutes.

TORTILLA SHELLS

¼ cup flour
⅓ cup water
⅛ teaspoon corn-free salt, to taste

Lightly coat or spray a small nonstick skillet with cooking oil.

In a medium bowl mix the flour and water. Stir until smooth. Stir in the salt.

Heat the skillet on medium-low to medium. Pour about half the batter into the skillet and spread it as thin as possible. Cover the skillet with the lid slightly to one side to allow steam to escape. Cook on medium-low to medium heat for 2 minutes.

Use a spatula to check the underside of the batter for doneness. When the batter has browned in spots, turn the tortilla and cook it on the other side, about 1 minute.

You will know that you have the right cooking temperature when the batter browns in spots on the first side in 2 minutes. If it does not, adjust the burner setting accordingly. Cooking the batter longer at a lower temperature will result in a glob, not a tortilla!

Repeat the cooking instructions with the other half of the batter.

Variations:
  ↳ A tortilla can be cooked with no oil in a nonstick skillet.
  ↳ Add about 1 tablespoon oil to the batter before cooking.

Yield: 2 small tortillas

CRACKERS

Do not preheat the oven.

1	cup flour
¼	teaspoon yeast
¼	teaspoon baking soda
½	teaspoon corn-free salt, to taste
⅓	cup cold water
1	teaspoon cooking oil

In a medium bowl combine the flour, yeast, baking soda, and salt. Stir well.

Add the cold water and oil. Stir until the dough is completely smooth.

Oil a baking sheet.

Spread the dough as thin as possible on the baking sheet. Flour a rolling pin and roll the dough very thin and flat. The dough must be spread evenly in order to cook evenly.

Score the dough (cut it by pressing with the end of a spatula) into cracker-size pieces.

Sprinkle the dough with more salt, if desired.

Put the baking sheet in the oven, and then turn on the oven to 400°. (Do not preheat; the cracker dough needs to dry at the lower temperatures while the oven heats.) Bake until light golden-brown and crisp, about 7 minutes.

After taking the baking sheet out of the oven, break the crackers at the scored lines and take them off the baking sheet immediately.

Variation: For lighter crackers, mix only the flour, yeast, and water. Cover this mixture, set it in a warm place (about 90°), and allow it to rise for 30 minutes to 1 hour. Then add the soda, salt, and oil. Bake as above in an oven that has not been preheated.

Yield: 20–25 crackers

BREAD
(using a bread machine)

1	cup water
1½	teaspoons corn-free salt
3	cups unbleached flour
2¼	teaspoons yeast

Pour the water into the machine's bread pan. Sprinkle in salt, then flour. Be sure that the flour mixture covers the water entirely. (Some machines call for salt to be added later.)

Make a depression in the center of the flour and add the yeast.

Put the bread pan into the machine. Use a small loaf setting. Use light, medium, or dark crust, as desired. Light or medium works best with all white flour. Makes a small loaf similar in flavor to French bread.

Variation: After you add the salt, add about 2 tablespoons cooking oil. The oil makes a softer bread, which lasts a little longer without refrigeration.

If you do not have a bread machine:

Rise 1: In a large bowl stir the yeast, warm water, and a cup of the flour. Do not add salt. Cover the bowl with a smooth cloth, not terrycloth, and leave in a warm place to rise for 1 hour.

Rise 2: Stir in the salt and other ingredients. Stir in the rest of the flour a little at a time. When the dough gets too heavy, knead by pushing down into the dough ball, then folding. Cover and allow the dough to rise until it has doubled in size, about 30 minutes.

Rise 3: Punch down the dough and shape it into a loaf. Oil a loaf pan or cake pan and place the loaf in it. Cover and allow the dough to rise for about 50 minutes. Preheat the oven to 350°. Bake at 350° for 25–30 minutes, until the crust is browned as desired. Small loaves will bake in less time.

Yield: 1 small loaf

Bread is made with flour, water, and yeast.
Everything else is a variation, even the salt!

Dough conditioners can make bread soft, fluffy, sometimes sweeter, and sometimes less crumbly. Preservatives make bread last longer. Nuts, fruit, and vegetable pieces add interesting flavors.

Unleavened bread is flour and water (see Tortilla Shells, page 19); yeast leavens the bread (makes it rise). Eggs or baking soda can also make bread rise. Quick breads, which have no yeast, often contain egg or soda or both to help with rising.

YUMMY YEAST BREAD
using a bread machine

1	egg
	Water (add enough water to the egg to make 1 cup)
2	Tablespoons cooking oil (or margarine or butter)
1½	teaspoons corn-free salt
3¼	cups flour (unbleached flour or see variations below)
2	Tablespoons sugar
1	teaspoon corn-free yeast, rapid-rise preferred

Put the egg in a 1-cup measure. Stir, but do not froth. Add enough water to measure barely 1 cup. Stir. Add the oil and stir.

Pour the mixture into the machine's bread pan. Sprinkle in the salt.

Sprinkle in the flour. Make sure it completely covers the water. (See below for flour variations.)

Add the sugar in two opposite corners.

Make a depression in the center of the flour. Put the yeast in this depression.

Put the bread pan into the machine. Use a small loaf setting. Use light, medium, or dark crust, as desired. A light or medium setting works best with all white flour.

Wheat contains gluten (yes, as in glue), which helps the bread stick together instead of just falling apart into crumbs. Rye, oats, rice, corn, barley, and other flours do not rise or stick together the same way as common white wheat flour (which usually contains a little barley).

Variations:

For more flavor (and nutrition), try this mixture instead of white flour:

2   cups unbleached flour
½   cup oat flour
¾   cup whole wheat flour

For a "country" flavor, try this mixture instead of white flour:

2¼ cups unbleached flour
½   cup rye flour
½   cup whole wheat flour

For a whole wheat flavor, try this mixture instead of white flour:

1   cup whole wheat flour
2¼ cups unbleached flour

Yield: 1 loaf of bread

The type of flour, amount of water, and amount of sugar all affect the way a bread bakes. For a full whole wheat or dark rye bread, use a different recipe. In this recipe, limited amounts of other flours may be substituted for part of the white flour.

CINNAMON TOAST

1	teaspoon ground cinnamon
2	teaspoons sugar
2	Tablespoons melted butter (or corn-free margarine or cooking oil)
2	slices corn-free sandwich bread

Place a rack in the oven's top rack position.

In a small bowl mix the cinnamon and sugar with the butter. Spread this mixture on the bread.

Place the bread slices on a baking sheet. Turn the oven to broil. Leave the oven door slightly open and toast the bread until it is golden-brown, about 1–2 minutes.

If you prefer, you can brown the bread in a medium-hot skillet.

Variations:

☙ **Nutmeg Toast:** Replace the cinnamon with ½ teaspoon nutmeg.

☙ **Allspice Toast:** Replace the cinnamon with ½ teaspoon allspice.

☙ **Spice Toast:** Use a combination of cinnamon, nutmeg, and allspice.

Yield: 2 servings

GARLIC BREAD
Preheat oven to 400°

1	teaspoon garlic powder or flakes
½	teaspoon onion powder or flakes (optional, to taste)
2	Tablespoons butter, corn-free margarine, or cooking oil
3–4	thick slices corn-free French or Italian bread (or use the bread recipe on page 21)

Preheat the oven to 400°.

In a small bowl mix the garlic powder and onion powder with the butter. Spread this mixture on the bread.

Place the bread slices on a baking sheet. Bake at 400° until the butter is melted through and the bread is golden-brown on both sides, about 7 minutes.

If you prefer, you can brown the bread on both sides in a skillet that is coated with oil or butter.

Variations:
Fresh Garlic: Substitute finely minced garlic for the dry powder.

Basil: Add about ½ teaspoon dried basil flakes (or 1½ teaspoons fresh minced basil). Bake as above.

Yield: 3-4 servings

TARRAGON BREAD

Follow the instructions for Garlic Bread above, except replace the garlic with dried tarragon flakes. If you prefer, use about 1 tablespoon fresh minced tarragon leaves instead of the dried flakes.

Variation: Add 1 teaspoon lemon juice to the oil and tarragon mixture.

> Corn-free French bread can be found in some grocery stores. Watch out for cornmeal on the bottom of the loaf, which may not be stated in the ingredients. Cornmeal is often used on the baking sheet to prevent sticking.

GRANOLA

Preheat oven to 350° • Cooking time: 22–25 minutes

1	42-ounce package quick rolled oats
1	teaspoon corn-free salt
1	12.5-oz. jar 100 percent pure maple syrup* (or honey)
⅔	cup cooking oil

Preheat the oven to 350°.

Measure the oats into a very large bowl. Sprinkle salt across the top, and then mix in slightly. Add the syrup or honey. Add the oil. Mix well.

Coat or spray two broiler pans or cake pans with cooking oil. Spread the granola mixture across the pans.

Bake the granola mix at 350°:

12–15 minutes (until light brown), then stir. Bake again.

5 minutes, or until light brown, then stir. Bake again.

5 minutes, or until light brown.

Remove to a large bowl, stirring occasionally before storing in a covered container. Plastic containers work and travel well.

*Note: Maple-flavored syrup contains corn.

Variation: For a milder flavor, increase the amount of rolled oats by an additional 3 cups and reduce the sweetener to only 1 cup.

Yield: 6–8 cups of granola

Crumbly granola can be used as a cereal with milk, rice milk, soy milk, or fruit juice. It can also be used dry for a snack or added to other baked goods, such as muffins or cookies.

POPRICE SNACKS

4	rice cakes, brown or white rice, plain or flavored
1	Tablespoon cooking oil (or less, to taste)
¼	teaspoon corn-free salt, to taste

Break the rice cakes into bite-sized pieces. Sprinkle on oil and salt. Stir. Heat briefly in a skillet or in the microwave. Serve warm.

Yield: 2 servings

Safe for the munchies!

RICE AND SEASONINGS

1	cup cooked rice (white or brown, instant or dry)*
1	teaspoon cooking oil
⅛	teaspoon corn-free salt, to taste
⅛	teaspoon pepper (optional, to taste)
1	teaspoon lime or lemon juice (optional)
⅛	teaspoon dried cilantro flakes (optional, to taste)

Fresh or frozen vegetables (optional):

⅓	cup broccoli florets
⅓	cup diced carrots
⅓	cup diced zucchini

Boil the rice (and hard fresh vegetables, if desired) in water according to package directions. Steam the rice, if you prefer.

Thaw frozen vegetables or cook fresh vegetables separately, if preferred, by boiling, steaming, or stir-frying. Begin cooking the hardest vegetables first: add the next hardest and so on; add the softest veggies last.

Add the oil, salt, seasonings, and veggies, if desired, to the rice. Allow the mixture to stand for 5–10 minutes to blend the flavors.

*Note: ½ cup instant rice or ⅓ cup dry rice makes about 1 cup of cooked rice.

Variations:

↪ Boil the rice in a broth (chicken or vegetable broth) or boil rice in a half-water/half-fruit-juice blend.

Instead of cilantro and lime juice, try one of these flavors:

↪ ⅛ teaspoon each powdered onion and/or garlic

↪ ⅛ teaspoon curry powder

↪ ¼ cup each peas and/or diced cooked onion and/or diced cooked mushrooms

↪ ¼ cup diced tomatoes; top the mix with grated Parmesan cheese

Yield: 2–3 servings, depending on the quantity of vegetables used

How well-done are vegetables? Crisp, bright-colored veggies may taste best, but if you have intestinal difficulties from reactions, then the peeled, soft, "over-cooked" vegetables may be easier for your system to process.

OAT BRAN MUFFINS

Preheat oven to 400° • Cooking time: 25–30 minutes

1	cup oat bran
¾	cup flour
2½	teaspoons corn-free baking powder (see page 11)
¾	teaspoon corn-free salt
½	cup brown sugar, to taste
⅔	cup cold milk (or water)
¼	cup cooking oil (or melted butter or corn-free margarine)
2	eggs, well-beaten

Preheat the oven to 400°.

In a medium bowl mix the oat bran, flour, baking powder, salt, and brown sugar. Add the cold milk and mix completely. Stir in the oil and beat for about a minute.

For lighter muffins, use a separate cup or bowl to beat the egg to fine foam. Fold in the egg.

Line or oil the muffin-tin cups. Fill them to two-thirds full with the muffin batter. Bake at 400° for 25–30 minutes. When the muffins are done, the centers are fully cooked.

Variations:

➬ **No-Wheat Oat Bran Muffins:** Instead of the ¾ cup flour, add 1 cup of oat bran (for a total of 2 cups of oat bran).

➬ **Low-fat Muffins:** Instead of whole eggs, use only egg whites. Reduce the oil to 2 tablespoons.

Yield: 14–15 muffins

RICE-PASTA MIX

1	cup quick rice (brown, white, or a mix)
½	cup uncooked angel hair noodles, broken into tiny pieces
1½	Tablespoons cooking oil (or butter)
2	cups water (or vegetable broth or corn-free chicken broth)
	Salt, pepper, seasonings to taste

In a medium-size frying pan add the rice, noodles, and cooking oil. Sauté over medium heat, stirring frequently.

Add the water and the seasonings, if desired. Simmer, partially covered, for about 6–8 minutes, stirring occasionally. Add 1–2 tablespoons water if the mixture gets too dry. Simmer until the rice and noodles are tender and the liquid is absorbed.

Serve warm as a side dish. Top with cherry tomato halves or sugar-snap peas, if desired. Or top with creamed meats or veggies, if desired.

Variations:

↪ Add about ½ cup of finely diced veggies, such as carrots, broccoli, celery, baby peas, onions, and/or mixed vegetables. Simmer about 10 minutes longer to blend the flavors.

↪ Add precooked meat, such as a can of chicken pieces or leftover cooked chicken, diced, or crumble-fried hamburger. Simmer about 10 minutes longer to blend the flavors.

↪ Stir in about ¼ cup slivered almonds after the mixture is cooked.

↪ After cooking, raise the heat and brown the mixture, stirring frequently.

Yield: about 3 servings

CHAPTER 3—VEGGIES and SALADS

Dressings and Dips

Salads

Vegetable Dishes

The symbol ▼ marks healthier recipe choices.

BASIC OIL AND VINEGAR

1–4   Tablespoons olive oil (or other corn-free salad oil)
1   Tablespoon balsamic vinegar (or other corn-free vinegar)

Mix the oil and vinegar. Your choice of quantities, oils, and vinegars will affect the flavor of the dressing, perhaps more than any seasonings added.

You may want to test the oil and vinegar basic for flavor before adding seasonings.

Yield: about 3 servings

Ratio of oil to vinegar:

A **very tart** dressing may have as much as 1 tablespoon of oil to 1 tablespoon of vinegar.

A **less tart** dressing may have 2, 2½, or 3 tablespoons of oil to 1 tablespoon of vinegar.

A **mild** dressing may have 4 tablespoons of oil to 1 tablespoon of vinegar. There is no "right" or "wrong" amount of oil to the vinegar. The question is, which do you like?

ℒ Different seasonings may go better with mild, average, or tart mixtures of oil and vinegar.

Oil:

ℒ Olive oil is the classic salad oil. It comes in dozens of flavors. If you love all kinds of olives, try a dark olive oil for a strong flavor.

ℒ If you don't care for olives, try a very light, mild olive oil. If you really detest olives, try a mixture of canola oil and olive oil. Or just leave out the olive oil and try canola oil, sunflower oil, safflower oil, sesame oil, or another salad oil.

ℒ Mild-flavored oils may go better with mild seasonings such as parsley or tarragon.

ℒ Avoid rancid oils. Even a slightly rancid oil will spoil the flavor of any dressing; olive oil in particular will spoil quickly at room temperature. Refrigerate oil, but bring it back to room temperature for adding and blending seasonings.

(continued on next page)

Vinegar:

❧ Avoid plain white vinegar. White vinegar is currently made with corn.

❧ You can choose apple cider vinegar, made from apples, or other vinegars made from rice, grapes (wine vinegar), or other foods. Be sure to read ingredients as some vinegar may be mixed with plain vinegar.

❧ Balsamic, one classic salad vinegar, is made from grapes. Its distinct flavor needs no further seasoning, but it can also carry strong herbs like oregano or rosemary. Balsamic vinegar comes in many flavors, all of them able to overpower mild seasonings. Its unique flavor comes from aging in wooden casks. Longer aging makes a stronger flavor and a higher price. Manufactured (not aged in wood) balsamic vinegar is milder and lower-priced.

Note: Lemon juice can be used for tartness instead of, or in addition to, vinegar.

Plain white vinegar is made with CORN.

OIL AND VINEGAR, Variations

3	Tablespoons oil
1	Tablespoon vinegar (to taste)
⅛	teaspoon corn-free salt (optional, to taste)
Pinch	pepper (optional, to taste)
⅛	teaspoon onion powder or flakes (optional, to taste)
Pinch	garlic powder or flakes (optional, to taste)

Mix the oil and vinegar. Add seasonings at least 2 hours before serving or, better yet, cover and refrigerate the mixture overnight to blend the flavors. Before serving, remove the dressing from the refrigerator and allow it to return to room temperature.

Variations:
⤳ Replace the onion with chives or finely ground shallot (milder).

⤳ Add ¼ teaspoon dried parsley flakes, ⅛ teaspoon dried dill weed, and about ⅛ teaspoon mustard powder (optional) or paprika (optional).

⤳ Add ¼ teaspoon dried oregano and ¼ teaspoon dried basil.

⤳ Add ¼ teaspoon each dried tarragon flakes and lemon juice. Optional: add ⅛ teaspoon black pepper.

⤳ Leave out the garlic and add about ¼ teaspoon dried cilantro flakes and ⅛ teaspoon black pepper. Optional: add lemon juice.

⤳ Add ⅛ teaspoon each dried parsley and thyme.

⤳ Add ¼ teaspoon rosemary, with or without the parsley and thyme above.

Yield: 3 servings

For fresh herbs, mince finely and use about 3 times the dried quantities shown. Refrigerate overnight or longer to blend the flavors.
To avoid mincing, suspend the herb branches in just the oil overnight or longer. Remove the branches before mixing the oil with vinegar.

PARSLEY-DILL VINAIGRETTE

3	Tablespoons oil
1	Tablespoon apple cider vinegar (or other corn-free vinegar)
¼	teaspoon dried parsley flakes
⅛	teaspoon dried dill weed
Pinch	corn-free salt (optional, to taste)
Dash	pepper (optional, to taste)
⅛	teaspoon onion powder or flakes (optional, to taste)
Pinch	garlic powder or flakes (optional, to taste)

Mix the oil and vinegar. Add the seasonings, cover, and refrigerate overnight or longer.

If you need the dressing sooner, add dried seasonings at least two hours before serving. (If you use fresh herbs, blend the flavors overnight or longer.)

Variations:
Tarragon Vinaigrette: In the vinaigrette above, replace the dill with ⅛ teaspoon dried tarragon flakes.

Rosemary Vinaigrette: In the vinaigrette above, replace the dill with ⅛ teaspoon dried rosemary.

Note: Use about 3 times the quantity for fresh herbs.

Yield: about 3 servings

MUSTARD VINAIGRETTE

¼	cup olive oil
1	Tablespoon balsamic vinegar
¼	teaspoon mustard powder (for a Dijon-like flavor, add a few drops of wine)
1	teaspoon minced tarragon
¼	teaspoon corn-free salt
⅛	teaspoon ground black pepper
1	teaspoon thyme (optional)
½	shallot, finely grated (optional)

In a small, nonreactive bowl (glass, ceramic, or plastic) whisk all ingredients until blended and creamy. Alternatively, combine all ingredients in a small jar, seal tightly with the lid, and shake until mixture is blended and creamy. Bottle and cover leftover vinaigrette; it can be kept refrigerated for a week or two. Return to room temperature before using.

Yield: 2–3 servings

RASPBERRY VINAIGRETTE

4	Tablespoons salad oil
1	Tablespoon apple cider vinegar (or a red or rose wine vinegar)
$\frac{1}{8}$	teaspoon garlic, to taste
Pinch	thyme, to taste
Pinch	oregano, to taste
Pinch	basil, to taste
Pinch	corn-free salt (optional, to taste)
Pinch	pepper (optional, to taste)
Pinch	sugar (optional, to taste)
6–8	crushed raspberries

Into a blender or mixing bowl measure the oil, vinegar, garlic, and desired seasonings.

Add the raspberries to the blender. If you are not using a blender, place the raspberries in another mixing bowl or sauce pan. Crush the raspberries with the back of a spoon or a small-hole potato masher, and then add the raspberries to the vinaigrette mixture.

Blend with the blender or beat with a fork or whisk. The finished mixture will look a little frothy, with no big chunks of raspberry.

Variation: Add ¼ teaspoon mustard powder before beating the mixture. For a little Dijon flavor, add a few drops of wine.

Yield: 3–6 servings

If desired, squeeze crushed raspberries through 3 layers
of cheesecloth to remove seeds.

CLASSIC FRENCH DRESSING

3 Tablespoons wine vinegar (or lemon juice or a mixture of both)
¼ teaspoon mustard powder
⅛ teaspoon corn-free salt (to taste)
Dash pepper
½ cup olive oil (or corn-free salad oil or a mixture of both)

Mix at least 2 hours before serving or, better yet, cover and refrigerate the mixture overnight to blend the flavors.

Whisk vinegar with the mustard powder, salt, and pepper. Slowly whisk in the olive oil. Keep leftover dressing refrigerated for up to a week.

Before serving, remove the dressing from the refrigerator and allow it to return to room temperature.

Variations:
↪ Use tarragon vinegar instead of wine vinegar/lemon juice.
↪ Add ¼ teaspoon tarragon instead of mustard powder.
↪ Add a pinch of cayenne pepper.

Yield: 4–6 servings

FRENCH DRESSING, Alternate

1 teaspoon tomato paste or purée (or 1 Tablespoon tomato juice)
½ cup salad oil (or mayonnaise)
¼ teaspoon tarragon (or paprika or mustard powder)
Dash black pepper
Dash onion powder (optional, to taste)
Dash garlic powder (optional, to taste)
¼ teaspoon brown or white sugar (optional, to taste)
1 Tablespoon apple cider vinegar (or lemon juice or a mixture of both)

In a medium bowl stir the tomato paste into the salad oil. Stir in the desired seasonings. Gradually stir in the vinegar.

Yield: 4–6 servings

RANCH DRESSING

2	Tablespoons water
1	Tablespoon nonfat dry milk
1	Tablespoon sugar
4	Tablespoons mayonnaise
⅛	teaspoon lemon juice
Dash	garlic powder
Pinch	onion powder
Pinch	corn-free salt

Mix the water, nonfat dry milk, and sugar. Gradually add this mixture to the mayonnaise, stirring to a smooth consistency. Stir in lemon juice and the garlic powder, onion powder, and salt.

Variation: Reduce the water to 1 tablespoon. Substitute 3 tablespoons buttermilk for the dry milk and lemon juice. Read ingredients and/or check with the manufacturer for corn-free buttermilk and container.

Yield: 2–3 servings

Double quantity:

2	Tablespoons nonfat dry milk
¼	cup water
2	Tablespoons sugar
½	cup mayonnaise
⅛	teaspoon lemon juice
⅛	teaspoon garlic powder
Dash	onion powder
Dash	corn-free salt

SOUR CREAM DIP

1   cup corn-free sour cream
½   teaspoon onion powder (or 2 teaspoons finely minced
       sweet onions)
1   Tablespoon finely chopped chives

Place the sour cream in a small bowl and stir in the onion powder and chives. Allow the mixture to stand, refrigerated, for several hours or overnight. Serve cold.

Variation: If you have no sour cream, add 1 tablespoon lemon juice to corn-free cream. As the dip stands after mixing, the lemon-acid will sour the cream.

Yield: 1 cup

BEAN DIP

1   can pinto beans (low-salt pinto beans may be corn-free)
1   Tablespoon cooking oil
½   teaspoon corn-free salt (optional, to taste)
½   teaspoon cayenne pepper (or chili powder—optional, to taste)

Drain the pinto beans and rinse them thoroughly. Heat the beans in a saucepan with a few tablespoons of water, the oil, salt, and cayenne pepper, if desired. Stir occasionally.

When the beans are hot, mash them with a potato masher.

Variation: For a hotter bean dip, add sliced or diced jalapeño peppers (or hotter habaneros or serranos). Discard stems and seeds. Dice or mince the peppers and stir them into the bean sauce. Do not touch your face or eyes while handling hot chili peppers. When handling raw hot peppers you may want to wear rubber gloves to protect your skin from pepper burns.

Yield: 2 servings

GUACAMOLE

3   ripe avocados
2–3   Tablespoons lime juice (or lemon juice—the juice of one lime
          or lemon)
1   ripe tomato, diced
½   teaspoon corn-free salt (to taste)
½   teaspoon onion powder (or 2 Tablespoons minced onion—
          optional, to taste)
2   teaspoons dried cilantro (or 2 Tablespoons finely minced fresh
          cilantro—optional, to taste)

Cut the avocados in half. Discard the pits and skin. Place the avocados in a mixing bowl.

Add the lime or lemon juice and mash the avocados, leaving some lumps.

Dice the tomato into very small pieces. Stir the tomato and all other ingredients gently into the mashed avocado. Be sure to leave some lumps of avocado.

Serve immediately, with veggies or chips for dipping. Or use guacamole as a side dish with other Southwestern foods.

If you need to store the guacamole for a few hours, do not add cilantro until just before serving. Cover the guacamole with plastic wrap pressed directly onto its surface. Keep at room temperature for up to an hour or in the refrigerator for up to 3 hours. Immediately before serving, add the cilantro. Taste and add more salt, if needed.

Variation: For hot guacamole, add chili powder, cayenne pepper, or fresh chili peppers, finely minced. For fresh chili peppers, such as jalapeño or the hotter serrano, discard stems and seeds and mince. Do not touch your face or eyes while handling hot chili peppers. When handling raw hot peppers you may want to wear rubber gloves to protect your skin from pepper burns.

Yield: 4 servings

Avocados come in two varieties. Guacamole is usually made with Hass, the dark avocados with rough skin. Florida avocados, with green smooth skins, can substitute if necessary. Chips can contain corn oil or other corn derivatives. Chose chips wisely!

SALSA

1	quart fresh diced tomatoes (or 1 32-oz. can diced tomatoes)
¼	large yellow onion, diced (about ⅓ cup)
1	large garlic clove, minced
1	green bell pepper, diced (skin, if desired)
1	yellow bell pepper, diced (skin, if desired)
2	tomatillos, husked and diced
3	small chili peppers, diced (skin, if desired)
1–2	small jalapeño peppers, sliced in rings (skin, if desired)
1	Tablespoon + ¾ teaspoon apple cider vinegar
¾	teaspoon sugar
1	teaspoon dried cilantro flakes (or about 2 Tablespoons fresh cilantro)
⅛	teaspoon red pepper powder
¾	teaspoon chili powder

Use canned, diced tomatoes or drop the fresh tomatoes in boiling water for about 2 minutes. Remove the tomatoes from the water and slip the skins off. Put the tomatoes in a large kettle and heat them on medium-low, uncovered. Dice and add onion. Mince and add garlic.

Cut the bell peppers in half and discard stems, seeds, and membranes. Dice the bell peppers. Add them to the tomato stew. If you prefer, skin the bell peppers first (see instructions below).

Discard the husk and stems of tomatillos. Dice and add the tomatillos.

Slice the jalapeños crosswise into rings. Dice the bell peppers and chili peppers.

Add the peppers, including the chilis and jalapeños, to the tomato stew. Add the vinegar, sugar, and dried seasonings.

Simmer the mixture on medium-low heat until the vegetables begin to feel tender when pricked with a fork. See the Salsa variations on page 45 for hotter salsa as well as the many ways to use salsa.

To Skin Peppers: Move an oven rack to the top position. Place the peppers on a baking sheet and put them in the oven on the top rack. Turn the oven on broil and leave the oven door open slightly. Broil the peppers, turning them until all sides are dark brown or black.

Remove each pepper from the oven when it is blackened. Place bell peppers in a covered pan for 20 minutes before skinning. Allow other peppers to cool enough to handle. You may want to use rubber gloves to handle peppers. *Do not touch your eyes or face* while handling strong chili peppers!

Peel the blackened skins off the chili peppers and jalapeños. Discard the stems and seeds.

For jalapeño rings, dig out the seeds without cutting into the peppers. Jalapeño rings can be removed by those who do not want to bite into straight jalapeño. Next, slice the jalapeños crosswise into rings. Dice the bell peppers and chili peppers.

Yield: about 1 quart

Commercial salsa normally contains corn or corn derivatives. For a quick variety, see Fast Salsa or Fish Salsa alternatives. The cooked salsa above takes more time (well worth it!). You can also customize any salsa for hotter taste.

FAST SALSA

⅔   cup diced tomatoes
⅓   cup diced onion (or green onion or shallots—optional, to taste)
¼   teaspoon cilantro flakes (or 1 teaspoon minced fresh cilantro)
Pinch black pepper
1   teaspoon lemon juice (optional, to taste)

Dice the tomatoes and onions. Mix the tomatoes and onion with the cilantro, pepper, and lemon juice. Refrigerate overnight, or at least 2 hours, if possible, to allow seasonings to blend. Serve cold.

Variations:

⤷ For even faster salsa, replace the diced onion with ¼ teaspoon onion powder or flakes.

⤷ Add ⅔ cup diced avocado, especially with cilantro, black pepper, and lemon juice.

⤷ Add a quarter of a green pepper, diced. (Discard stem, seeds and membranes.)

⤷ For hotter flavor, add hotter chili peppers, either dried or fresh diced. **Dry Options:** paprika (mild), or red pepper, or hotter peppers crumbled from whole dried peppers. **Fresh Options:** green chili (Anaheim, mild), jalapeño (hot), serrano or habanero (hotter) make salsa hot.

Discard stems, seeds, and membranes, and slice or dice the hot chili pepper. *Do not touch your face or eyes* while handling hot chili peppers. You may want to use rubber gloves for handling the hotter varieties. If you prefer the peppers peeled, see directions "To skin peppers" under the Salsa recipe, page 42.

⤷ Add a mixture of the various chili-pepper flavors, such as green chili plus bell peppers or green chili plus jalapeño peppers.

⤷ Use ¼ teaspoon dried oregano instead of, or in addition to, cilantro flakes. This makes more of a pasta-sauce flavor, especially if you leave out the lemon juice.

Yield: 2 servings

The seeds and membranes of a chili contain most of the capasaicin, the chemical that makes the chili "hot." A few people eat hot chili peppers, seeds and all—very few!

If the chili taste is burning your mouth, put out the fire with iced tea. Lemon works almost as well. Water does not help!

SALSA, Variations and Uses

For hotter salsa, add hotter chili peppers. Keep the milder ones for the variety of their flavors. A few popular varieties include:

Mild: bell peppers, especially yellow, orange, or red, and chili peppers (Anaheim)

Medium hot: jalapeño peppers

Hot: habanero peppers

Very Hot: serrano peppers

For a fast salsa, use chili peppers raw or dried. You can buy hot, dried chili peppers and crush them to add small amounts of strong flavors. If you used fresh, raw chili pepper, discard the stems, seeds, and membranes and dice the pepper.

Fast salsa can be simmered to blend the flavors, if you have the time. Sauté the onion with butter or cooking oil. Add 2–3 tablespoons water and diced chili peppers, as desired. Simmer while you dice the tomatoes. Add all the remaining ingredients and simmer until flavors blend to taste.

WARNING: Do not touch the eyes or face while handling hot chili peppers! For more information about other hot chili peppers, see Dr. Richter's Fresh Produce Guide, or search the Internet for chili pepper or Scoville units (a measure of chili hotness).

USES FOR SALSA

⤳ Use salsa as a dip for chips or veggies.

⤳ Combine salsa with corn-free sour cream and use as a dip.

⤳ Season tortillas, burritos, fajitas, and other Southwestern dishes.

⤳ Make scrambled eggs, add cooked meat bits. Cover with corn-free shredded cheese. Add salsa.

⤳ Add salsa to a crock pot with stewing beef or game meat such as venison, elk, or buffalo.

⤳ Season a vegetable stir-fry.

⤳ Season baked or broiled chicken.

⤳ Season baked or broiled fish.

SALAD TRAY

Broccoli florets: Rinse thoroughly. Cut the florets from the stems; save the stems for soup.

Carrot sticks: Scrub and/or peel. Cut lengthwise, crosswise, or diagonally into small slices.

Cauliflower florets: Rinse thoroughly. Cut the florets from the stems.

Celery sticks: Scrub. Remove strings or peel the backs. Cut lengthwise into small slices.

Cherry tomatoes: Rinse. Remove any long stems; serve whole.

Red radishes: Scrub. Remove the tops and bottoms. Serve whole or cut into slices or decorative shapes.

Bell peppers (green, red and/or yellow): Rinse. Cut out the stem and base; cut in half and remove the seeds. Slice into strips.

Button mushrooms: Clean with a damp paper towel or soft brush. Trim off ¼-inch of the stem bottom. Do not soak mushrooms or they will turn mushy.

Cucumbers: If there is a waxy coating, peel it off. (The coating contains corn.) Slice crosswise. If the cucumber is older, cut it in half lengthwise and drag a spoon through the center to remove the seeds.

Grape tomatoes (or baby Roma tomatoes): Wash; serve whole.

Green onions (or scallions): Wash. Slice off the base and trim the tops short.

Zucchini (small): Cut off the ends. Clean zucchini with a soft brush; do not peel. Slice crosswise.

Choose about 5 or more favorite vegetables. Rinse the raw, whole vegetables thoroughly in cold water. Avoid commercial vegetable-cleaning products since they contain corn.

Prepare small pieces that can be eaten raw as finger-food. For serving, place one or several dressings and/or dips (see recipes on pages 33–45) in small bowls in the center of a large tray or plate. Add a small spoon for each dip.

Arrange veggies around the dips by alternating colors and shapes. Provide small plates for guests to fill with their choices of salad, dressings, and dips.

Variations: For decoration try Seaphire, Teardrop or Pear tomatoes, or Enoki mushrooms.

To prevent discoloring, you can dip veggie pieces in water with lemon juice. Use 2–3 tablespoons lemon juice in 1 quart of water.

TOSSED SALAD

2   cups lettuce pieces
Add any or all of the following, as desired:
1   cup spinach leaves or romaine lettuce
1   tomato, diced or sliced (or several cherry tomatoes)
1   carrot, shredded or sliced
⅓   cup shredded red cabbage
2   radishes, sliced
1–2 green onions or shallots, sliced

To wash an entire head of iceberg lettuce, cut out the stem and run cold water into the head while pulling the leaves slightly loose to rinse the lettuce well. Remove any outer leaves that are dry, torn, or discolored. Turn the head cut-side down and stand it in a colander to drain.

If you plan to use only part of the lettuce, cut off a chunk and wash only that part. As with most vegetables, the rest of the lettuce will keep better if it is not washed.

When the lettuce has drained, tear or cut it into pieces and place the pieces in a large bowl. Prepare other veggies and add them, as desired.

Toss the salad with a salad fork and spoon. Dressings may be tossed with the salad or served on the side. Serve the tossed salad in the salad bowl or on individual plates.

Note: See the recipes for corn-free salad dressings, pages 33–39.

Variations:
Personal Salads: Place the lettuce in the salad bowl and other vegetables in separate bowls to allow guests to create the salad of their choice.

Bed of Greens: Place larger leaves on separate plates and serve the tossed salad on top of the greens.

Dinner Salad: Add corn-free, sliced luncheon meats, shredded cheese, chicken chunks, tuna chunks, or hard-boiled eggs, sliced or diced. See recipe for Hard-boiled Eggs, page 120.

Yield: 2–3 servings

To keep cut vegetables and fruit from discoloring, use a rinse made of 2–3 tablespoons lemon juice or vinegar in about 1 quart of cold water. Those sprinkle-on crystals are ascorbic acid, usually made from corn.

TOSSED SALAD CHOICES

Greens (about 1 cup per person—choose one or several):
Iceberg lettuce
Spinach leaves
Delicate-flavored lettuce leaves, such as romaine, green leaf, red leaf, or a butterhead (Bibb or Boston)
Greens with more character, such as endive, radicchio, kohlrabi, kale, escarole, or collard greens
Dandelion leaves
Colors (choose one or several):
Shredded carrots
Shredded red or green cabbage
Diced tomato, cherry tomatoes, Roma tomatoes, or grape tomatoes
Diced or shredded radish
Broccoli florets, cut small
Cauliflower florets, cut small
Onion bits, sliced or diced small, or shredded

Wash the greens, drain, and tear or cut them into bite-sized pieces. Add other veggies as desired. Serve the greens in a salad bowl, either laid under other veggies or tossed with them.

For several guests with widely varied tastes, try serving the greens in two or more bowls, grouped by stronger and milder flavors. For a fast meal (and faster clean-up), serve the salad directly on the dinner plate instead of using separate salad bowls.

Variations:
⤷ For a gourmet touch, serve the tossed salad with a fresh-pepper grinder and choices of salad dressings on the side. Some people prefer the greens to be torn by hand; others like the crisp flavor of greens cut with a knife, especially head lettuces.

⤷ Create your own "house salad" by adding your favorite veggies to the greens and perhaps your own variation of a dressing.

⤷ Add to taste: alfalfa sprouts; avocado (ripen by placing in a paper bag; check daily); bean sprouts; mushrooms

---

In some countries, salad can mean lettuce only.

COLE SLAW

2	Tablespoons mayonnaise (or salad dressing)
2	Tablespoons milk (or water, lemon juice, or apple cider vinegar)
2	teaspoons sugar (optional, to taste)
Pinch	paprika (or mustard—optional, to taste)
1	cup shredded cabbage, light or dark
¼	cup shredded carrots (optional)

In a medium bowl combine the mayonnaise and milk and stir until the mixture reaches a smooth, creamy consistency, adding more milk if necessary. Stir in the sugar and paprika, if desired. Stir in any addition seasonings desired (see variations below).

Shred the cabbage and carrots and combine with the dressing. Add any other vegetables desired (see variations below). Stir. Chill before serving.

Variations:
Seasonings—Add one or more:

½	teaspoon minced onion
¼	teaspoon celery seed
Dash	salt and/or pepper

Veggies—Add one or more:

¼	cup shredded red cabbage
½	tomato, diced

Tart Dressing—Stir all ingredients together and use in place of sweet dressing.

2	tablespoons salad oil
1	tablespoon balsamic vinegar (or lemon juice or apple cider vinegar)
⅛	teaspoon dill seed
⅛	teaspoon onion flakes
Pinch	corn-free salt

Yield: 2–3 servings

Cole slaw comes in many flavors, sweet or tart, in salad dressing or oil-and-vinegar. Choose your favorite—or try them all.

CARROT-RAISIN SALAD

2   Tablespoons mayonnaise (or salad dressing)
1½   teaspoons sugar (optional, to taste)
1   Tablespoon milk (or water, lemon juice, or apple cider vinegar)
Pinch teaspoon paprika (optional, to taste)
1   cup shredded carrots
2–3   Tablespoons raisins

Place the mayonnaise in a small bowl and stir in the sugar. Stir the milk into the mayonnaise and sugar mixture, a little at a time, until the mixture reaches a smooth, creamy consistency. Stir in the paprika, if desired.

Scrub the carrots and cut off the ends. Peel if desired and shred. Combine the carrots, raisins, and dressing. Stir and chill before serving.

Yield: 2–3 servings

CAESAR SALAD

2–3   Tablespoons olive oil (or salad oil or combination)
⅛   teaspoon garlic powder (or 1 small clove of garlic, finely minced)
1   small bunch chilled romaine lettuce, about 12–14 ounces, or
         mix with other salad greens
2–3   Tablespoons grated Parmesan cheese
         Salt and pepper (to taste)
1   soft-boiled egg (coddled: 1 min.)
1½   Tablespoons lemon juice (or wine vinegar)
1   cup garlic croutons

Combine the oil and garlic and set aside. For more blended flavors, combine these in the morning, or a day or two before, and refrigerate.

Wash the romaine lettuce and drain it well in a colander or on paper towels. Cut off the hard stem and tear or cut the lettuce into bite-sized pieces. Place them in a large salad bowl.

Set an egg out at room temperature. Bring water to boil and use a spoon to gently lower the egg into the boiling water. Boil for 1 minute; the yolk and part of the white will still be runny. If you prefer, you can substitute a diced, hard-boiled egg.

Drizzle the garlic-olive oil mixture on the salad greens. Sprinkle on salt, pepper, and lemon juice. Toss the salad to coat every leaf to glistening.

Sprinkle the egg across the salad. Toss the salad again.

Sprinkle on Parmesan cheese and garlic croutons (see box below).

Variations:

↪ Garnish the salad with 4 anchovy fillets.

↪ **Garlic lovers:** double or triple the amount of garlic called for. Sauté fresh garlic.

↪ For a more tangy salad, add a little wine vinegar or more lemon juice.

↪ Add a dash of dry mustard with the other seasonings.

Yield: 2 servings

> CROUTONS—To make garlic croutons, butter 2 slices of bread on both sides. Place one slice on top of the other and cut in both directions to make cubes. Place these on a baking sheet and sprinkle on garlic powder as generously as you like. Brown the croutons on 450° or broil, stirring occasionally. If you prefer, you can brown the croutons in a skillet on the stove top.

SPINACH SALAD

2	hard-boiled eggs
5–6	slices corn-free bacon, fried crisp and crumbled into bits
1	large bunch (6–8 oz.) spinach, well-washed
3	Tablespoons cooking oil (mild-flavored, such as canola)
2	Tablespoons apple cider vinegar (or lemon juice)
1	Tablespoon brown sugar (optional)
1	teaspoon powdered onion (or 1 Tablespoon finely chopped fresh onion—optional)
Pinch	salt, pepper, garlic (optional, to taste)

Peel the hard-boiled eggs and dice them with a knife or egg slicer.

The bacon can be diced before frying or crisp-fry the bacon and drain it; then cool and crumble into bits.

Wash the fresh spinach well and drain. Trim off and discard stems. Tear the leaves into bite-sized pieces and place in a large salad bowl. Chill the salad while making the dressing.

To make the dressing: Combine the oil and vinegar. If using sugar, melt it into the oil and vinegar over low heat. Add any seasonings desired. Drizzle the hot dressing over the salad for "wilted" greens or serve the dressing on the side.

Sprinkle on the bacon bits and diced eggs. Serve immediately.

Variations:

Hot Bacon Dressing: After frying the bacon, drain off the excess bacon grease. Omit the oil. Add vinegar (and any seasonings desired) to the hot, bacon-greased pan. Stir over low heat to melt any sugar. Drizzle the hot bacon dressing over the salad and toss to coat the spinach. Top with diced eggs and serve immediately.

Low-fat Variation: Omit the salad oil and bacon. Sprinkle lemon juice directly onto the greens and add seasonings, or mix the seasonings into lemon juice or apple cider vinegar before adding to the salad. Finish with diced egg whites.

Yield: 2 servings

CAUTION: Some bacon contains dextrose, a corn derivative.
Be sure to read ingredients!
White vinegar is made from corn. Use apple cider vinegar or lemon juice.

BELL PEPPER & PASTA SALAD

1	16-oz. bag pasta (spiral or bow-tie noodles)
1–2	Tablespoons cooking oil
1	red bell pepper, sliced
1	green bell pepper, sliced
1	apple, sliced (optional)
1	Tablespoon lemon juice (optional)
⅛	teaspoon onion powder (optional, to taste)

Boil the pasta in water and 1–2 tablespoons of cooking oil to prevent sticking. When the pasta is done, drain it and rinse it in cold water.

Cut the stems out of the bell peppers. Slice the peppers in half and remove the seeds and membranes. Slice or dice the peppers.

Cut the apple in half and remove the core, stem, and bottom. Slice or dice the apple.

Put lemon juice on the apple to keep it from browning or dip the apple slices in a mixture of about 1 tablespoon lemon juice to 1 cup of water.

In a large bowl mix the pasta, bell pepper, apple, and onion powder. Chill.

Stir in a dressing (see below) or serve the dressing on the side.

Sweet-Tart Dressing: Mix about ½ cup mayonnaise with 4–5 tablespoons of apple cider vinegar or lemon juice. Stir in 4 teaspoons sugar.

Vinaigrette Dressing: Mix ½ cup olive oil or salad oil with 3–4 tablespoons of apple cider vinegar or lemon juice. Stir in a dash each of seasonings such as oregano, basil, garlic, pepper, and/or rosemary.

Variation: Instead of onion powder, add 1 tablespoon diced onion (bermuda or sweet onion) or chopped green onions (scallions).

Yield: 4–5 servings

PEA-BEAN SALAD

1	15½-oz. can garbanzo beans
1	10-oz. package frozen peas, thawed
¾	cup raw peanuts (optional)
⅓	cup mayonnaise
1	Tablespoon water (or vinegar, lemon juice, or milk)
⅛	teaspoon paprika (optional, to taste)
Pinch	corn-free salt (optional, to taste)
Pinch	sugar (optional, to taste)

Rinse the garbanzo beans well. Thaw the peas in a saucepan or microwave. Combine the beans, peas, and peanuts, if desired.

Combine the mayonnaise with the water and any seasonings desired. Stir into the bean-pea mixture.

Chill; serve cold. Refrigerate any leftover portion immediately.

Variations:

↪ Instead of raw peanuts, use salted, roasted peanuts, if preferred. Or use diced ham and/or hard-boiled egg slices.

↪ Use black-eyed peas instead of garbanzo beans.

Yield: 3–4 servings

Any food with mayonnaise needs to be kept cold. Mayonnaise spoils easily, with no flavor or color change for warning.

Beans will digest more easily if they are well-rinsed before cooking or eating.

POTATO SALAD

4–5	large red potatoes
5	eggs, hard-boiled
½	cup chopped onion (or 1 teaspoon onion powder—optional)
2	celery stalks, diced
1	medium cucumber, diced (optional)
⅓	cup mayonnaise (or salad dressing)
2	teaspoons apple cider vinegar (plain vinegar is made from corn)
2	teaspoons dill weed (more if you want the flavor of dill pickle)
½	teaspoon mustard powder
1	teaspoon celery seed (optional, to taste)
½	teaspoon corn-free salt (optional, to taste)
¼	teaspoon pepper (optional, to taste)
1	Tablespoon sugar (if you want the flavor of sweet pickle)
Pinch	paprika (optional—for garnish)

Wash the potatoes and cut out eyes. Peel the potatoes now or after cooking and cooling, if desired. For faster cooking, cut the potatoes in half. Boil the potatoes until slightly soft in the center when pricked with a fork, about 20 minutes. Then cool the potatoes enough to handle. Peel the potatoes and cut them into half-inch (12 mm) cubes. Put the cubes in a large mixing bowl.

Simmer the eggs in water with salt to prevent leaks from eggshell cracks. Simmer for 9–12 minutes, until the eggs are solid with the yolks slightly tender. When the eggs are done, cool them enough to handle. Peel the eggs and slice them. Add the eggs to the bowl with the potatoes, reserving some egg slices for garnish, if desired.

Commercial pickles and mustard paste usually contain corn derivatives. For the flavor of pickles, use cucumber in the salad or pickle the cucumber (see recipe, page 76) at least a day before. For the flavor of mustard, use mustard powder. For a Dijon flavor, add a little wine.

(continued on next page)

(continued from previous page)

Dice the onion, celery, and cucumber. Add to the potatoes and egg. Chill the mixture in the refrigerator for 5–10 minutes.

Meanwhile, in a separate bowl mix the vinegar and seasonings. Taste and adjust the seasonings, if you like. Chill the dressing.

Stir the dressing gently into the potato mixture. Cover and refrigerate the potato salad for at least 1 hour and up to 1 day before serving. Serve cold with a garnish of egg slices and paprika, if desired.

Variations: Add diced red or green bell pepper, grated carrots, garlic, and/or bacon bits.

Yield: 4–5 servings

Large red potatoes are popular for potato salad; round white potatoes may work even better. Small (red) new potatoes can be a lot of extra work to peel. If you prefer, try Yukon gold or other types of potatoes.

BREAD TRAY WITH VEGGIES

Preheat oven to 425° • Cooking time: 20–30 minutes

¾	cup water
1	teaspoon sugar
1	teaspoon yeast
2	cups flour, divided
1	egg
2	Tablespoons cooking oil
¾	teaspoon corn-free salt

In a large mixing bowl mix the water, sugar, yeast, and 1 cup flour. Set this mixture in a warm place (80–90°) for about a half hour. The mixture will become frothy and rise to about twice the original size. If it has not risen enough, stir the mixture briskly and leave it in the warmth another 15–20 minutes.

Preheat the oven to 425°. Oil and flour a cake pan.

Stir the yeast mixture until smooth. Add the egg, oil, and salt. Stir until smooth. Stir in the remaining 1 cup flour.

Pour the batter into the cake pan and spread it as thin as possible. Bake the batter at 425° for about 20–30 minutes. Bread tray will be golden-brown when done.

If desired, brush oil on the bread tray while it's still warm.

Spread the bread tray with a topping to hold the vegetables in place. Add bite-sized vegetable pieces and press them down slightly to keep them in place. Topping possibilities include:

↪ Bean Dip (page 40) and yellow, orange, red, or green bell peppers

↪ Cream cheese or mayonnaise and tomatoes, bell peppers, broccoli, celery, cauliflower. (Season the mayo with paprika or mustard powder, if desired.)

↪ Peanut butter and celery and/or carrots

↪ Applesauce, cinnamon, apple pieces, and/or banana slices

↪ Mashed potatoes (page 64) and tomatoes, bell peppers, broccoli, and/or carrots. Season with dill and/or mustard powder.

To make a warm place: turn on the oven to the lowest setting. As soon as you can barely feel warmth in the oven, turn the oven off. (If the air in the oven feels toasty-warm, it is too hot for yeast; open the oven door and let it cool a little.) If you use the oven as a warm place, don't forget to remove the batter before preheating.

CREAMED VEGETABLES

1   cup vegetables (choose one or two) with a dash of seasonings:
      asparagus (with parsley, celery seed, and/or diced hard-boiled egg)
      broccoli florets (with garlic, olive oil, ginger, and/or sesame seeds)
      carrots (with parsley, onion, or brown sugar)
      cauliflower florets (with dill weed, cumin, garlic or nutmeg, lemon)
      mushroom pieces (with herbs)
      okra (with celery, lemon, basil, oregano, tomato and/or vinegar)
      onion or small pearl onions (with mustard powder, diced tomato, and/or shredded carrot)
      peas (with onion, garlic, ginger or nutmeg, sugar)
      potatoes (with onion, garlic, herbs, and/or diced tomato)
1   recipe White Sauce (see page 160)

Use small veggies or dice them. Boil the vegetables in a small amount of water, or sauté mushrooms or onions. Peas do not need to be cooked ahead.

Drain the veggies and reserve the liquid. Set the veggies aside.

Make the White Sauce in a skillet. Use the reserved veggie liquid to make the White Sauce, adding enough cold water to make 1 cup.

Add the cooked vegetables to the White Sauce. Add one or more seasonings, to taste. Simmer for about 5 minutes to blend the flavors.

Variation: Add about ¼ cup shredded cheese, to taste, as a topping or melted into the White Sauce. You may need to shred your own. Prepackaged shredded cheese can be coated with a dusting of cornstarch—though some brands use potato starch—to prevent sticking.

Yield: about 2 servings

FRESH, CANNED, or FROZEN VEGGIES

Fresh or frozen, any salad or veggies packaged in small pieces may be dusted with cornstarch to prevent clumping. Wash well, but don't use a ready-made fruit and vegetable rinse. It may contain corn derivatives, such as ascorbic acid and other harmful chemicals.

Use plain cold water to wash salad stuff or veggies, fresh or frozen. If you need a rinse to prevent discoloring, use a mixture of water and lemon juice (about 1 quart water to 2–3 tablespoons lemon juice).

Fresh vegetables ripen faster and spoil faster when kept next to each other in airtight spaces, such as airtight plastic bags or boxes. A green plastic bag, called an Evert-Fresh Bag, can store veggies or fruit weeks longer without spoiling. If your grocery store does not carry them, see the Evert Corporation under Resources, page 266.

Raw or cooked? Each way of eating veggies has its own values. For example, veggies and fruit both contain natural ascorbic acid (vitamin C). Raw salads and vegetable preserve this because cooking (heat) destroys vitamin C. Sunlight also destroys vitamin C, so raw veggies and fruit at a picnic need to hide in shade.

Cooked veggies can provide more of other vitamins. For example, vitamin A (from green and red veggies) may be absorbed better if the vegetable is cooked to a beautiful bright green. However, if you have intestinal reactions, then raw and lightly cooked veggies may be irritating to the gut tissue. You may need soft-cooked, longer-cooked veggies while the gut heals.

Canned veggies often contain ascorbic acid or other corn derivatives. Salt is a common additive; check with the manufacturer to find out if it's iodized (with corn derivatives).

Sauces in canned or frozen veggies can also contain corn derivatives. It's safer to use vegetables from a package with one ingredient only, the vegetable, such as "Ingredient: green beans," "Ingredient: carrots," or "Ingredient: peas." Well, okay, the label might read, "Ingredients: peas and carrots." But you get the idea.

Watch out for cornstarch, corn syrup, and/or ascorbic acid (usually made from corn) in any packaged vegetables or vegetable wash or freshener. Loose pieces are often dusted with cornstarch to prevent clumping. This packaging cornstarch does not have to be mentioned in the ingredients.

(continued on next page)

Vegetable juice—is it really? Try reading ingredients on the different cans that say "Tomato Juice" or even "100 percent Tomato Juice." You may be surprised to find ingredients like corn syrup or ascorbic acid (made from corn). Look for that single ingredient: tomato juice.

When rinsing veggies to make your own vegetable juice, be sure to use plain cold water or a mixture of water and a little lemon juice.

Raw frozen peas make great snacks. Even kids love 'em. Be sure to rinse first; they are probably packaged with a fine dusting of cornstarch.

FREEZING VEGGIES

Vegetables that freeze well may be cut into small slices or pieces first. These include bell peppers, carrots, green beans, onion, peas, and zucchini. Preparation for freezing varies, but most fresh veggies need to be washed and some need to be blanched.

When you wash a vegetable, use plain cold water or a mixture of water and lemon juice (about 1 quart water to 2–3 tablespoons lemon juice). Commercial vegetable and fruit washes usually contain corn derivatives.

To blanch a veggie, boil it for about 1–3 minutes, longer for harder veggies.

To prepare veggies for freezing:
Bell Peppers: Discard stem, seeds, and membranes; slice or dice.
Carrots: Wash, discard stems, peel, and slice or dice. Blanch.
Green beans: Wash, discard stems, and slice. Blanch.
Onions: Discard stem, peel, and dice.
Peas: Shell the peas. Blanch.
Zucchini: Wash, discard ends; slice or dice.

Assemble pint or quart plastic boxes. Plastic bags may contain corn-starch to prevent sticking; the boxes may be safer for you. Prepare 1 or 2 quarts of vegetables in season. (See above.)

Place the veggie pieces on a baking sheet to dry. Place a paper towel under them, if desired, to help absorb moisture. Remove any paper towels once the veggies are dry. If desired, set the baking sheet with veggies directly into the freezer to cool and freeze quickly.

Select the size of plastic boxes according to the quantities you will want to use. (Avoid plastic bags, which be made partly of corn.) Place the cooled or frozen veggies in the boxes.

Spread the boxes around inside the freezer to freeze more quickly. Once frozen, the veggie boxes may be stacked for more convenience.

Yield: 1–2 quarts of frozen veggies

To use frozen veggies: Thaw the veggies in the refrigerator or at room tempera-ture. Avoid mushy zucchini; thaw it in a strainer so it can drain. Frozen zuc-chini can turn very soft; use it for cooking in soups, casseroles, or zucchini bread. Use other thawed veggies like fresh veggies in recipes such as soups, casseroles, steamed vegetables, creamed vegetables, stir-fry, etc.

MASHED OR BOILED POTATOES

2   large potatoes, + "1 for the pot" (russet or Idaho)
         Butter (or corn-free margarine or salad oil, to taste)
         Corn-free salt and pepper, to taste

Fill a large saucepan about halfway with water and begin heating the water on medium.

Peel the potatoes. Cut out the eyes and any bad spots.

Cut potatoes into pieces. (To prevent discoloring, drop the pieces into water as soon as they are cut.) Smaller pieces will cook faster; larger pieces will hold their shape better and remain firmer. Add enough water to cover the cut potato pieces.

Cover the pot, lower the heat, and let the potatoes simmer until they are soft, about 15–35 minutes. Time will vary depending on the size of potato pieces, heat used, and altitude.

For mashed potatoes, set aside about 1 tablespoon of the boiling water per potato. Drain off the rest of the water through a colander. (Optional: save the potato water for a soup base.)

For boiled potatoes, season and serve. Or cube the boiled potatoes and chill them for use in a potato salad.

For mashed potatoes, put the drained potatoes back in the pot along with 1 tablespoon of milk or reserved water per potato. Add about 1 tablespoon of butter, corn-free margarine, or salad oil per potato. Add salt and pepper to taste. Add other seasonings, as desired (see variations below). Mash and stir well. Serve hot.

Variations:

ᕙ Use red or white potatoes instead of russet. Peel or just scrub them—your choice. See also Roasted Potatoes (page 63) for cooking red or white potatoes.

ᕙ Season the mashed or boiled potatoes with parsley flakes or diced fresh parsley.

ᕙ Garnish the potatoes with diced tomato and/or sautéed onion.

ᕙ Season the potatoes with other favorites, such as tarragon or rosemary or garlic.

ᕙ Season the potatoes with a combination of flavors such as cilantro, pepper, and lemon; or chili powder or curry mix; or a salsa.

Yield: 2–3 servings

ROASTED OR MASHED POTATOES
Preheat oven to 375° or use stove top

1	pound large red potatoes (3–4) (or white potatoes or small new potatoes)
2	Tablespoons olive oil (or other salad oil, to taste)
	Corn-free salt and pepper, to taste

Wash the potatoes well and cut out large eyes and any bad spots. Cut large potatoes in half. Boil the potatoes for about 15 minutes and then drain. To peel: run cold water over the potatoes and slip the skins off with a flat knife.

Oven Roasting: Preheat the oven to 375°. Coat or spray a baking sheet with oil. Place the potatoes on the baking sheet in a single layer, cut side down. Drizzle the oil over the potatoes and sprinkle on seasonings if desired; see variations below. Roast the potatoes for about 10–15 minutes. Push a fork well into a potato to test; potatoes will be soft when done.

Stove-top Roasting: Use a large saucepan with a lid that closes tightly and does not allow steam to escape. Place the potatoes in the saucepan in a single layer, cut-side down.

Add enough water to cover about half of the potatoes.

If you want to peel the potatoes, boil them for about 15 minutes; then remove the potatoes from the pan and run cold water over them. Use a flat knife to slip off the skins. Place the potatoes back in the saucepan.

Drizzle oil over the potatoes and sprinkle on seasonings desired (see variations below). Cover the pan tightly and roast the potatoes for an additional 10–15 minutes. (That's a total of 25–30 minutes.)

Roasting times vary depending on the size of potatoes, the heat used, and the altitude. The potatoes will be soft throughout when they are done. Serve warm.

To test for doneness, push a fork well into a potato; it will be soft when done.

Variations:
Rosemary or dill: Sprinkle on 1 teaspoon dried rosemary or ½ tablespoon finely chopped fresh rosemary before roasting. Or use dill weed instead.

(continued on next page)

(continued from previous page)

Tarragon or Parsley: After roasting, sprinkle on 2 teaspoons dried tarragon or parsley. If you prefer, use ½ tablespoon finely chopped fresh tarragon or parsley. Add pepper to taste.

Mashed Potatoes

Put the cooked potatoes and 4–5 tablespoons of milk or water in a saucepan. Add salt, oil and/or seasonings, as desired. Mash and stir well. Serve hot.

Variations:

↪ Season the mashed potatoes with a combination of seasonings and flavors, such as cilantro, pepper, and lemon; or chili powder or curry mix; or a salsa.

↪ **Potato Salad:** Plain roasted potatoes can also be cubed and chilled for use in a potato salad.

Yield: 2–3 servings

BAKED POTATOES

Preheat oven to 400° • Cooking time: 20–30 minutes

2   large potatoes*

Scrub the potatoes well. Cut out the eyes and any bad spots. With a fork, prick each potato only twice, just through the skin, to prevent explosion. Limit the depth and number of pricks to retain moisture.

Place the potatoes on an oven rack with space between them. For more moist baked potatoes, wrap each potato in aluminum foil.

For faster baking, cut each potato lengthwise and wrap each half in aluminum foil to prevent loss of moisture.

Bake at 400° until the potatoes are soft inside. Insert a fork to test the potato's doneness or pick up the spud with an oven mitt and see if it gives when you squeeze it. Larger potatoes will need more time to bake. Higher altitude also adds to baking time.

For softer baked potatoes, use an oven mitt to squash the warm potato inside its skin before serving.

*Note: Russet potatoes bake well.

Variations:
↪ Top the potato with cooked Brussels sprouts, broccoli florets, diced tomatoes, and/or other veggies.
↪ Top the potato with fat-free chicken broth, with or without veggies.
↪ Top the potato with creamed vegetables or creamed meat. For fewer calories, the White Sauce can be made with whole wheat flour, skim milk or water, and half the amount of oil (see page 160).

Yield: 2 servings

An old saying tells how many potatoes to use:
"One per person, plus one for the pot."

BITE-SIZED BAKED POTATOES

Preheat oven to 400° • Cooking time: 15–20 minutes

2	potatoes (preferably russet)
1	Tablespoon cooking oil (or olive oil)
½	teaspoon corn-free salt (optional)
	Seasonings (optional, see choices below)

Preheat the oven to 400°.

Wash and peel the potatoes; dice into bite-sized chunks. Stir the potato chunks in the cooking oil, or spray them with a corn-free cooking oil spray.

Generously oil a baking sheet so that the potatoes don't stick. Spread the potatoes on the baking sheet. Sprinkle the salt over the potatoes, if desired.

Bake the potatoes at 400° for 8–12 minutes. Then turn them with a spatula. After turning the potato chunks, sprinkle them with dried seasonings, if desired. (Some seasonings turn bitter if heated too long or at too high a heat.) Choose your own favorites or see below.

Bake the potatoes for another 7–8 minutes. When the potatoes are done, they will be soft in the center and golden brown on some of the sides.

Serve hot. If desired, serve with ketchup (see recipe for corn-free ketchup, page 77) or cold, diced tomatoes on the side.

Seasoning suggestions:

2	teaspoons basil leaves and/or 1 teaspoon oregano
2	teaspoons cilantro and/or a dash of black pepper
1	teaspoon lemon-pepper and/or 2 teaspoons tarragon
2	teaspoons dill weed and/or powdered mustard
1	teaspoon rosemary and/or thyme

Note: Tarragon plus lemon and black pepper hints at the flavor of béarnaise, especially with a few drops of vinegar and/or red wine added.

Yield: 2 servings

Potatoes can be seasoned like an omelet—any way you like! Onion and garlic are standard. For variety, try paprika, chili powder, or hotter peppers. For delicate flavors, try tarragon or other herbs.

Test a new savory seasoning by trying it on potatoes, mashed, baked, or in chunks. Cook the potato first, since many seasonings turn bitter with prolonged or high heat. See Chapter 14, "Seasonings," for more ideas.

ARTICHOKES

2	artichokes
2	Tablespoons cooking oil (optional)
Pinch	corn-free salt (optional)
Pinch	pepper (optional)
2	Tablespoons lemon (optional)

Rinse the artichokes well. Cut off the top and the stem near the base and the top. Tear off any brown or deeply split leaves on the outside. With kitchen scissors, trim off the pointy tips of remaining leaves.

Set the artichokes, leaves pointed up, in a medium-size saucepan. Almost cover the artichokes with water. Spread open the leaves and sprinkle in the oil, lemon, and seasonings, if desired.

Cover the pan. Bring the water to a boil, then lower the heat and simmer for 30–40 minutes. The insides of the outer leaves will be soft when the artichoke is done.

Turn the artichokes stem side up to drain and cool slightly.

To eat an artichoke, tear off a leaf and draw the base of the leaf between your teeth (to get the soft insides). When you tear off enough leaves to reach the center of the artichoke, cut out the "choke." You can eat the heart of the artichoke with a fork.

Variation:
Steamed Artichokes: Steam the artichokes, stem side up, in about 1 inch of water. Make sure the pan has a lid that seals tightly. Add a few drops of lemon juice to melted butter or margarine, and serve as a garnish with plain steamed artichokes.

Yield: 2 servings

Artichoke flavor stays with your tongue long after you've finished eating it! This flavor can overpower more delicate flavors. When planning a menu, you may want stronger seasonings to follow the artichokes.

ASPARAGUS

1   **small bunch asparagus**

Rinse the asparagus under cold water. Break off the tough bottom part of each stem.

Lay the asparagus in a skillet and barely cover it with water. Cover the skillet, and heat to boiling. Simmer for a few minutes.

Many people consider asparagus done when it turns bright green. Some prefer to cook it longer, to a pale green color.

Variations:
- Serve with melted butter, corn-free margarine, or cooking oil.
- Serve with hollandaise sauce.

Yield: 2–3 servings

GREEN BEANS AND TOMATO SAUCE

1	8-oz. can green beans (or 1 cup fresh green beans)
⅓	cup tomato paste
⅓	cup water

Use any type of green beans you prefer: fresh, canned, frozen, crosscut or French cut. If you use fresh green beans, rinse the beans and cut off the stems and tops. Boil or steam fresh green beans for 2–3 minutes.

In a medium-size skillet combine the green beans, tomato paste, and water. Add a seasoning variation, if desired (see below). Heat while stirring the tomato paste and water until smooth. Serve immediately.

Variations:
↦ **Add one or several of the following seasonings:**

⅛	teaspoon corn-free salt (optional, to taste)
Pinch	pepper
½	teaspoon onion powder or flakes; if you prefer fresh onion, use about 2 tablespoons diced onion
¼	teaspoon garlic powder or flakes; if you prefer fresh garlic, use about 1 small clove, diced

↦ **Add one of these dried seasonings. If you prefer fresh herbs, see below.**

⅛	teaspoon basil
⅛	teaspoon marjoram
⅛	teaspoon thyme
⅛	teaspoon oregano
⅛	teaspoon dill weed

↦ Oil a small baking dish and add the green bean–tomato mixture. Top with corn-free shredded cheese, broken crackers, or moist bread crumbs. Bake at 350° until the topping turns golden-brown, about 10–12 minutes. Serve hot.

Yield: 2 servings

If a recipe calls for dried herb flakes and you prefer fresh, use about triple the amount of finely chopped fresh herbs. Dried herbs that are older will be milder. See Chapter 14, "Seasonings and Spices," for more information about fresh seasonings.

ONION RINGS

$\frac{1}{2}$	cup milk (or water)
$\frac{1}{4}$	cup flour
$\frac{1}{8}$	teaspoon corn-free salt
1	yellow onion
	Cooking oil to $\frac{1}{2}$-inch deep in the pan

Stir the milk, flour, and salt until smooth to make a thin batter.

Discard the onion peel, stems, and skin. Slice the onion across so that the slices will come apart into rings.

Prepare a plate covered with a few layers of paper towels.

In a deep saucepan heat about a half-inch of oil. Use a spatter lid to prevent a sticky stove! When the oil is hot enough, a drop of the batter will sizzle and brown quickly.

Use a fork to dip an onion ring into the batter. Transfer the ring to the hot oil. It will float on the surface. Continue dipping and transferring a few more rings until the surface is almost full of onion rings.

Turn the rings until they are browned on both sides. Transfer the rings to the plate covered with paper towels. Sprinkle with salt and let them cool a bit before serving.

Yield: about 2 servings

BELL PEPPER RINGS

Follow the above recipe, except substitute a green bell pepper for the onion. Rinse the bell pepper. Discard the stem, seeds, and membranes. Cut the pepper crosswise to make rings. Continue with the recipe above.

Variations:
Okra Rings: Rinse and cut off the caps. Slice the okra into circles.
Zucchini Sticks: Cut off the stems and peel. Cut the zucchini into finger-sized sticks.
Cheese Sticks: Cut mozzarella cheese into finger-sized sticks.
Continue with the above directions.

Serve onion rings or other batter-fried appetizers with salsa for a dip.

CANDIED YAMS (SWEET POTATOES)

Preheat oven to 375° or 350° with meringue • Cooking time: 20–30 minutes

2	Tablespoons + 1 Tablespoon cooking oil (or butter)
¼	teaspoon corn-free salt (optional, to taste)
3	Tablespoons + 1 Tablespoon brown sugar (or maple syrup—to taste)
1	15-oz. can yams (or sweet potatoes)*

Preheat the oven to 375° for glazed yams or 350° for yams with meringue topping.

Coat or spray a baking pan or dish with cooking oil.

For mashed yams, mix all of the ingredients, reserving 1 tablespoon each of oil and sugar for topping. Place the mixture in the baking dish. For sliced, mix the oil, salt, and sugar (reserving topping amounts). Layer the slices into the baking pan, alternating with the oil-brown sugar mixture.

Top with the remaining tablespoon of oil and brown sugar, sprinkled over the mashed or sliced yams or potatoes. Bake at 375° until the topping caramelizes into a glaze, about 30 minutes.

If you prefer, add the meringue topping (see below).

*Note: Canned sweet potatoes or yams may contain corn syrup. Be sure to read the ingredients!

Variation:

↪ **Meringue:** Whip 2 egg whites and ¼ teaspoon cream of tartar to a fine froth. Beat in ¼ cup sugar, a little at a time. Beat to very stiff peaks. Pile this gently onto the yams. Pull up points or swirl for decoration, if desired. Bake at 350° until the topping begins to turn golden-brown, about 30 minutes.

↪ Add cinnamon, nutmeg, and/or allspice to the yams. Or add orange zest or orange juice.

Yield: 2–3 servings

FRESH SWEET POTATOES OR YAMS

Preheat oven to 375° • Cooking time: 45 minutes

1   sweet potato or yam per person

Wash the sweet potatoes or yams and prick the skins with a fork. Bake at 375° until tender, about 45 minutes. Cool, then peel, and cut into smaller pieces or mash.

You can continue with the Candied Yams recipe on page 71, or cook these like white potatoes. See potato recipes on pages 62–66.

Yams or sweet potatoes? In the U.S., the word *yams* may refer to both sweet potatoes and yams. However, they are two different plants, from two different continents. Try both and see which you like best.

SUMMER SQUASH

Preheat oven to 350° • Cooking time: 10–15 minutes

1	medium yellow squash (crookneck or straight)
2	Tablespoons cooking oil
	Corn-free salt (optional, to taste)
1½	Tablespoons brown sugar (optional, to taste)

Preheat the oven. Coat or spray the inside of a medium-size baking dish with cooking oil.

Peel the squash, if desired. Slice it crosswise into pieces about ⅛-inch thick. Arrange the pieces side by side in the baking dish. Sprinkle with oil, salt, and brown sugar.

Bake at 350° until the squash is tender, about 10–15 minutes. Alternatively, you can cook this dish in a covered skillet on the stove-top, stirring occasionally.

Variations:

↪ Add a pinch of nutmeg and/or allspice before adding the oil and brown sugar.

↪ Use zucchini (1 medium, 8-inch or 9-inch unpeeled, sliced) instead of, or with, other summer squashes.

Yield: about 2 servings

WINTER SQUASH

Preheat oven to 350° • Total cooking time: 60 minutes

1	cup winter squash (acorn, butternut, hubbard, pumpkin, etc.)
2	Tablespoons cooking oil
	Corn-free salt (optional, to taste)
1½	Tablespoons brown sugar (optional, to taste)

Coat or spray the inside of a medium-size baking dish with cooking oil. Discard the seeds, fibers, and hard skin of a winter squash. Cut or scoop into bite-sized pieces and boil for about 30 minutes.

Place in the prepared baking dish. Sprinkle with oil and other seasonings, as desired. Bake at 350° until the squash is tender, about 30 minutes more.

Variations:

Acorn Squash: Cut in half, remove seeds and fibers, and place the unpeeled halves cut-side down in the baking pan. Add about ¼ inch of boiling water. Bake at 400° for 30 minutes. Then turn the squash cut-side up and fill with partly cooked meat and/or onions. Bake for another 30 minutes. Serve with applesauce as a topping, if desired.

↳ Mash the boiled squash with orange juice and bake until tender.

Yield: about 2 servings

Summer squash (yellow crookneck, zucchini, and others) is usually eaten young, skin and all. Eat winter squash mature, after discarding the hard seeds, fibers, and skin.

TOMATO SAUCE

1   6-oz. can tomato paste
6   oz. water
       Seasonings, to taste

In a small saucepan heat the tomato paste while stirring in an equal amount of water a little at a time. Stir in complementary seasonings such as onion, garlic, basil, oregano, and thyme. Milder seasoning choices include celery, celery seed, chives, dill weed, or tarragon.

Yield: 1 ½ cups

STEWED TOMATOES

3–4   large tomatoes
       Seasonings, to taste

Boil the tomatoes in water for 8–10 minutes. Discard the water and chill the tomatoes under cold water. Pull off the skins with a sharp, nonserrated knife. Cut the tomatoes into a saucepan. Include any liquid, but do not add water. Simmer for about 10 minutes. Season, as in the Tomato Sauce recipe above.

Yield: 2 cups

Tomato sauce and stewed tomatoes often contain citric acid, usually made from corn. Tomato sauce comes in a plain variety, with one ingredient: tomatoes. Your grocer can order this if it is not already on the shelf.

SWEET PICKLE RELISH

3	cups finely diced small Kirby cucumbers (3–4 inches)
1	cup finely diced bell peppers (optional)
½	cup finely diced onions (optional)
½	cup finely diced celery (optional)
⅓	cup corn-free salt, kosher salt or pickling salt
3	cups water
2	cups apple cider vinegar
½	cup sugar
1	Tablespoon mustard seeds (optional, to taste)
½	teaspoon celery seeds (optional, to taste)
1–2	garlic cloves, minced (optional, to taste)
¼	cup minced dill weed

Cut about ½ inch off both ends of the cucumbers to avoid bitterness. Finely dice the cucumbers, bell peppers, onions, and celery. Combine the vegetables, salt, and water. Let the mixture stand for 3 hours.

Drain the salt water and rinse the vegetables thoroughly in cold water. Drain well and set aside.

Boil the vinegar and sugar long enough to dissolve the sugar. Add the other seasonings and the vegetables you have soaked in brine, rinsed, and drained. Bring the mixture to a boil, stirring occasionally.

Lower the heat and simmer the mixture to the desired consistency, about 15 minutes.

Assemble enough glass jars to hold about 5 cups of relish. Cool the relish or else heat the glass jars before filling the jars. Store the relish in glass jars in the refrigerator. (Since this recipe does not call for a sterile canning process, the relish will need refrigeration.)

You may serve this relish right away; however, the flavors will blend more as the relish stands, refrigerated, for a few days or a week or more. It will keep, refrigerated, for weeks or months.

Variation: For dill relish, leave out the sugar in the recipe above.

Yield: 5 cups

Most commercial pickles contain corn syrup and vinegar made from corn. You can make sweet relish quickly. (Whole pickles will take longer.)

KETCHUP

1	6-oz. can tomato paste
½	cup water (or pineapple juice)
6	Tablespoons sugar (or brown sugar)
2½	Tablespoons apple cider vinegar
⅛	teaspoon corn-free salt (optional, to taste)
Pinch	onion powder (optional, to taste)

Place the tomato paste in a small bowl and stir in a little of the water, and then stir in the rest.

Add the sugar, vinegar, salt, and onion powder and stir well.

Refrigerate this ketchup in glass jars. It can keep, refrigerated, for weeks or months.

Yield: 1½ cups

ZUCCHINI

1   large zucchini, sliced (or 2 small)
1   medium-size tomato, diced (optional)
½   yellow onion, diced (optional)
      Salt and pepper (optional, to taste)

Coat or spray the inside of a medium-size skillet with cooking oil.

Peel the zucchini, if desired. Slice it crosswise into pieces about ⅛-inch thick and lay the pieces side by side in the prepared skillet.

If adding tomato, discard the stem and dice. If you prefer the tomato peeled, drop it into boiling water for a minute or two and then slip off the peel. Add on top of the zucchini.

If adding onion, discard the stem and peel. Dice and add on top of the zucchini.

On medium heat, cook until the veggies are tender, about 10–15 minutes. Season as desired.

Variations:

↬ Add half of a green bell pepper. Discard the stem, seeds, and membranes. Dice and add with the other veggies. After the softer veggies are tender, stir occasionally. Cook the dish slightly longer if you are using bell pepper.

↬ For hot flavor, add half of a jalapeño pepper. Discard stem, seeds, and membranes. Slice the jalapeño crosswise. Cook the dish slightly longer if you are using jalapeño.

↬ Use yellow crookneck squash instead of zucchini. Cut the larger slices in half to get similar-size pieces.

Yield: 2–3 servings

BREADED ZUCCHINI

Slice a zucchini, as above. Before placing the pieces in a skillet, dip them in flour or a mixture of water, flour, and egg. Fry the breaded zucchini on medium to medium-low heat until golden brown.

> These soft summer squashes do not usually need to be peeled. However, you may prefer to discard the peels and seeds of older squashes.
> Zucchini tastes very different from other summer squashes.

CHAPTER 4: FRUIT and FRUIT SALADS

The symbol ▼ marks healthier recipe choices.

FRESH FRUIT TRAY

Apple Slices: Rinse thoroughly; discard stems and core. Slice the apple and immediately dip the slices in water with lemon juice to prevent discoloring. (This ascorbic acid mix is corn-free.)

Banana Slices: Peel, slice, and give the slices toothpick handles.

Strawberries: Rinse thoroughly. Leaves can stay on for a fruit tray.

Grapes: Green, Concord, or red. Rinse thoroughly. Grapes can stay on the stem, but cut the stems to make smaller bunches of grapes. Try the tiny, sweet champagne grapes (July to September).

Cherries: Rinse thoroughly. Stems can stay on for a fruit tray.

Pineapple Wedges: Cut the skin and center out of the pineapple; cut the rings into wedges. Or cheat and use canned pineapple wedges—not packed in corn syrup.

Honeydew Melon: Slice the melon; discard the center with seeds. Slice and cut into chunks or use a melon baller to make bite-sized melon balls.

Choose 5 or more favorite fruits that can be prepared in bite-sized pieces.

You can use small fruits whole (berries, grapes, cherries). Apples and bananas need to be sliced. Apples also need to be dipped in acid-water to prevent browning. You can cut other fruits (melons, pineapple) into balls or wedges and give them toothpick handles.

Rinse the raw fruits thoroughly in cold water. Avoid commercial vegetable-cleaning products since they contain corn. Prepare small whole fruits and/or small pieces that can be eaten raw as finger food. Arrange fruits on the tray by alternating colors and shapes. Serve cold.

Provide more toothpicks, napkins, and small plates. Crackers also go well with fruit trays.

Yield: about 1 cup of fruit per person

To prevent discoloration, you can dip fruit pieces in water with lemon juice. Use 2–3 tablespoons lemon juice in about 1 quart of water.

Variations:

ᕫ Orange and tangerine slices come prepackaged by nature. Peel the orange, separate the sections and you have orange slices for the fruit tray. Watch out, though—they drip, so be sure to provide napkins.

ᕫ **Blueberries (May to September), and/or Raspberries (June to September):** Rinse and sort out bad ones. Remove any stems.

ᕫ **Cantaloupe (June to November) and/or Watermelon (May to August):** Prepare like honeydew melon.

ᕫ **Cherries (May to August) and/or Rainier Cherries (May to June):** Rinse thoroughly. Stems can stay on for a fruit tray.

ᕫ More unusual choices include mango, papaya, guava, kumquats, and star fruit.

For more information about choosing, storing, and preparing fruit, see *Dr. Richter's Fresh Produce Guide* by Henry Richter, Ph.D.

FRESH, CANNED, AND FROZEN FRUIT

Fresh: Fruit tastes great and offers the most vitamins per calorie if eaten fresh. Peeled fruit is safe to eat. Otherwise, wash the fruit with cold water or a mixture of water and lemon juice (about 1 quart water to 2–3 tablespoons lemon juice). Commercial products for washing fruit contain ascorbic acid, usually made from corn.

Storage: Fruits ripen and spoil faster when kept next to each other in airtight spaces, such as airtight plastic bags or boxes. A green plastic bag, called an Evert-Fresh Bag, can keep fruit or veggies weeks longer without spoiling. If your grocery store does not carry them, see Evert Corporation under Resource Guide, page 266.

Canned: Fruit is often canned "in heavy syrup." Guess what kind of syrup. Yes, corn syrup. Even fruit canned without syrup may contain ascorbic acid to replace the vitamin C destroyed by the canning process. Ascorbic acid in the U.S. today is usually made from corn. You're safer if you use fruit with one ingredient only, the name of the fruit, e.g., "Ingredient: peaches," "Ingredient: pineapple." You get the idea.

Frozen: Fruit can be frozen in syrup or in pieces. You may have issues with both. Pieces of frozen fruit may have a fine dusting of cornstarch to prevent sticking. Wash these very thoroughly or freeze your own. See Freezing Fruit on page 84.

Juice: Much of fruit's soluble fiber is lost when it is juiced. If you have digestive reactions from food intolerance, you need soluble fiber. Still, as beverages go, fruit juice can have more fiber and vitamins than soda pop. Since you may be replacing soda pop with fruit juice, consider the options.

↳ **Fresh fruit juice:** Wash and squeeze your own. Safe, right? Not if you use commercial fruit washes, which contain ascorbic acid, probably made from corn. Use cold water or a mixture of water and lemon juice (1 quart water to 2–3 tablespoons lemon juice).

↳ **Canned fruit juice:** Is it really juice? Many fruit drinks are made from water, corn syrup, and a little fruit flavoring. Check the label for one ingredient: fruit juice.

↳ **Frozen fruit juice:** Again, is it really juice? Like regular fruit juice, frozen fruit drinks can also be made from water and corn syrup. Again, look for a single ingredient.

↳ **Powdered fruit juice:** Again, is it really juice? As above, check the label.

Watch out for corn syrup and/or ascorbic acid (usually made from corn) in any fruit product, fruit wash, or fruit freshener.

FREEZING FRUIT

1–2   quarts small berries in season (strawberries, blueberries,
           raspberries, blackberries, cranberries, etc.)
Pint or quart plastic boxes

Wash the berries, preferably in a colander. Discard stems and any berries that are bad. Cut out any bad spots; otherwise, leave the berries whole.

Place the berries on a baking sheet to dry. Use a paper towel under them, if desired, to help absorb moisture. Remove any paper towels once the berries are dry. If desired, set the baking sheet with berries directly into the freezer to cool and freeze quickly.

Select the size of plastic boxes according to the quantities you will want to use. (Avoid plastic bags, which may be made partly of corn.) Place the cooled or frozen berries in the boxes.

Spread the boxes around inside the freezer to freeze more quickly. Once frozen, the berry boxes may be stacked for more convenience.

Variations:

⤷ To freeze cherries or peach slices, add a little sugar to retain color. To pit cherries, make a small cut at the stem end and pick out the pit with the end of a vegetable peeler.

⤷ To freeze fruit with syrup, clean and cut the fruit. Then cover it with sugar, to taste. Allow the sugared fruit to stand, refrigerated, for 15–20 minutes. This will create the syrup. Place the fruit and syrup in short plastic boxes, such as sandwich boxes. Spread the boxes around inside the freezer to freeze quickly. You can stack the boxes later.

⤷ Freeze orange slices (sections) for popsicles!

Yield: 1–2 quarts frozen berries

TO USE FROZEN BERRIES: Thaw the berries in the refrigerator or at room temperature. Use the berries like fresh berries in recipes such as berry muffins, pancakes, syrups, etc. For berries with syrup, add sugar to frozen or thawed berries. Let the mixture stand (about 15–20 minutes), and the mixture will create berry syrup, such as strawberries or peaches with syrup for shortcake.

LEMONADE

1	cup water
¼–⅓	cup sugar, to taste
2	lemons
	Ice cubes

Boil 1 cup of water. Melt the sugar in the boiling water.

Juice the lemons. You should have about 6 tablespoons of fresh-squeezed juice.

Fill a 1-quart jar (32 ounces) with ice cubes. Add the lemon juice and sugar-water. Fill the rest of the jar with cold water.

Serve cold.

Variation: Add the juice of 1 lime for a lemon-lime flavor.

Yield: 4 servings

> Lemonade from the grocery store usually contains corn syrup.
> You may need to make extra of this recipe because you and your friends will
> get spoiled to the delicious taste of fresh lemonade!

SWEET ORANGE ICE

4	ice cubes
6–8	ounces orange juice, preferably fresh-squeezed
1	Tablespoon nonfat dry milk (or 2 Tablespoons corn-free yogurt, sherbet, soy milk, or rice milk—optional)
1	Tablespoon sugar (optional, to taste)

Put the ice cubes in a blender and pulse the blender to break up the ice.

If you are using fresh-squeezed orange juice, juice the oranges. They can be cut in half and squeezed by hand, but it works better to use an electric juicer or a hand juicer. Add the orange juice.

Add the dry milk and sugar, if desired. Pulse, whip, chop, and blend until the ice is crushed and the mixture is smooth.

Yield: 1 serving

> For fresh-squeezed orange juice, use juice oranges, which are smaller and
> heavier than eating oranges.

BANANA-STRAWBERRY SMOOTHIE

4	ice cubes (about ¾ cup crushed ice)
⅓–½	banana
4–8	ounces strawberries
4	ounces blueberries (optional)
1	Tablespoon nonfat dry milk (or 2 Tablespoons corn-free yogurt, sherbet, soy milk, or rice milk—optional)
1	Tablespoon sugar (optional, to taste)

Put the ice cubes in a blender and pulse the blender to break up the ice.

Add the banana. Rinse the strawberries and discard the stems. Add the strawberries. Add the blueberries, dry milk, and sugar, if desired.

Pulse, whip, chop, and blend until the ice is crushed and the mixture is smooth.

Yield: 1 serving

CUSTOM-MADE SMOOTHIE

4	ice cubes
½	cup fruit (banana, berries, fruit juice, guava, mango, etc.)
½	cup another kind of fruit (juice, chunks, berries, etc.)
1	Tablespoon nonfat dry milk (and/or sugar—optional, to taste)

Prepare as above.

Variations: Try Banana-Apple, Lemon-Strawberry, or Banana-Pineapple-Coconut.

Yield: 1 serving

APPLE SALAD

3	Tablespoons mayonnaise
1	Tablespoon lemon juice (or vinegar or milk—optional, to taste)
1	Tablespoon sugar (optional, to taste)
¼	teaspoon paprika (or mustard powder—optional, to taste)
2	apples, diced
1	stalk celery, diced
⅓	cup chopped walnuts (optional)
¼	cup raisins (optional)

In a medium bowl combine the mayonnaise, lemon juice, sugar, and paprika. Stir until creamy.

Cut the apples and stir them into the dressing immediately to prevent discoloration.

Stir in the celery, walnuts, and raisins, as desired.

Chill at least 5 minutes before serving.

Note: This salad is best with a crisp, crunchy type apple. Use softer apples for cooking.

Yield: 2 servings

Many grocery store produce sections contain the booklet *Dr. Richter's Fresh Produce Guide*. This little gem can tell you all about different kinds of apples as well as many other fruits, vegetables, and herbs.
It's an excellent resource to help you prepare fresh, corn-free food.

9 double?

TUNA-APPLE SALAD

4	Tablespoons mayonnaise
1	Tablespoon lemon juice (apple vinegar or water—optional, to taste)
¼	teaspoon paprika (or mustard powder—optional, to taste)
⅛	teaspoon dill weed (optional, to taste)
1	teaspoon sugar (optional, to taste)
1–2	apples, diced
1	6-oz. can tuna

In a medium bowl combine the mayonnaise, lemon juice, paprika, dill weed, and sugar. Stir until creamy.

Cut the apples and stir them into the dressing immediately to prevent discoloration. Add the tuna. (For a milder fish flavor, break up the chunks of tuna.) Stir.

Serve immediately.

Note: Salad is best with a crisp, crunchy type of apple. Use softer apples for cooking.

Variations:

↪ Add ¼–½ cup diced broccoli florets.

↪ Add a pinch of salt, pepper, and/or other fish-friendly seasonings (see the Spice Chart Appendix on page 257).

Yield: 2 servings

Though this salad tastes best fresh, you can carry it for lunch. Use a tightly sealed container and keep it chilled, not frozen. The salad will keep overnight, refrigerated, but the flavor may change.

STRAWBERRY SHORTCAKE

Preheat oven to 450° • Baking time: 10–12 minutes

24	ounces strawberries, fresh or frozen (unsweetened)
3–5	Tablespoons sugar (to taste)
1	cup flour
1½	teaspoons corn-free baking powder (see page 11)
¼	teaspoon corn-free salt
1	Tablespoon sugar
1	Tablespoon cooking oil
⅓	cup cool water (or milk)
	Milk (optional)
	Whipped cream (optional)

Cut the leaves and tops off of the strawberries and slice larger berries. Add the sugar and stir. Cover and refrigerate while making the shortcake; the fruit and sugar mixture creates strawberries with juice.

Preheat the oven to 450°.

In a separate bowl combine the flour, baking powder, salt, and sugar. Stir. Add the oil and stir. At this point, the mixture will form uneven crumbles of flour and oil.

Add the water or milk. Stir the dough until it forms a ball and cleans the sides of the mixing bowl. (If the dough does not clean the bowl, see the note below.)

Form the dough into 4–6 balls and drop them onto an ungreased cookie sheet.

Bake at 450° for 10–12 minutes, until lightly golden-brown.

Serve the shortcake warm, topped with strawberries and their juice. Milk and/or whipped cream can be added.

Note: Dough that is too wet will be sticky and will not clean the sides of the bowl as it is stirred. Sprinkle 1 tablespoon of flour over the dough if the dough is too wet. Dough that is too dry will break apart and fail to form a ball as it is stirred. Sprinkle 1 tablespoon of water over the dough if the dough is too dry.

Yield: 2 servings

CRANBERRY SAUCE

1–2   oranges (optional)
1   12-oz. package cranberries
1   apple, diced (optional)
½–1   cup sugar (or brown sugar—to taste)
⅓   cup honey (optional)

If you are using oranges, peel them and cut them into quarters. Discard the seeds.

Rinse the cranberries; remove any stems and bad berries. Place the cranberries and orange pieces in a blender a few at a time, and use the pulse feature to chop (not blend) the fruit.

If you are using an apple, peel and core it. Dice the apple into small pieces.

In a serving bowl place the fruit along with the sugar and honey, if desired, stir, and chill.

Variations:

⤷ Add 1 cup chopped pecans or walnuts.

⤷ Add a pinch of cinnamon and a pinch of nutmeg. Or use ¼ teaspoon allspice.

⤷ Add ½ cup chopped dried fruit, such as raisins or dried apricots.

⤷ Add ½ cup chopped raspberries.

Yield: 8–12 servings

COOKED CRANBERRY SAUCE

Use the quantities above but omit the honey. Boil the sugar in 1 cup of water until it dissolves.

Lower the heat and simmer all ingredients, stirring occasionally, until the cranberries burst (about 30 minutes). Remove from the heat and allow the sauce to cool before serving.

Most commercial cranberry jells and sauces contain corn syrup.
For plain cranberry condiment, buy fresh cranberries and add sugar.
Either chop the berries in a blender and add sugar or cook them in water and sugar until the cranberries burst.

GRAPEFRUIT BOWL

1	grapefruit
1	orange (optional)
6–8	sweet cherries, in season (optional)
6–8	sweet red or green grapes, in season (optional)
6–8	melon balls, in season (optional)
1	avocado (optional)

Wash the grapefruit well in cold water. Cut the grapefruit in half crosswise, halfway between the stem and the bottom end. Remove the seeds. In each half grapefruit, slice along the membranes and skin to remove all the grapefruit wedges. Slice the wedges in half and place them in a bowl. Set aside.

Remove the center and radial membranes from both halves of the grapefruit skin to make bowls of the skin. If desired, cut the top edge of each bowl in a decorative zigzag.

If you are using two or more other fruits, reduce the quantities to fit into the grapefruit bowls.

If you are using an orange, peel the orange and break it in half. Remove the seeds and center membranes. Separate the orange slices and cut them in half. Stir them gently with the grapefruit pieces.

Prepare and add other fruit pieces, as desired. For cherries and grapes, remove stems and cut in half. For melon (honeydew, cantaloupe, and/or watermelon), cut balls with a melon baller. Stir gently into the grapefruit mixture.

If you are using avocado, cut it in half, remove the pit, peel, and slice. Cut the slices in half. Sprinkle with grapefruit or lemon juice to retain color. Do not stir avocado with other fruit pieces; it will disintegrate.

Spoon the fruit pieces into generous mounds in the grapefruit bowls. If you are using avocado, spoon in a few pieces of avocado after each spoonful of other fruits. Serve immediately.

Variations:

↪ Garnish the fruit with shredded coconut.

↪ For a sweeter fruit mix, stir about 1 tablespoon sugar, to taste, with the grapefruit pieces before adding other fruits.

Yield: 2 servings

MANDARIN ORANGE SALAD

½   cup sliced almonds
3   Tablespoons sugar
¼   cup cooking oil
2   Tablespoons apple cider vinegar
2   Tablespoons sugar
½   teaspoon corn-free salt
Dash   pepper
¼   teaspoon dried parsley flakes (or 1 Tablespoon fresh
     chopped parsley)
½   head romaine lettuce (about 1 cup of torn or cut pieces)
½   head iceberg lettuce (about 1 cup of torn or cut pieces)
1   cup chopped celery
2   green onion stalks (scallions), chopped (optional)
1   11-oz. can mandarin oranges, drained

In a dry skillet heat the almonds and sugar, stirring constantly until the sugar melts and coats the almonds. Remove from the heat and chill the nuts in an airtight container.

In a small bowl mix the oil, vinegar, sugar, salt, pepper, and parsley. Set aside.

Chop or tear the lettuce into pieces; chop the celery and scallions. Combine.

The salad greens may be chilled for up to 20 minutes. If chilling, wait until serving time to add the oranges, almonds, and dressing.

Drain the mandarin oranges.

Add the oranges, almonds, and dressing to the greens. Toss and serve immediately.

Yield: 6 servings

AVOCADO SLICES

2   avocados
2–3   lettuce leaves
1   Tablespoon lemon or lime juice
Dash   corn-free salt (optional)
Dash   sugar (optional)

Chill the ripe avocados.

Rinse the lettuce leaves and lay each in a salad bowl.

Cut the avocados in half and remove the pits. Slice the avocado halves, and lay the slices on a leaf of lettuce in the salad bowls. Sprinkle lemon or lime juice over the avocado slices immediately to prevent browning. Sprinkle on salt and sugar, if desired.

Serve cold.

Yield: 2–3 servings

Avocados come in two varieties. Hass avocados are dark and rough-skinned. Hass avocados make great guacamole. Florida avocados are green and smooth-skinned. They may contain less fat and calories. Some people prefer Florida avocados for eating slices.

CHERRY SYRUP

½   cup cherry liquid (drained from 1 can of red tart pie cherries)
¾   cup sugar
⅛   teaspoon lemon juice (optional, to retain color)

Place the cherry liquid in a saucepan. Stir in the sugar.

Quickly bring the mixture to a boil over medium heat, stirring frequently. Raise or lower the temperature slightly, as needed. Stir constantly and boil the mixture until it foams.

Continue stirring and boiling for about 1 minute, until the mixture does not pour off a spoon like water but like a very thin syrup. Do not overcook; the syrup will thicken more as it cools.

Stir in any seasoning variations desired (see below).

Allow the syrup to cool at room temperature. Serve warm.

Store leftover syrup in the refrigerator and warm to serve, if desired.

Yield: ½ cup

Variation: Add a pinch of cinnamon or nutmeg or mint after adding the berries.

STRAWBERRY, RASPBERRY, or BLUEBERRY SYRUP

equipment needed: cheesecloth to strain out the berry seeds

1¼   cups fresh strawberries, raspberries, or blueberries

Crush the berries using a blender or with the back of a spoon or a small-hole potato masher.

Fold the cheesecloth over 3 or 4 times. Strain the crushed berries through several layers of cheesecloth to remove skins and seeds.

Follow the Cherry Syrup recipe above, substituting ½ cup of this berry juice in place of the cherry liquid.

Variation: Combine favorite berries for your own special syrup.

When the syrup is boiling, the sugar is very close to burning. It needs constant attention and stirring. When the syrup is done, it will take several minutes to cool enough to touch or taste.

CHAPTER 5: PROTEINS / MAIN DISHES

Beef

Chicken and Turkey

Fish

Eggs

Pork

Lamb

Beans

The symbol ▼ marks healthier recipe choices.

HAMBURGERS

1   **pound ground beef, ground chuck roast, or other ground meat**
¼ – ½ **teaspoon corn-free salt (optional, to taste)**
⅛– ¼ **teaspoon pepper (optional, to taste)**

Salt (and any seasonings) may be mixed into the raw meat before form-ing hamburger patties or sprinkled on uncooked meat in the pan.

Form the meat into 4 hamburger patties.

Heat a medium-size skillet until a drop of water dances (hotter than a drop that sizzles). Place the hamburgers in the hot skillet and brown them briefly on each side. Turn down the heat to medium or medium-low.

Do not cover the pan unless you prefer the flavor of steamed meat. Use a spatter-lid (a round screen with a handle), or else the spattering grease will coat your stove-top.

After the meat is cooked partway, turn the hamburger patties with a spatula. If you are using meat with a high fat content, be sure to drain the excess fat from the pan occasionally.

Let the hamburgers cook to the preferred taste—rare (mostly pink in-side), medium (a little pink inside), or medium-well (almost no pink in-side). To test, separate the center of the hamburger with a fork, and check the color.

Serve with bread and condiments such as lettuce, sliced onions, and tomatoes. For ketchup or mustard, see variations below.

Variations:

◑ Commercial ketchup usually contains corn syrup. See corn-free Ketchup on page 77.

◑ Add ¼ teaspoon mustard powder, to taste. For a Dijon flavor, add a little cooking wine. (Commercial mustard paste usually contains corn de-rivatives.)

◑ Add 1 teaspoon onion powder or flakes (optional). Use fresh diced onion, if preferred. Or you can add sliced onions to the pan to sauté with the meat.

◑ Add ¼ teaspoon garlic powder or flakes. Use 1 fresh minced garlic clove, if preferred.

◑ Add ½ teaspoon chili powder, or tarragon, or rosemary.

Yield: 4 servings

CRUMBLE-FRIED HAMBURGER

1	pound ground beef, ground chuck roast, or other ground meat
¼–½	teaspoon corn-free salt (optional, to taste)
⅛–¼	teaspoon pepper (optional, to taste)

Heat a skillet until a drop of water dances (hotter than a drop that sizzles). Break the meat apart and place the meat chunks in the hot skillet. Use the end of a spatula to cut the meat chunks into smaller pieces.

Sprinkle the salt, pepper, and any other seasonings on the meat, as desired (see variations below).

Turn down the heat to medium or medium-low. Do not cover the pan unless you prefer the flavor of steamed meat. Use a spatter-lid (a round screen with a handle), or else the spattering grease will coat your stove top.

When the meat begins to brown, use the end of the spatula to cut it into smaller and smaller pieces. Stir and turn the meat. Continue cutting and stirring until the meat is the size desired, large or small chunks, or fine crumbles.

If you are using meat with a high fat content, be sure to drain the excess fat from the pan occasionally.

Let the crumble-fried hamburger cook to the preferred taste—rare (light brown), medium (brown), or medium-well (dark brown).

Variations:

⤳ Add 1 teaspoon onion powder or flakes (optional.) Use fresh diced onion, if preferred. Or you can add sliced onions to the pan and let them sauté with the meat.

⤳ Add ¼ teaspoon garlic powder or flakes. Use 1 fresh minced garlic clove, if preferred.

⤳ Add ½ teaspoon chili powder.

⤳ Add ½ teaspoon tarragon or cilantro. Pepper goes well with both of these.

Yield: 3–4 servings

For lower calories, use meat with 7 percent fat.

You can use Crumble-fried Hamburger with hash-brown potatoes or in spaghetti sauce, macaroni, or soups. Try it with White Sauce (page 160) over biscuits, on a bed of rice, or with mashed potatoes or yams.

BEEF STEW

1–2   pounds stewing beef
       Water
5   large red potatoes, peeled and cut up (optional, to taste)
3   carrots, sliced (optional, to taste)
1   stalk of celery, peeled and sliced or diced (optional, to taste)
       Pepper and other seasonings, to taste

Use a crock pot or a large kettle with a lid that seals tightly. Cut any pieces of gristle or large pieces of fat from the stewing beef. Cut any over-large pieces in half. Place the beef pieces in the crock pot or kettle. Cover the meat with water. Add salt to taste. Cover the pot and begin heating on medium while you prepare the veggies.

Wash, peel, and cut the potatoes into large chunks. Wash, peel, and slice the carrots. Add the pieces to the stew as they are ready. Prepare any other vegetables desired, and add them to the stew. Stir and add more water to almost cover the stewing meat and veggies.

Turn the heat down and barely simmer for several hours. A stove-top kettle may be faster, 1–3 hours. A slow-cooking crock pot can stew for 4–6 hours unattended.

When the stew is done, the meat is brown through and falling apart, the vegetables are soft, and potatoes may begin to melt into the stewing liquid.

When the stew is almost done, add pepper and/or other seasonings as desired. Serve in bowls with bread or biscuits on the side.

Variations:

↩ Fresh onion or garlic can be added when the temperature is turned down. If you prefer to use pepper or herbs (such as parsley, sage, rosemary, thyme, basil, oregano, tarragon, cilantro, etc.), add them 10–15 minutes before the stew is done. Pepper and many herbs can turn bitter or lose flavor when heated too long or at too high a temperature.

↩ Add a few tablespoons of red wine (cooking wine).

↩ Add 1 bell pepper, sliced or diced, to taste. Wash the pepper and discard stem, seeds, and membranes. Slice or dice the pepper and add it to the stew. If desired, add chili powder or cilantro and pepper 10–15 minutes before the stew is done.

Yield: 4–6 servings

COVERED ROAST BEEF

Preheat oven to 375° • Total cooking time: 3–5 hours

2½ pounds roasting beef
  Seasonings such as salt, pepper, onion, garlic, bay leaf, herbs
  (optional)

Turn on the oven to 375°. Remove and discard any strings on the beef. Wipe the beef with a damp cloth to remove any small chips of bone. If desired, remove larger pieces of fat.

Heat a pan for browning the meat. At the correct temperature, water droplets sprinkled into the pan will dance, not sizzle. Brown the beef on all sides; when done, it will lift easily.

Put the beef in a small roasting pan, fat side up. Cover the pan tightly and roast at 375° for about 1 hour. If the lid does not seal tightly, the roast will need a few tablespoons of water added to replace the steam lost.

After an hour, turn the oven down to 275°. Sprinkle the meat with salt, pepper, onion, and/or garlic, if desired. Put bay leaves on top, if desired. Continue roasting for about 2 more hours (rare, firm, pink in the center) or 3 more hours (medium) or 4 more hours (well done, very tender, meat falling apart). If you start with frozen beef, add a half-hour or more to the roasting time.

Discard bay leaves before serving. Serve au jus (with meat juices) or add gravy and/or Yorkshire pudding. (See the next few pages for gravy and Yorkshire pudding recipes.)

Note: To use a meat thermometer, insert it into the center of the roast. A rare roast (pink in the center) will read at least 140°. A medium reading is about 160°.

Variations:
↩ **Seasonings:** Fresh onion or garlic can be added when the temperature is turned down to 275°. If you prefer to use herbs (such as parsley, sage, rosemary, thyme, tarragon, cilantro, etc.), add them 10–15 minutes before the roast is done.

Roasting meat creates its own juices. Vegetables add to the juice.
If the roasting pan lid does not seal tightly, add a few tablespoons of water to replace the steam lost. If you prefer more meat juices, see Beef Stew on the previous page.

↪ **Pot Roast:** Add chunks of larger vegetables (such as potatoes, carrots, onions, celery, etc.) when the temperature is turned down to 275°.

↪ **Stove top:** Use a large kettle with a lid that seals tightly. Heat the roast on the stove top instead of in the oven. Start with the burner on medium or medium-low heat, until the meat juices form and simmer. Then turn the burner down to a very low heat, just enough to keep the juices barely simmering for the remaining roasting time.

Yield: 5 servings

CLASSIC ROAST BEEF

Preheat oven to 450° • Total cooking time: 1½–2 hours

3	**pounds tender roasting beef, such as standing or rolled rib or rump roasts**
1	**clove garlic**
	Fresh ground black pepper (optional)

Lower the oven rack below halfway. Preheat the oven to 450°.

Choose a roasting pan or dish just large enough to hold the meat easily, fat side up. Coat or spray the pan or dish lightly with cooking oil.

Discard any strings tied around the meat. Wipe the meat with a damp cloth, or rinse it quickly in cold water to remove any bits of bone. If desired, rub the meat with a clove of garlic or fresh ground black pepper.

Place the meat in the roasting pan, fat side up. Place the meat in the oven and roast for 20 minutes. Then lower the temperature to 325°. Roast for another 75–80 minutes.

A meat thermometer inserted into the center of the roast, not touching bone or fat, will read 130°–140° for a rare to medium-rare roast.

If you prefer medium to medium-well, see variations below.

Serve au jus (with meat juices), or add gravy and/or Yorkshire pudding.

Variations:

↪ For more seasonings, marinade the meat before roasting.

↪ For au jus, remove the meat from the pan and place it on a serving platter, covered to keep warm. Skim the fat off the top of the meat drippings. Add about a half cup of red wine or water to the drippings and simmer this on the stove top. Salt, pepper, and season to taste.

↪ This uncovered and unbasted method works best for rare and medium-rare roast. If you prefer meat that is not pink in the center, consider Covered Roast Beef on page 100.

(continued on next page)

(continued from previous page)

⤷ For longer roasting times, you may want to baste the meat occasionally. Draw the meat drippings (from below the fat) into a basting tube and drizzle the liquid over the meat. If the roast starts drying out, in spite of basting, you may need rescue it by covering it. The meat thermometer will read about 160° for a medium roast. For medium-well, the center of the roast will be light brown, not pink.

Yield: 3–6 servings (boneless cuts will yield more meat)

GRAVY

2	cups meat drippings from Roast Beef or Roast Beef Stew (see pages 99–100)
2	Tablespoons flour (or arrowroot powder)
¼	cup cold water

Half-fill a medium-size skillet with meat drippings (about 2 cups or less). Mix the flour with ¼ cup cold water. Stir until smooth. Pour this mixture slowly into the meat drippings, while stirring. Be sure to mix completely before further heating.

Bring to a boil, stirring constantly to avoid lumps.

⤷ **Alternate method:** Bring the drippings to a boil and stir in the flour-water mixture a spoonful at a time while maintaining the boil and stirring constantly to avoid lumps.

YORKSHIRE PUDDING

Preheat oven to 425° • Cooking time: 20 minutes

1	cup flour
1	cup cold water (or milk)
½	teaspoon corn-free salt
2	eggs
½	cup hot meat drippings

Preheat the oven to 425°. In a medium bowl stir the flour, cold water or milk, and salt until smooth. Stir in the eggs; do not overbeat.

Classic Yorkshire pudding is oven-baked and served with roast beef. Pour ½ cup hot meat drippings into a small baking pan. Pour the batter into the middle of the pan. Leave the roast in the oven and raise the temperature to 425°. Bake the batter at 425° until puffed, golden-brown, and crisp, about 20 minutes.

Variations:

Without roast: Coat a small baking pan with 2 tablespoons of cooking oil. Add 1 tablespoon water. Pour the batter into the middle of the pan. Bake at 425° for about 20 minutes.

Stove-top: Coat a medium-size frying pan with 2 tablespoons cooking oil. Pour the batter into the middle of the pan. Set a lid on the pan, off to one side, to allow moisture to dissipate. Cook on low to medium-low heat for about 8 minutes. Turn the batter after the egg is no longer liquid. Cook until the pudding is puffed, golden-brown, and crisp, about 8 minutes more.

Yield: 2–4 servings

CHICKEN WITH APPLES

1	can corn-free apple juice concentrate (frozen, undiluted)
2	boneless, skinless chicken breasts, diced
1–2	Tablespoons oil (for browning)
2	cooking apples, such as Granny Smith
1	teaspoon lemon juice
	Corn-free salt (optional, to taste)

Set the apple juice concentrate out to thaw.

Dice the chicken breasts to 1-inch cubes or slightly smaller. You may find it easier to cut the chicken if it is partially frozen.

Heat a medium skillet and add the oil and chicken pieces.

Brown chicken lightly in the oil. Add apple pieces, apple juice concentrate, and lemon juice. Stir. Add salt to taste, and stir.

Simmer the mixture for 10–15 minutes, until the chicken pieces are white throughout with no pink.

Variations:

↳ For 3–4 servings, use 3–4 chicken breasts and apples instead of 2.

↳ Add ½ onion, to taste. Cut up the onion and sauté the pieces in the oil with the chicken. Or use 1 tablespoon dried onion powder and add it with the chicken pieces.

↳ Add 2 garlic cloves, to taste. Mince the garlic and sauté the pieces in the oil with the chicken. Or use ¼ teaspoon garlic powder and add it with the chicken pieces.

Yield: 2 servings

Raw chicken may contain bacteria. Be sure to cook the chicken through and clean your hands, all counters, and all utensils thoroughly after contact with raw chicken.

STOVE-TOP CHICKEN DUMPLINGS
Cooking time: 35–40 minutes

1   10-oz. can corn-free chicken broth
2   cans cold water (20 oz.)
5   Tablespoons flour
1   recipe Dumpling Batter (see below)
¼   teaspoon corn-free salt (optional, to taste)
⅛   teaspoon pepper (optional, to taste)
2   Tablespoons cooking oil (or corn-free margarine—optional, to
        taste)
2   5-oz. cans chicken pieces (or use leftover diced, cooked chicken)

In a large skillet or saucepan, stir together the chicken broth, cold water, and flour until smooth. Bring the mixture to a boil while stirring frequently. Remove from heat. Stir in salt and pepper to taste.

Make Dumpling Batter (below), and then put the skillet back on the heat. Stir in the oil and chicken pieces. Drop in the dumpling batter by spoonfuls.

Cover the mixture and simmer for 35–40 minutes, until the dumplings are cooked through. Stir occasionally and add water, if needed.

Variations:
↘ Spray a baking dish with cooking oil. Add the mixture. Bake at 250° for about 30 minutes, until the top is golden brown.

↘ Add 2–6 oz. frozen peas, frozen diced carrots, and/or onions. Simmer for another 5 minutes.

Yield: 4 servings

DUMPLING BATTER

1½   cups flour
½   teaspoon corn-free salt
3   teaspoons corn-free baking powder
2   Tablespoons cooking oil
⅔   cup cool water (or milk)

In a mixing bowl combine the flour, salt, and baking powder and stir. Add the oil and stir. The mixture will form uneven crumbles of flour and oil. Add water or milk. Stir until mostly smooth.

ROAST CHICKEN
Preheat oven to 375° • Total cooking time: 1½–3 hours

3–5   **pounds roasting chicken**
       Butter (or cooking oil)
       Salt and/or seasonings (see page 108)

If you want to stuff the chicken, begin with the Chicken Stuffing recipe, page 107.

Remove the giblets and any extra pieces of fat. Rinse the chicken inside and out. If desired, stuff the cavity loosely.

Set the chicken in a small roasting pan, breast side up. Coat the meat with melted butter or cooking oil. Tuck the wing tips under. If you want, cross the drumsticks and tie them together. (Cotton string can scorch; use linen kitchen string.) Untie the drumsticks for the last half hour of roasting.

Sprinkle or rub the meat with salt. Avoid a seasoning rub with herbs or black pepper; they can scorch or turn bitter in the oven. If you are using spices or chili peppers in a sauce or stuffing, you may want to rub those seasonings on the meat. For choices, see page 108.

To reduce spatters, make an aluminum foil tent over the meat loose enough to allow steam to escape. Avoid touching the meat with the foil. Or for more moist meat, wrap the chicken tightly in the foil.

Roast at 375° for 1–2 hours. Baste occasionally, if desired.

Larger quantities take longer; preheating shortens the roasting time slightly. When the meat is done, leg joints move easily and the meat will be white or brown throughout, with no pink inside. Pepper may taste better if you add it at the table or about 10 minutes before the chicken is done. Cool for about 10 minutes before carving. Serve (and store) stuffing separately.

Variations: You can roast chicken plain, with just salt. If you use a poultry seasoning, read ingredients to avoid chemicals made from corn. See page 108 for some of the many herbs, spices, and mixtures to try with chicken.

Yield: 3–5 servings

CAUTION: Avoid plastic roasting bags; they are usually contain corn.

CHICKEN STUFFING

4	cups dry bread or light toast (about 5 slices)
¼	cup minced onion (about a fourth of an onion—optional, to taste)
½	cup chopped celery (about 4 stalks—optional, to taste)
¼	cup butter (or cooking oil)
½	teaspoon corn-free salt (optional, to taste)
¼	teaspoon pepper (optional, to taste)
½	teaspoon dried parsley flakes (or 1½ teaspoons minced fresh parsley—optional, to taste)
¼	teaspoon thyme (or dried sage, marjoram, or rosemary—optional, to taste)

Stack the dry bread slices and cut them into cubes.

In a large skillet sauté the onion and celery in the oil, stirring occasionally. Stir in some of the bread cubes or crumbs. Brown the bread lightly, stirring occasionally. Turn off the heat.

Add the salt, pepper, parsley, and other seasonings to the skillet and stir well. Stir in the rest of the bread. Sprinkle on between 1 tablespoon and ½ cup of meat juices or water, depending on your preference for dry or moist stuffing.

Stuff the chicken before roasting. If you prefer, you can heat the stuffing (in a separate dish or pan) in the oven or on the stove top. Just boil a cup of water, remove it from heat, add the above mixture, and stir.

Variation: Instead of the seasonings above, use corn-free poultry seasoning or a mixture from the next page.

Yield: Stuffing for a 4-pound chicken

CAUTION: Always wash hands and utensils and any surfaces that come into contact with raw chicken. Raw chicken can harbor very unfriendly bacteria; fortunately, cooking kills the critters.

CHICKEN SEASONINGS: Choose one or several from one group. You may want to match the rub on the meat to one or several of the stuffing seasonings.

Onion, Garlic: Sprinkle chicken dishes and/or stuffing with onion and/or garlic powder before roasting. For better flavor, sauté diced onion and/or minced cloves of garlic.

Parsley, Herbs, Veggies: Use parsley, celery, and/or carrot. Or try parsley, sage, rosemary, and thyme (just like the song). Basil, marjoram, and savory also go with chicken. More unusual choices include bay leaf or dill and mustard powder.

Southwestern: With onion, add cilantro, paprika, and stronger chili peppers. Or use a salsa (see pages 42–45) to season the chicken in the oven or at the table.

Italian: Add basil, oregano, onion, and/or garlic. Spaghetti sauce works too.

French: Try chicken with tarragon, pepper, and lemon juice.

Asian: Add soy sauce, ginger, and five-spice powder, or an Oriental seasoning mix.

Indian: Use a curry powder or try garam masala with lemon juice, paprika, ginger, cumin, garlic, onion, and cayenne.

Onion and garlic are popular seasonings worldwide, nearly as common as salt and pepper. Herbs and mild flavors usually taste like foods from northern climates. Hotter places tend to use hotter spices.

BREADED AND ROASTED CHICKEN PIECES
Preheat oven to 325° • Cooking time: 40–50 minutes

3	chicken breasts, thighs, or drumsticks (16–20 ounces)
1	egg (optional)
½	cup flour
1	teaspoon corn-free salt (optional, to taste)
	Cooking oil

If you are using frozen chicken pieces, thaw them first. Remove skin, if desired, and extra pieces of fat. If you are using egg, stir the egg and dip the chicken pieces in it first.

Place the flour and salt in a bowl or paper bag. Put the chicken pieces in the flour one at a time. Turn each or shake the bag until the chicken piece is coated with flour and salt.

Put the chicken pieces on an oiled broiler pan or baking dish. Drizzle a little cooking oil over them. Roast the chicken (uncovered) at 325° for 40–50 minutes.

Baste with a little more oil every 15 minutes or so. After the last basting, sprinkle on seasonings, as desired (see variations below). The chicken is done when the meat is white, with no pink inside.

Variations:

↪ After the last basting, sprinkle on seasonings such as pepper, onion and/or garlic powder or flakes. Parsley flakes and paprika also go well with breaded chicken.

↪ Parsley, sage, rosemary, and/or thyme can go with or without pepper, onion, or garlic.

↪ For a Southwestern taste, add onion powder, black pepper, cilantro, and stronger chili powders. Or drench the chicken pieces with a salsa (see pages 42–45).

Yield: 3 servings

Commercial breading usually contains corn. Skinless, boneless breasts and other pieces can be purchased fresh or frozen but are often processed with additives. Read ingredients!

Raw chicken can harbor salmonella and other harmful bacteria. Be sure to wash your hands and any utensils and surfaces which may have come in contact with the raw meat. You may want to use an antibacterial soap or spray also.

TURKEY ROAST

Allow thawing time, possibly a day or more
Preheat oven to 325° • Cooking time: 4–5 hours

1   **8- to 12-pound roasting turkey**
        Butter (or cooking oil)
        Corn-free salt and seasonings

If the turkey is frozen, allow time to thaw it completely (see box below).

If you want to stuff the turkey, prepare the stuffing before handling the raw meat.

To clean the turkey, remove the giblets and any loose fat. Rinse the turkey in cold water, inside and out. If desired, rub salt in the cavity.

To stuff the turkey, set the head end in a bowl and spoon the stuffing loosely into the cavity.

If desired, rub the meat with butter or oil and salt. Avoid a seasoning rub with herbs or black pepper; they can scorch or turn bitter in the oven. If you do use spices or chili peppers in a sauce or stuffing, you may want to rub one or several of those seasonings on the meat. For a Turkey Glaze instead, see page 113.

Place the turkey in the roasting pan breast side up. Make a loose tent from aluminum foil over the meat to prevent spattering but still allow steam to escape. Avoid touching the meat with the foil. Lower the oven rack for a large turkey.

Roast the turkey at 325° for 4–5 hours. Time will vary with the size and temperature of the turkey. Uncover the turkey for the last 20–40 minutes of roasting. When the meat is done, leg joints move easily and the meat is white or brown throughout with no pink inside.

Remove the roasting pan with turkey from the oven, replace the foil cover, and allow the meat to stand for 5–10 minutes before carving. Serve (and store) stuffing separately.

Yield: 8–12 servings

Turkey is often sold frozen. Check with your butcher or the package for thawing directions and times. You can thaw a turkey for a day or more in the refrigerator (use a drip pan) or at room temperature (wrap in about 3 layers of newspaper). You can also thaw a turkey in cold water, changed frequently, in hours instead of days. Cook the turkey as soon as it is thawed.

CAUTION: Avoid plastic roasting bags; they are usually made from corn.

FOIL-WRAPPED TURKEY*

Total cooking time: 2¼–3 hours

Preheat the oven to 450°. Follow the instructions for Turkey Roast except roast the turkey in an aluminum foil wrap for faster cooking time and more moist meat. Before placing the turkey in the roasting pan, place it breast side up on aluminum foil. To wrap the turkey, bring the foil together at the top and fold down to touch the meat. To close, press the foil ends up. Cook up to 3 hours. For the last 20 minutes of cooking time, unfold and open the foil wrap.

*Note: Use foil wrap for juicy meat. Cook the foil-wrapped turkey longer at lower temperatures (300°–325°) for even more tender meat.

CAUTION: Wash hands, utensils, and any surfaces that contact raw poultry.

TURKEY STUFFING

6	cups cubed dry bread or light toast (about 8 slices of bread)
⅓	cup butter (or cooking oil)
⅓	cup finely minced onion (about ⅓ onion)
1	cup chopped celery (about 8 stalks)
1	teaspoon corn-free salt (optional, to taste)
½	teaspoon pepper (optional, to taste)
1	teaspoon dried parsley flakes or about 1 Tablespoon minced fresh parsley (optional, to taste)
½	teaspoon thyme, dried sage, marjoram, or rosemary (optional, to taste)

Stack the dry bread slices and cut them into cubes. Cut up the onion and celery.

In a large skillet meat the butter and sauté the onion and celery, stirring occasionally. Stir in some of the bread cubes or crumbs. Brown the bread lightly, stirring occasionally. Turn off the heat.

Add the salt, pepper, parsley, and other seasonings to the skillet and stir well. Sprinkle on between 2 tablespoons and ⅔ cup of meat juices or water, depending on your preference for dry or moist stuffing.

Stuff the turkey before roasting. If you prefer, you can heat the stuffing (in a separate dish or pan) in the oven or on the stove-top. Just boil a cup of water, remove it from heat, add the above mixture and stir.

Variation: Instead of the herb seasonings above, use corn-free poultry seasoning. Be sure to read ingredients; avoid chemicals made from corn.

Yield: Stuffing for an 8- to 10-pound turkey

TURKEY GLAZE

1	cup corn-free red currant jam
¼	cup apple cider vinegar
2	Tablespoons sugar (or honey)
¼	teaspoon corn-free red cooking wine (optional)*
⅛	teaspoon garlic (and/or mustard powder—optional)

You can substitute fresh currants or cranberries for the jam. Make them into syrup (see syrup recipe on page 94), and use this in place of the red currant jam.

In a medium saucepan combine all ingredients. Heat until boiling, stirring occasionally. Then reduce the heat and simmer for 2 minutes, stirring frequently.

During the last hour or two of roasting, brush the turkey with some of the glaze three separate times. Serve the remaining glaze on the side.

*Note: European red wines are typically corn-free; American wines may not be.

CREAMED TUNA

1½   cups cold milk (or skim milk or water)
3–4   Tablespoons flour
1   Tablespoon cooking oil (optional, to taste)
½   teaspoon corn-free salt (optional, to taste)
¼   teaspoon pepper (optional, to taste)
1   6-oz. can low-salt tuna

Pour the cold milk into a skillet and stir in the flour with a spatula. Mash out any lumps. Heat the mixture to a boil, stirring constantly and scraping the pan while heating. Boil until the mixture thickens into sauce. Add oil and salt and pepper, if desired.

Drain and add the tuna. Use a spatula to cut the tuna into smaller chunks. Stir.

Simmer lightly for a minute or two. Serve warm over noodles, rice, bread, potatoes, Baking Soda Biscuits (see page 14), or vegetables (for example, green beans, cooked carrots, or peas).

Variations: Add one or several of the options below (to taste):
¼   cup fresh or frozen peas
¼   cup diced tomatoes
¼   cup cooked, cut up Brussels sprouts
½   teaspoon onion powder or flakes
¼   teaspoon garlic
¼   teaspoon dill weed
¼   teaspoon rosemary
1–2   teaspoons sugar

Yield: 2 servings

Read ingredients! Terms like "vegetable broth" may mean that the product contains soy or corn. Sometimes a low-sodium variety will be free of other additives. When using low-salt varieties, a recipe may need more salt.

BAKED FISH

Preheat oven to 350°–400° • *Cooking time: 20–30 minutes*

2   5-oz. fish fillets
       Butter (or margarine, olive oil, or cooking oil)
       Corn-free salt, to taste

Coat lightly or spray a shallow baking dish with cooking oil.

Arrange the fillets to cover the bottom of the dish. Dot the fillets with butter or oil. Salt lightly, to taste. Add one of the variations below, if desired.

Bake the fillets at 350°–400° for 20–30 minutes. Fish will flake easily when it is done.

Bones come away easily when fish is done.

Variations:

↳ Sprinkle on pepper, lemon, onion powder or minced onion, and parsley before baking. Bake at 350° to preserve the seasoning flavors.

↳ Coat the fillets liberally with rosemary and/or thyme before baking. Bake at 350° to preserve the seasoning flavors.

↳ Add milk before baking, ½ cup of milk to 1 pound of fillets.

↳ Before baking, sprinkle on onion flakes, pepper, and dill weed. Coat the fillets with mayonnaise. Arrange sliced lemon rings or orange rings on top.

Yield: 2 servings

For baking, choose a fat fish, such as mackerel, herring, lake trout, salmon, tuna, whitefish, or catfish. Mackerel, herring, lake trout, salmon, sardines, and tuna are high in omega-3 fatty acids, which may reduce the risk of coronary heart disease.

BROILED FISH
Cooking time: 5–8 minutes

2   5-oz. fish fillets
       Butter (or margarine, olive oil, or cooking oil)
       Corn-free salt, to taste

Turn the oven to the broil setting.

Coat lightly or spray a shallow baking dish with cooking oil.

Arrange the fillets to cover the bottom of the dish. Dot the fillets with butter or oil. Salt lightly, to taste. Add one of the variations below, if desired.

Raise the oven rack to the top position. Set the fillets in the oven, 2–3 inches from the top flame or top heating elements. Leave the oven door open slightly.

If you are using a lean fish, baste often with melted butter, margarine, olive oil, or cooking oil. Do not turn the fillets.

Broil for approximately 5–8 minutes or until the fillets are golden brown. Fish is done when it flakes easily.

Note: If black pepper is desired, add it after the fish is done broiling. Pepper can turn bitter in high heat.

Variation: Sprinkle fillets with minced onion before broiling.

Yield: 2 servings

For broiling, choose a fat fish. Lean fish are better poached or steamed.
If you do broil a lean fish, baste often.

Fat fish	Lean fish
Mackerel	Bass
Salmon	Haddock
Lake trout	Pike
Herring	Red snapper
Tuna	Halibut
Whitefish	Cod
Catfish	Perch

SALMON with ORANGE MARINADE

Preheat oven to 400° • Cooking time: 20 minutes, after marinating 1 hour

1	small onion, diced (optional, to taste)
2	cups soy sauce
½	cup orange juice
2	teaspoons garlic powder
2	teaspoons ginger powder (optional, to taste)
4	6-oz. salmon fillets

Dice the onion. Stir together the soy sauce, orange juice, garlic powder, and ginger powder and onion, if desired. Add the salmon fillets and marinate for 1 hour or longer.

Preheat the oven to 400°.

Wrap each fillet in aluminum foil to hold in the sauce. Bake at 400° for about 20 minutes or on a hot grill. When the salmon is done, it will be flaky but moist.

Serve hot with salsa (see below) if desired.

Yield: 4 servings

SALSA for SALMON

1	tomato, diced
3	green onions, diced (shallots)
½	mango, diced (or ½ cup sliced strawberries)
½	cup diced cucumber
2	Tablespoons cilantro flakes (or ½ cup chopped fresh cilantro)

Dice the tomato, onions, mango, and cucumber. In a serving dish, combine all ingredients and stir.

Yield: 1½ cups

SALMON CAKES

Preheat oven to 400° • Cooking time: 10–12 minutes

2	cans salmon (preferably sockeye), drained
¼	teaspoon tarragon (and/or basil)
¼	teaspoon onion powder
¼	teaspoon garlic powder
Dash	corn-free salt, to taste
Dash	pepper (optional, to taste)
Pinch	mustard powder (optional, to taste)
1	Tablespoon rice flour (or whole wheat flour)
1	egg (or egg white—optional)
1–2	Tablespoons olive oil (or cooking oil)

Preheat the oven to 400°.

Drain the canned salmon. Stir the salmon and seasonings together. Add 1 tablespoon rice flour for thickening. If desired, stir in a beaten egg. Make this mixture into cakes (patties).

Put a little more rice flour onto a plate. Dip the salmon cakes into the flour, coating both sides.

Heat the olive oil in a skillet. Add the salmon cakes and grill them on both sides until golden brown.

Coat or spray a baking pan or dish with olive oil or cooking oil. Add the salmon cakes and bake at 400° for 12–14 minutes. Salmon cakes will be hot in the center when they are done.

These salmon and halibut recipes come from an Alaska halibut fisherman who advises care in choosing fish cuts. Fresh fish does not smell "fishy." It is firm to the touch, not soft. Shop at a fish market, if possible. A fish fillet is boneless. It comes from beside the ribs. A fish steak has a bone down the center; it comes from closer to the tail. If you choose a side of fish, use needle-nose pliers to pull out the bones.

Variations:

⤳ Dice and boil a small potato. Add the potato to the salmon mixture.

⤳ Use fresh seasonings, if desired. Mince the onion and garlic and sauté in a skillet coated with olive oil or cooking oil. Mince fresh tarragon and/or basil. (Do not sauté herbs.) Add these seasonings to the salmon mixture and cook as above.

↪ Add southwestern flavor with chili peppers:

½	red bell pepper, diced
½	yellow bell pepper, diced
1	jalapeño pepper, seeded and diced (optional)

Slice the peppers in half and discard the stems, seeds, and membranes. Dice half of each bell pepper. (The leftovers can be sliced and frozen for future use.) Dice the jalapeño pepper.

Sauté the peppers lightly. If you are using fresh onion and garlic, sauté the peppers with them. Add to the salmon mixture and cook as above. Serve with salsa, if desired.

Yield: 2–3 servings

SALMON SNACKS

8	ounces salmon steak or fillets
1	cup soy sauce
¼	cup brown sugar
1	teaspoon garlic powder, to taste
Dash	ginger, to taste

Cut the salmon into bite-sized pieces.

In a medium-size skillet, mix together the soy sauce, brown sugar, garlic powder, and ginger. Add the salmon pieces and simmer on medium to medium-low heat until the salmon is cooked through. Fish is done when it flakes easily.

Serve the Salmon Snacks with dips and/or salsa, possibly with a vegetable or fruit tray.

Variation: Instead of soy sauce, use orange juice or another fruit juice. Reduce the amount of brown sugar.

Yield: 2 servings

SCRAMBLED EGGS

3–4   eggs
1   Tablespoon milk (or water)
Pinch corn-free salt (optional, to taste)
Pinch pepper (optional, to taste)

Coat or spray a nonstick skillet with cooking oil. Break the eggs directly into the pan and add the milk. Stir thoroughly.

Cook the eggs on medium heat, stirring frequently and scraping off the pan surfaces. The eggs are done when they are no longer liquid. Season as desired and serve immediately.

Variations:

↪ Substitute 2 egg whites for one egg to lower the cholesterol.

↪ Add your favorite variety of mixed vegetables to the raw eggs.

↪ For a heartier egg flavor, leave out the milk or water.

↪ Add a pinch of an egg-friendly seasoning such as basil, bell pepper, celery seed, chives, cumin, dill weed, mustard powder, onion, paprika, parsley, rosemary, or tarragon.

Yield: 2 servings

**If you don't know the flavor of an egg-friendly seasoning,
try it out on scrambled eggs.**

**Toast or potatoes help to balance a scrambled egg meal.
Add orange juice or orange slices as well.**

HARD-BOILED EGGS

6–12 eggs
Pinch corn-free salt

Gently place the eggs in a large saucepan and add water to cover. Add salt to prevent large leaks if an eggshell cracks.

Heat to a boil on medium-low heat.

Boil the eggs for 9–12 minutes on medium-low heat. The water should boil gently, not just simmer. Do not use a very vigorous boil, which may crack the eggshells.

Hard-boiled eggs are done when they turn solid, with the yolks still slightly tender.

When the eggs are done, pour off the hot water and immediately plunge the eggs into very cold water. This helps make the eggs easier to peel. As the water warms, pour it off and replace it with more cold water.

After the eggs have been chilled with cold water, refrigerate any that will not be used immediately. To peel a hard-boiled egg, crack the shell and then roll the egg on a hard surface to crack it all over. Peel off the shell and rinse.

> **WARNING: Do NOT attempt to microwave an egg in its shell! The hot eggshell can explode, even after you remove it from the microwave.**

SOFT-BOILED EGGS

1–2   eggs per person, for immediate use

Follow the above instructions for Hard-boiled Eggs on the opposite page, but boil for only 4–5 minutes. Soft-boiled eggs are done when the whites turn solid with the yolks still a thick liquid.

Serve soft-boiled eggs immediately in an egg cup, which stands the egg up on end.

Tap around the top of the eggshell with a spoon and lift off the top piece of shell. Salt, if desired. Use a small spoon to dip out the soft-boiled egg.

Variation: Mash the soft-boiled eggs with a fork and salt them lightly. Serve on a piece of buttered toast.

> **Allow more time to boil eggs at higher altitudes, such as mountain resorts or high-altitude cities like Denver. Water boils at a lower temperature in the lower air pressure at high altitude.**

FRIED EGGS

1–2   eggs per person
      Corn-free salt (optional, to taste)
      Pepper (optional, to taste)

Coat or spray a skillet with cooking oil. Heat on medium.

Break the eggs into the hot skillet by opening the cracked shell just far enough to let out the egg white. Allow the white to sizzle for a bit and begin turning white. Then drop the egg yolk gently on top. Add salt and pepper to taste.

For sunny-side up, cook the egg as is until the white is no longer clear.

For over-easy, cook the egg until most of the white is no longer clear. Then use a spatula to gently turn the egg over. Cook until the white is no longer clear.

For over-hard, cook the egg until most of the white is no longer clear. Then use a spatula to gently turn the egg over. Cook until the white is no longer clear, and the yolk is firm.

Serve immediately. Serve with toast or bread, if desired.

Variation: After the eggs are cooked, pour salsa over them. Allow this mixture to stay in the pan, on the heat, long enough to warm the salsa.

For a nonfat protein, use only the egg whites.

POACHED EGGS

1–2   eggs per person, for immediate use
       Corn-free salt and/or pepper, to taste

Stove-top method:

In a small saucepan place enough water to cover the eggs out-of-shell.

Break the eggs gently into the water. The goal is to not break the yolks! Bring the water to a gentle boil, on medium-low heat, and boil for 4–5 minutes.

Poached eggs are done when the white is solid and the yolks a thick liquid. Serve immediately.

Use a slotted spoon to gently lift the egg into a serving dish, such as a small soup bowl. Again, the goal is to not break the yolks.

Microwave method:

Place enough water in a small microwaveable bowl to cover an egg or two out-of-shell.

Break the eggs gently into the water. The goal is to not break the yolks! Prick the yolks on top with a sharp fork to prevent (or at least delay) explosions.

Microwave the eggs on low for a minute or two. You will need to experiment with your machine to find the exact time. The goal is to get the eggs to cook before the yolks explode.

Poached eggs are done when the white is solid and the yolks a thick liquid. Serve immediately.

Use a slotted spoon to gently lift the egg into a serving dish, such as a small soup bowl. Again, the goal is not to break the yolks.

Variations:

↳ Serve with a little tomato sauce such as ketchup (See corn-free Ketchup, page 77), spaghetti sauce, or pizza sauce.

↳ Season with a pinch of an egg-friendly flavor such as basil, cumin, dill weed, mustard powder, onion, rosemary, or tarragon.

↳ For a nonfat protein, use only the egg whites.

Allow more time to boil eggs at higher altitudes, such as mountain resorts or high-altitude cities like Denver. Water boils at a lower temperature in the lower air pressure at high altitude.

FRENCH TOAST

2	eggs
¼	teaspoon corn-free salt
½	cup milk (or water)
½	teaspoon sugar (optional)
6	bread slices

Stir together the eggs, salt, milk or water, and sugar. Dip both sides of the bread slices into the egg mixture. Coat the bread completely but do not allow it to soak.

Coat or spray a medium-size skillet with cooking oil. Fry the egg-coated bread slices on medium-low heat on both sides, until light brown. Serve hot.

Variations:
 ↳ Add ¼–½ teaspoon vanilla (to taste) to the egg mixture.
 ↳ Serve with fruit syrup, maple syrup, or brown sugar.
 ↳ Serve with a tomato sauce.
 ↳ Add a pinch of an egg-friendly and bread-friendly seasoning to the egg dip. Try basil, cumin, dill weed, mustard powder, onion, rosemary, or tarragon.

Yield: 2–3 servings

PORK SPARE RIBS

2	pork spare ribs (about 1½ pounds)
1	tomato, diced (or ½ cup salsa—optional)
1	teaspoon cooking oil
Dash	corn-free salt (optional, to taste)
Dash	pepper (optional, to taste)

Spray or barely coat a skillet with cooking oil. Heat the skillet and add the ribs. Brown them briefly.

Put the ribs in a crock pot, or a stove-top kettle with a lid that seals well. Add the tomato or salsa. If you do not use tomato or salsa, add ½ cup of water. Stir in the oil, salt, and pepper.

In the crock pot, cook the mixture on high for about a half hour. Then cook all day (6–8 hours) on low. In a kettle, the ribs can simmer for fewer hours. Pork is done safely when the meat is brown throughout with no pink.

Yield: 2 servings

Do not eat pink pork! It can cause trichinosis.

PORK CHOPS

2	pork chops (about 1 pound)
2	Tablespoons flour
Dash	pepper
⅛	teaspoon corn-free salt (optional, to taste)
Dash	garlic powder (optional, to taste)
Dash	onion powder (optional, to taste)

Rinse the pork chops in cold water to remove any bits of bone. Pat them dry.

In a large bowl mix the flour and seasonings. Dip each pork chop in the mixture and coat both sides.

Barely coat the cooking surface of a large skillet with oil.

Put the pork chops in the skillet. Cook the chops on medium heat for about 12 minutes and then turn them over. Cook for about 8 minutes more. Pork chops are done when there is no pink in the center of the meat.

Yield: 2 servings

For safety, always cook pork thoroughly. Never eat pork rare.

PORK ROAST

Preheat oven to 325° • Cooking time: 2–3 hours

1–3   pounds pork loin roast
Corn-free salt and pepper, to taste

Cherry-Almond Glaze
1   12-oz. jar corn-free cherry preserves (or use cherry syrup recipe,
        page 94)
¼   cup apple cider vinegar
¼   teaspoon corn-free red cooking wine (optional)
2   Tablespoons sugar (or honey)
¼   teaspoon cinnamon
¼   teaspoon nutmeg
¼   teaspoon cloves
¼   cup toasted slivered almonds (see Toasted Almonds, page 203)

Preheat the oven to 325°.

Wipe the meat with a damp towel and pat it dry. Rub the roast all over with salt and pepper. Place the roast in a shallow roasting pan. Roast, uncovered, at 325° for 2–2½ hours.

In a large saucepan combine the glaze ingredients, except for the almonds. Heat until boiling, stirring occasionally. Then reduce the heat and simmer for 2 minutes, stirring frequently. Add the almonds and keep the sauce warm.

Spoon some sauce over the roast to glaze. Bake for an additional 30 minutes. Baste several times to keep the meat moist. Pork is done when brown through; for safety, leave no pink inside.

Serve the roast with the remaining sauce as a side dish.

Variations:

No Glaze: Rub the meat with preferred seasonings. Flavors that complement pork include salt, pepper, onion, basil, coriander, fennel, lemon balm, rosemary, and sage. Baste the roast several times during the last 30 minutes of cooking.

Onion Glaze: Sauté 2 onions, sliced, in 2 tablespoons butter or cooking oil. Stir in 2 tablespoons balsamic vinegar and 2 tablespoons dark brown sugar. Salt and pepper to taste. Cook, stirring frequently, until the onions are tender and the sugar turns to a glaze. Add ½ cup raisins, if desired. Use in place of Cherry-Almond Glaze in the recipe above.

Yield: 2–6 servings

ROAST LEG OF LAMB

Preheat oven to 325° • *Total cooking time: 3+ hours*

3	pounds leg of lamb
	Corn-free salt, to taste
	Pepper, to taste
5	Tablespoons butter, melted (or salad oil)
4	cups hot water
2	cups dry rice

Rinse the meat in cold water. Put it in a baking pan or dish, fat side up, uncovered.

Sprinkle salt and pepper on the meat, to taste. Brush or pour the melted butter over the meat. Insert the meat thermometer, if you are using one, into the thickest part of the meat, but not touching bone.

Roast, uncovered, at 325° for about 2½ hours.

Lower the temperature to 300°. Add the water and rice. Add seasonings, as preferred (see variations below). Cook until the rice is tender, 20–30 minutes.

Check for doneness. When lamb is done, an oven thermometer inserted into the center of the meat, not touching bone, reads 175°–182°.

Remove the roast from the oven and roasting pan. Keep it hot and let it stand for 10–15 minutes before carving.

Variations:

Avgolemono: For avgolemono, return the rice to the oven still in the roasting pan. In a separate small bowl, beat 2 eggs to a fine foam. Beat in 3 tablespoons lemon juice (juice from 1–2 lemons). Pour this mixture over the hot rice and return it to the oven for a few more minutes. Serve the rice in a separate serving dish.

Seasonings: Parsley, black pepper, mint, and/or oregano go well with lamb roast, as do the rice or the avgolemono. Garlic also goes well with lamb. Celery and/or onion are other choices. Yet more options are brown sugar, cinnamon, cardamom, and/or black pepper.

Yield: 7–8 servings

LAMB CHOPS

1   lamb chop per person
       Garlic powder (or garlic salt, to taste)

Have the lamb chops sliced thin, about ¾ of an inch or slightly less.

Rinse the meat in cold water. Place the lamb chops in a baking dish or on a broiler pan. Sprinkle or rub the meat with garlic powder, to taste.

Move the oven rack to the top position. Turn the oven on broil and leave the oven door slightly open. Broil the lamb chops for 4–6 minutes. Turn the chops over and broil for another 3–4 minutes.

Variations:

↪ Use cloves instead of garlic for the seasoning.

↪ Instead of broiling, grill the lamb chops.

↪ Season with mint, with or without garlic.

↪ Instead of broiling, bake the lamb chops in a covered baking dish. The chops can bake on top of a bed of veggies or rice, in a small amount of liquid. See Roast Leg of Lamb (page 128) for adding avgolemono to rice.

DRY BEANS

2   cups dry beans (black beans, black-eye peas, kidney beans,
        navy beans, pinto beans, or other beans)
6   cups cold water for soaking

Rinse the beans in cold water and sort out any bad ones.

Beans need to soak and soften before cooking. Cover the beans with plain cold water and soak them overnight. In a pinch, you can boil the beans for 5–10 minutes and allow them to soak for an hour or two.

Discard the soaking water, and rinse the beans again. To prevent the beans from toughening, do not add salt, tomato, or other acidic foods at this time.

Cover the beans with fresh water and simmer for 1½–2 hours, until the beans are soft. Beans can be simmered on the stove top or in a crock pot.

Use these cooked beans in place of canned beans in any recipe, such as Baked Beans (page 132), Pork and Beans (page 132, variations), chili beans, refried beans, bean salsa, and so on. Add the needed vegetables, meat, and/or sweeteners and continue to simmer or bake the bean dish until the flavors blend as desired. Add seasonings in the last 10–30 minutes before the bean dish is done. Many seasonings fade or turn bitter with long cooking times.

Yield: 6 cups cooked beans

Classic recipes may call for re-using the soak-and-simmer water. Starting with fresh water helps to reduce the flatulence that beans can cause.

DRY LENTILS or SPLIT PEAS

1   cup lentils or split peas, 8 ounces
2   cups water for simmering

Rinse the lentils in cold water and sort out any bad ones. Add water, bring to a boil, and simmer for about 30 minutes.

Use these cooked lentils or peas in recipes such as Lentils and Couscous (page 134), Lentil Soup (page 184), or Split-Pea Soup (page 182). They can also be chilled and added to salads.

Yield: 2 cups of cooked lentils or split peas

Black beans, also called turtle beans or frijoles negros, are often used in Hispanic dishes. Kidney beans, or red beans, normally come in chili. Some prefer chili made with pinto beans. Navy beans, also called white beans, are the basis of classic Boston baked beans. Pinto beans, as refried beans, are often served with Southwestern dishes such as burritos, tacos, and tostada. Lentils and split peas make good soups.

BAKED BEANS

Preheat oven to 325° • Cooking time: 2 hours or longer

2	slices bacon
¼	onion, sliced or diced
1	15-oz. can white beans (navy beans)*
⅛–¼	cup brown sugar (or corn-free molasses or maple syrup, to taste)
¼	teaspoon corn-free salt, to taste
¼–½	teaspoon mustard powder, to taste
1–2	cups water

Cook the bacon, pour off most of the drippings, and drain. Place the bacon slices on paper towels to cool. Slice the onion and sauté the pieces in the remaining bacon drippings.

Crumble the bacon bits. Layer the ingredients into a baking dish or crock pot: beans, bacon bits, onion, beans, bacon bits, onion.

Measure the brown sugar or other sweetener. Stir the salt and mustard powder into the sweetener. Pour the sugar-seasoning mixture over the top. Add water to cover the beans. Bake uncovered at 325° for 2–3 hours or longer to blend the flavors. In a crock pot, the beans can cook for 4–6 hours. Add water, if needed.

*Note: Two-thirds cup dry white beans makes about 2 cups of cooked beans.

Variations:

Dry Beans: Start with ⅔ cup dry, small white beans or navy beans for 2 cups of cooked beans. If you use dry beans, you may want to start them soaking the night before. They will need to be soaked and cooked for several hours before they are ready to replace the canned beans shown above. Use the package directions or see Dry Beans on page 130.

Pork and Beans: Add one 6-oz. can of tomato paste to the beans before layering them into the baking dish.

Yield: 2 servings

PINTO BEANS and TORTILLA CHIPS
Preheat oven to 350°

2–3	tortillas*
1	can pinto beans (low-salt pinto beans may be corn-free), drained and rinsed
1	Tablespoon cooking oil
½	teaspoon corn-free salt (optional, to taste)
⅓	teaspoon pepper (optional, to taste)

Brush the tortillas with oil on both sides. Salt the tortillas lightly and stack them. Cut the stack in half three times, making six triangle wedges from each tortilla.

Coat or spray a baking sheet with cooking oil. Spread the tortilla pieces on the baking sheet. Bake at 350° about 10 minutes, turning once.

Drain the pinto beans and rinse them thoroughly. Heat the beans in a saucepan with a few tablespoons of water, the oil, salt, and pepper. Stir occasionally.

When the beans are hot, mash them with a potato masher.

*Note: Read ingredients. You may need to make your own tortillas (see page 19). See also Nachos with Meat (page 150), Nacho Chips with Cheese Dip (page 148), and Tostada (page 173).

Variations:

Low-fat: Do not oil or bake the tortillas. Warm them in the oven or microwave. Put the bean sauce in the center of a tortilla. Fold the tortilla over the sauce, then fold in one side. Fold the top down, and you have a bean burrito snack.

Fast Snack: Omit the tortillas and dip the bean sauce with corn-free potato chips or crackers.

Veggies: Add diced tomatoes or minced onions to the bean sauce.

Hot Flavor: Add dry powdered seasonings such as mild paprika, mild or hot red pepper (cayenne), or hot chipotle pepper. If you prefer, add diced fresh pepper such as mild bell pepper, warmer Anaheim or jalapeño, hot serrano, or very hot habanero.

Yield: about 2 servings

LENTILS AND COUSCOUS

1	15-oz. can plain cooked lentils
	Corn-free salt and pepper, to taste
1	cup plain, dry couscous
	Butter (or cooking oil)
1	small tomato, diced (optional)
¼	cup cooked broccoli tips, diced (optional)
¼	cup shredded or finely minced carrots (optional)

Drain and rinse the lentils. Put them in a saucepan, add seasonings to taste (see variations below), and heat the lentils on medium, stirring occasionally.

Start water boiling for the couscous. If you prefer tender pasta, use a little more water than the package suggests. Add butter or cooking oil and salt, according to package directions. After the water boils, remove it from the heat, add the couscous, stir, and cover the pan. Allow the couscous to stand for 5 minutes. Adjust oil and salt to taste.

Dice the tomato. Steam or boil other veggies.

Mix the lentils and couscous. Mix in the vegetables or use them as a garnish.

Serve warm.

Variations:

- Add onion and garlic. Use dry powder or flakes or sauté fresh onion and/or garlic.
- Add a little ginger powder and garnish with sesame seeds.
- Add your favorite curry powder or garam masala.
- Add chili powder and/or diced green bell peppers or hotter chili peppers.
- Add a can of chicken pieces or ½ cup of leftover, cooked diced chicken.
- Add about ¼ pound crumble-fried ground beef, lamb, or pork.
- Instead of canned lentils, use 2 cups (16 ounces) of dry lentils and begin by soaking them overnight. See Dry Beans on page 130.

Yield: 2 servings

Like any pasta, couscous can be cooked al dente (crunchy) or tender. You may prefer the flavor of couscous packaged in cardboard boxes to the varieties packaged in plastic jars.

TOFU CUBES

1 package firm or traditional tofu
Corn-free salt, pepper, and/or seasonings to taste

Slice the tofu into ½-inch cubes.

Coat or spray a skillet with cooking oil. Heat the skillet and add the tofu cubes. Season to taste, if desired (see variations below).

Stir frequently. Brown the tofu cubes lightly on all sides.

To serve, add the tofu cubes to other dishes, such as soups, salads, stir-fry veggies, or spaghetti.

Variations:

↳ Tofu will accept any savory seasoning. See your favorite recipes, mild or hot, Italian, Southwestern, Asian, Indian, whatever. Season the tofu with your favorite spice or combination.

↳ Use paprika to color the tofu cubes like cheese.

↳ Make Stir-Fry Veggies (see page 167), and add tofu cubes after the softest vegetables.

↳ Add tofu cubes to Clear Sauce (see page 161). Add canned chicken pieces or leftover cooked chicken pieces. Add your favorite poultry seasoning/s such as onion, garlic, parsley, sage, rosemary, thyme, diced celery, and diced carrot. For many other possibilities, see Chicken Stuffing and Seasonings, page 107. Serve over biscuits, noodles, or mashed potatoes.

↳ Add tofu cubes to a tomato sauce (tomato paste mixed half-and-half with water). Season with onion, garlic, oregano, basil, and/or other spaghetti seasonings. Serve over noodles or potatoes.

↳ Make a Tossed Salad (see page 47), and add tofu cubes, browned or uncooked.

↳ Make Homemade Spaghetti (page 154) and add small tofu cubes instead of crumble-fried hamburger.

Yield: Cubes for 1–3 other dishes

Tofu = soybean paste. Hummus = garbanzo bean paste.
Tahini = sesame seed paste.

TOFU OVER RICE

1	cup cooked rice (white or brown, instant or dry)*
½	package traditional or firm tofu (6–8 ounces)
⅛	teaspoon corn-free salt (optional, to taste)
⅛	teaspoon pepper (optional, to taste)
	Seasonings to taste (see below)
1	tomato, diced (for garnish)
	Fresh herbs (for garnish)

Cook the rice according to package directions. While the rice is cooking, cut the tofu into ½ to ¾-inch cubes.

Coat or spray a medium-size skillet with cooking oil. Heat the skillet and add the seasonings. Place the tofu cubes in the skillet and sauté lightly.

Serve the tofu cubes on top of the rice. Garnish with diced tomatoes and/or green herbs such as parsley, oregano, or cilantro.

*Note: (½ cup instant rice or ⅓ cup dry rice makes about 1 cup of cooked rice.)

Variations:
⤷ Cook about 2 tablespoons of wild rice first. Wild rice takes longer to cook than white or brown rice. Add the wild rice to the rice and continue with the recipe above.

⤷ While the rice is cooking, sauté sliced water chestnuts. Then cut and add the tofu and continue with the recipe above.

⤷ After the rice is cooked, add frozen peas. Heat and stir just long enough to heat the peas.

⤷ Add ⅓ cup of any or all: diced red or green bell pepper, broccoli florets, cut small, and diced carrots. Allow 5–10 minutes to blend flavors.

⤷ If you prefer fried rice, prepare 1½ teaspoons water beaten into 1 egg. Add the rice to the skillet with the tofu cubes and stir. Turn up the heat, add a little oil and heat while stirring. When the tofu and rice are very hot, add egg-and-water mix quickly. Keep stirring until the mixture is evenly browned, and then remove it from the heat. Serve hot.

Yield: 2–3 servings, depending on the quantity of vegetables used

CHAPTER 6: PROTEINS / MILK / CHEESE

The symbol ▼ marks healthier recipe choices.

GRILLED CHEESE SANDWICH

per sandwich:
   2   slices bread*
  1–2   slices cheese

Coat or spray a medium skillet with cooking oil, corn-free margarine, or butter.

Heat the skillet over medium-low to medium heat. Lay a slice of bread in the pan, a slice of cheese on top, and then another slice of bread. Cover and brown the bread on one side; then turn the sandwich and brown the bread on the other side.

When the sandwich is done, the cheese will be melted, but it will not run into the pan. If the cheese runs, next time try a slightly hotter temperature to brown the bread faster.

*Note: (Read ingredients! Or make your own bread; see recipes in Chapter 2, "Breads and Grains.")

Variations:
↪ Try adding a pinch of cheese-friendly seasoning to the cheese layer. Some choices include: basil, celery seed, chives, cumin, dill weed, nutmeg, oregano, paprika, parsley, sage, or thyme.

↪ Leave the sandwich open-faced. Instead of the top slice of bread, add slices of tomato and grated carrots.

↪ Use cheddar cheese slices (mild, medium, or sharp).

↪ Use Swiss cheese slices. Serve with apple or peach slices on the side.

↪ Use Colby cheese slices or Colby-Jack (also called CoJack).

↪ Use Monterey Jack cheese slices or Pepper-Jack. Serve with red grapes on the side.

↪ Use mozzarella cheese slices. Warm an Italian sauce, such as spaghetti or pizza sauce, and pour some over the sandwich.

Prepackaged sliced cheese usually has a fine cornstarch dusting to prevent the cheese from sticking to plastic or other slices of cheese. To eliminate corn totally, buy cheese in blocks and slice your own.

COTTAGE CHEESE SNACKS

½   cup corn-free cottage cheese
⅛   teaspoon cinnamon, to taste
1   teaspoon sugar

Stir the cottage cheese, cinnamon, and sugar together for a quick snack.

Variations:
➥ Put the mixture in an oven-safe or microwaveable bowl. Broil or microwave until the cottage cheese just begins to bubble and change to a pudding-like texture. Serve warm.

➥ Spread the mixture on two slices of bread. Place these open-face sandwiches on a piece of aluminum foil and toast them under the oven broiler.

Yield: 1 serving

COTTAGE CHEESE AND CUCUMBER

½   tomato, diced (or cherry tomatoes—optional)
½   cup corn-free cottage cheese
6 –8   slices cucumber

Dice the tomato and stir it into the cottage cheese. Garnish with cucumber slices.

Yield: 1 serving

MACARONI and CHEESE

2	ounces cheese, shredded by you or packaged with potato starch
½	cup milk, divided
½	cup dry noodles
¾	teaspoon flour
¾	teaspoon cooking oil
1	teaspoon corn-free salt (optional, to taste)
1	Tablespoon butter (or corn-free margarine or oil)
½	teaspoon corn-free salt (optional, to taste)

Shred the cheese and measure the milk. Set them aside at room temperature to warm up.

In a medium saucepan boil water for the noodles. When the water boils, add the noodles and a few drops of oil to help prevent sticking. Simmer according to package directions, stirring occasionally.

Meanwhile, place the flour and half the milk (¼ cup) in a small skillet. Stir the flour into the milk until the mixture is very smooth. Add the oil and stir. Heat the mixture on low to medium-low, stirring occasionally until it boils. Then simmer and stir constantly. The mixture will turn to a smooth, creamy consistency. If desired, stir in about a teaspoon of salt.

Lower the heat and add a few shreds of cheese. Stir until the cheese melts in and the mixture is smooth again. If the mixture bubbles, pull the skillet off the heat and turn the heat down a little. Stir, then return the skillet to the heat. The goal is to keep the mixture just warm enough to melt the cheese but not hot enough to bubble.

Add a spoonful of the remaining milk and stir over low heat until smooth.

(continued on next page)

You'll need to buy cheese in bricks. Prepackaged sliced and shredded cheese are dusted with a fine powder of cornstarch to prevent the pieces from sticking. The plastic is also coated with cornstarch. If you are extremely sensitive, consider discarding thin slices from the cheese-brick from all six of the surfaces that have contacted the plastic packaging.

Repeat, alternately adding cheese and milk. Stir each addition until smooth. When all of the cheese and milk is in the mixture, take the mixture off the heat.

As soon as the noodles are cooked, drain them and return them to the saucepan. Stir in 1 tablespoon butter, margarine, or oil and ½ teaspoon salt, if desired. Stir in the warm cheese sauce over low heat. Serve warm.

Yield: 2 servings

Your cheese choices include cheddar, Colby, Colby-Jack, Monterey Jack, Swiss, mozzarella, and others. You may need to avoid American and Velveeta, which often include corn-derivatives.

NO-YEAST QUICK PIZZA CRUST

2	cups flour
1	teaspoon corn-free salt
½	teaspoon sugar
3	teaspoons corn-free baking powder (see page 11)
1½	Tablespoons cooking oil (or olive oil)
1	cup water

Mix the flour, salt, sugar, and baking powder. Add the oil and stir. Add the water and stir; batter will remain slightly lumpy. Spread the batter on the baking pan. Add the toppings and bake.

Restaurant pizza dough is often baked on top of cornmeal to prevent sticking.

PIZZA

Preheat oven to 425° • Cooking time: 15–18 minutes

½   pound hamburger, crumble-fried (optional, see page 98)
       Oil
⅓   cup tomato paste
⅓   cup water
¼   teaspoon oregano (optional, to taste)
⅛   teaspoon each seasonings such as basil, onion, garlic,
           black pepper, as desired
2   cups grated mozzarella cheese (about 8 ounces of brick cheese)
       Toppings, as preferred

Crumble fry the hamburger if you are using it for a topping.

Oil a pizza pan or a cake pan. Make a pizza crust dough from the recipe on the previous page or use the recipe on the next page for a relatively fast yeast crust. If you use a ready-made pizza crust, be sure to read the ingredients. (Pizza crust often contains corn additives.) Place the pizza crust dough on the pan.

Preheat the oven to 425°.

Combine the tomato paste and water with oregano and other seasonings, to taste. Spread this sauce on the pizza crust with the back of a spoon.

Sprinkle the crumble-fried hamburger over the sauce, if desired.

Grate the cheese and sprinkle it over the sauce and hamburger.

Add other toppings as desired, such as mushrooms, onions, anchovies, pineapple chunks, spinach pieces, bell pepper pieces, etc. For an Italian option, try tuna fish instead of hamburger.

Bake at 425° for 15–18 minutes, until the crust and cheese are slightly browned.

Yield: 4 servings

Read ingredients! Ready-made pizza and pizza dough may contain corn flour, corn starch, corn syrup, and/or cornmeal. In a restaurant, pizza dough is often baked on top of cornmeal to prevent sticking. Preshredded cheese may be packaged with corn starch, which is not always shown on the label.

YEAST BREAD PIZZA CRUST

Preheat oven to 425° • Cooking time: 15–20 minutes

¾	cup water
1	teaspoon sugar
1	teaspoon yeast
2	cups flour, divided
1	egg
2	teaspoons cooking oil
¾	teaspoon corn-free salt

Mix the water, sugar, yeast, and 1 cup of the flour. Set this mixture in a warm place (80°–90°) for about a half-hour. The mixture will become frothy and rise to about twice its original size. If it has not risen enough, stir the mixture briskly and leave it in the warmth another 15–20 minutes. Then remove it from the warmth.

Preheat the oven to 425°. Coat or spray oil on a cake pan and add flour.

Stir the mixture until smooth. Add the egg, oil, and salt. Stir until smooth. Then stir in the remaining 1 cup flour.

Pour the batter into the cake pan and spread it as thin as possible. If the batter is too thick, the crust will not cook through.

Add the pizza sauce and toppings. See the previous page for sauce and topping recipes.

Bake the batter at 425° for 15–20 minutes. The crust will be golden-brown and the cheese melted when done.

Variation: Replace half the white flour with whole wheat flour. Add some water; the whole wheat flour absorbs more water.

Yield: Crust for 1 pizza

CHEESE SAUCE

2	ounces cheese, shredded by you or packaged with potato starch
½	cup milk
¾	teaspoon flour
¾	teaspoon butter (or corn-free margarine or cooking oil)
1	teaspoon corn-free salt (optional, to taste)
	Seasonings (optional, to taste)

Shred the cheese and measure the milk. Set them aside at room temperature to warm up.

Meanwhile, place the flour and half the milk (¼ cup) in a small skillet. Stir the flour into the milk until the mixture is very smooth. Add the butter and stir. Heat the mixture on low to medium-low, stirring occasionally until it boils. Then simmer and stir constantly. The mixture will turn to a smooth, creamy consistency. If desired, stir in about a teaspoon of salt.

Lower the heat and add a few shreds of cheese. Stir until the cheese melts in and the mixture is smooth again. If the mixture bubbles, pull the skillet off the heat and turn the heat down just a little. Stir, then return the skillet to the heat. The goal is to keep the mixture just warm enough to melt the cheese but not hot enough to bubble.

Add a spoonful of the remaining milk and stir over low heat until smooth. Repeat, alternately adding cheese and milk. Stir each addition until smooth. When all of the cheese and milk is in the mixture, take the mixture off the heat.

Variations:

↷ Try with cheddar cheese, mild, medium or sharp, or a combination of cheddar and other cheeses. For a milder cheese sauce, try Colby, Monterey Jack, Colby-Jack, or mozzarella.

↷ For Alfredo sauce, use fresh Parmesan cheese.

↷ Add paprika, to taste.

↷ Add chili powder, to taste. See also Nacho Cheese Dip, page 148.

↷ Add red cooking wine to a Swiss/cheddar mix; use with red meats.

↷ Add oregano and/or basil to a mozzarella cheese sauce.

Yield: ½ cup

To avoid corn-derivatives, avoid American and Velveeta cheeses (try Colby-Jack instead) and buy cheese in bricks, not shredded or sliced.

SPINACH-CHEESE CASSEROLE
Preheat oven to 350° • Cooking time: 30–40 minutes

2	10-oz. boxes frozen spinach (thawed) (or fresh spinach)
1	cup cottage cheese
½	cup cream cheese
2	teaspoons onion powder (or ½ onion, diced)
½	can sliced mushrooms (about 3 ounces, optional, to taste)
½	teaspoon corn-free salt (to taste)
¼	teaspoon pepper (to taste)
	Other seasonings (optional, to taste)
2	eggs

Preheat the oven to 350°.

Thaw the frozen spinach or clean and cut fresh spinach. Warm the cream cheese until it is soft.

Stir together the spinach, cottage and cream cheeses, onion powder, mushrooms, and the salt, pepper, and other seasonings, if desired. For a lighter result, beat the eggs to a froth before adding. Add the eggs and stir well.

Coat or spray a baking dish with cooking oil. Add the spinach mixture and bake at 350° for 30 minutes. The casserole is done when it is slightly browned on top and firm in the center.

Variations:

↳ For a crisp topping, sprinkle bread crumbs on the spinach before baking.

↳ Line a pie pan with pie crust dough (see recipe under desserts) and bake the mixture as spinach pie.

Yield: 3 servings

LASAGNA

Preheat oven to 350° • Cooking time: 20 –30 minutes

1	pound hamburger
½	medium onion, chopped (or about ½ teaspoon onion powder or flakes—optional, to taste)
2	cloves garlic (or about 1 teaspoon garlic powder or flakes—optional, to taste)
1	26-oz. jar corn-free spaghetti sauce (or make Homemade Spaghetti sauce—see page 154)
1	Tablespoon dried oregano (optional, to taste)
1	Tablespoon basil (optional, to taste)
	Corn-free salt and pepper, to taste
9	lasagna noodles (about 8 ounces)
16	oz. mozzarella cheese
16	oz. cottage cheese
4–8	oz. cheddar cheese (optional)

Crumble fry the hamburger, (see page 98). If you are using fresh onion and/or garlic, add them to cook with the hamburger. When the hamburger is brown, add the spaghetti sauce and oregano, basil, salt, and pepper to taste. Simmer for about 10 minutes.

Meanwhile, boil the noodles according to package instructions.

Shred or slice the hard cheeses. When the noodles are done, drain the noodles. Preheat the oven to 350°. In a cake pan or baking dish, spread a thin layer of the tomato sauce.

Arrange a single layer of the lasagna noodles (3 noodles) next. Add a layer of the tomato sauce and then sprinkle on a layer of mozzarella cheese. Add a layer of cottage cheese in scoops; it does not need spread out since the heat of baking will spread it.

Repeat the layers: noodles, sauce, and cheese.

(continued on next page)

You can usually find corn-free spaghetti sauce. Authentic Italian dishes do not have corn. If you do not find a safe commercial spaghetti sauce, see the Spaghetti recipes, pages 152–55.

Top with a layer of noodles and a layer of shredded hard cheeses. Bake at 350° for 20–30 minutes, until the cheese melts and browns. (Low-fat cheese will not brown as dark.)

Allow the lasagna to cool for at least 5 minutes before cutting. Cool more before serving.

If desired, top the dish with Cheddar cheese.

Variation:

Ricotta: Use 8 ounces of ricotta cheese in place of other cheeses.

CAUTION: Ricotta cheese usually contains corn derivatives in small amounts. If you react to such ingredients, do not use ricotta which has them. Check with your doctor.

Yield: 8 servings

NACHO CHIPS with CHEESE DIP

4	ounces Colby-Jack or Monterey Jack cheese
½	cup skim milk, divided
¾	teaspoon flour
¾	teaspoon cooking oil
	Dry chili-pepper powders, to taste: paprika, red pepper, etc.
2–3	tortillas (see box on opposite page)
¼	teaspoon corn-free salt

Shred the cheese and measure the milk. Set them aside at room temperature to warm up.

Meanwhile, place the flour and half the milk (about ¼ cup) in a small skillet. Stir the flour into the milk until the mixture is very smooth. Add the oil and stir. Heat the mixture on low to medium-low, stirring occasionally until it boils. Then simmer and stir constantly. The mixture will turn to a smooth, creamy consistency.

Lower the heat and add a few shreds of cheese. Stir until the cheese melts in and the mixture is smooth again. If the mixture bubbles, pull the skillet off the heat and turn the heat down just a little. Stir, then return the skillet to the heat. The goal is to keep the mixture just warm enough to melt the cheese but not hot enough to bubble.

Add a spoonful of the remaining milk and stir over low heat until smooth.

Repeat, alternately adding cheese and milk. Stir each addition until smooth. When all of the cheese and milk is in the mixture, take the mixture off the heat.

Stir in seasonings and peppers, as desired. See variations on next page.

Brush the tortillas with oil on both sides. Salt the tortillas lightly and stack them. Cut the stack in half three times, making six triangle wedges from each tortilla.

Preshredded and sliced cheese usually contains cornstarch to prevent sticking. Use shredded cheese with potato starch instead, or shred or cut your own from a cheese brick.

Coat or spray a baking sheet with cooking oil. Spread the tortilla pieces on the baking sheet. Bake at 350° about 10 minutes, turning once. When the pieces are lightly brown and crisp, they can be used for nacho chips.

Serve the warm chips with nacho dip on the side or drizzled over the chips.

Variation: Add slices of chili peppers, such as green bell peppers, green chilies (Anaheim), jalapeño, habanero, etc. For chili preparation and cooking directions, see Salsa and Fast Salsa recipes, pages 42–44.

Yield: 2 servings

Commercial tortillas may contain cornstarch or other corn additives. If you cannot find safe tortillas, try Tortilla Shells, page 19.

NACHOS with MEAT

Preheat oven to 350° • Cooking time: 10–12 minutes

1	recipe Tortilla Shells (see page 19)
1	recipe Nacho Cheese Dip (see page 148)
½	pound hamburger (or diced chicken)
	Chili powder, onion, garlic, and/or cayenne, to taste
½	can pinto beans (or black beans), refried
1	teaspoon oil
	Corn-free salt, to taste
1	tomato, diced
¼	onion, diced (optional)
1	jalapeño pepper, sliced (optional)

Make the Tortilla Shells and Nacho Cheese Dip ahead of time.

Crumble-fry the hamburger (see page 98) or chicken pieces with chili powder and other seasonings, to taste.

In a separate pan warm the refried beans. Stir in about a teaspoon of oil, and salt to taste. Mash the beans with a potato masher.

Warm the wheat Tortilla Chips in the oven at about 350°, if desired. Top the middle of the chips with beans then hamburger mix, diced tomatoes, and onion. Drizzle on the cheese sauce. Top with jalapeño pepper slices, if desired. Toppings need to leave some chips uncovered around the edges.

If you prefer, you can serve the chips and toppings in separate bowls. Guests can then create the nacho dish of their choice using only the toppings they choose.

Serve nachos with the beans, hamburger, and cheese sauce warm. All guests can eat nachos from the same dish, or you can serve nachos in individual dishes. If desired, serve salsa and/or guacamole on the side. See salsa and guacamole recipes on pages 41–44.

You eat nachos with your fingers by dipping chips into the toppings.

Variations:

↳ For milder nachos, omit the jalapeño peppers. If desired, use diced green bell pepper instead.

↳ For hotter nachos, serve diced habanero or serrano peppers on the side.

Yield: 2–3 servings

CHAPTER 7: CASSEROLES AND COMBINATIONS

The symbol ▼ marks healthier recipe choices.

FAST SPAGHETTI with MEAT

1	pound ground beef
1	15- to 18-oz. jar corn-free spaghetti sauce (or use Homemade Sauce, see page 154)
8–10	oz. spaghetti, linguini, or flat noodles
½	teaspoon olive oil (or cooking oil)
	Parmesan cheese (optional—for garnish)

Place the ground beef in a large skillet and crumble-fry the meat on medium to medium-high, stirring occasionally and using a spatula to break the meat into small pieces (see page 98).

When the meat is browned through, lower the temperature to very low and stir in the spaghetti sauce. Stir in desired seasonings (see variations below).

In a large saucepan bring 2–3 quarts of water to boil. Add the pasta. Add the oil to prevent the noodles from sticking. Boil the pasta to the desired tenderness, stirring occasionally.

Drain the pasta in a colander.

Serve the pasta and sauce in separate serving dishes or serve the pasta with sauce on top on individual plates. Serve with shredded Parmesan cheese for garnish, if desired.

The spaghetti sauce will keep, refrigerated, for several days. Flavors will blend, and the sauce may taste even better the next day. Leftover pasta does not keep. Make it fresh for leftover sauce or use the leftover sauce over potatoes, rice, or biscuits.

When is pasta done cooking? If you cut a partly cooked noodle in two, the center has a darker color. Some say the pasta is done the instant this changes to one smooth color. Others prefer to cook the pasta longer and softer.

Variations:

Tomato: Add up to a whole tomato, diced, especially with extra basil.

Oregano: Add up to 2 tablespoons dried oregano for stronger flavor.

Garlic: For garlic lovers, add ½ teaspoon of garlic powder or flakes or about 2 garlic cloves, pressed, sliced, or minced.

Onion: Add about ½ cup of diced onion.

Basil: Add up to 1 tablespoon dried basil or 3 tablespoons fresh chopped basil.

Garden: With or without the meat, add any one or all of such favorite veggie pieces as tomatoes, onions, mushrooms, zucchini, green bell peppers, celery, and/or carrots.

Cheese: Add Romano, Parmesan, provolone, ricotta, and/or cottage cheese.

Yield: 3–4 servings

For a lower-calorie meal, use 7-percent-fat meat and serve the sauce over rice, not pasta.

HOMEMADE SPAGHETTI

1	6-oz. can tomato paste
1¼	cups water, divided
1	teaspoon dried oregano, to taste
1	teaspoon dried basil (optional, to taste; see seasoning variations, page 152–53)
½	teaspoon sugar (or brown sugar—optional, to taste)
1–2	fresh tomatoes, diced
1	teaspoon onion powder or flakes or 1 Tablespoon fresh minced onion (optional, to taste)
¼	teaspoon garlic powder or flakes or 1 small clove of garlic, minced (optional, to taste)
½	teaspoon corn-free salt (optional, to taste)
1	pound ground beef
6–8	oz. spaghetti, linguini, or flat noodles
½	teaspoon olive oil (or cooking oil)
	Parmesan cheese

In a medium saucepan place the tomato paste and a little of the water. Stir until the tomato paste is smooth. Continue to stir in the rest of the water, a little at a time. Stir in the oregano, basil, and sugar. Heat over medium-low, stirring occasionally.

Stir in the diced tomatoes. Turn the heat down to very low and allow the seasonings to blend while preparing the rest of the ingredients. Stir occasionally.

Lightly coat or spray a large skillet with olive oil or cooking oil. Sauté the onion and garlic, if desired. Crumble-fry the ground beef in the skillet with the onion and garlic (see page 98).

When the meat mixture is cooked, add the sauce mix to it. Keep the mixture on low heat to blend the flavors, 5–20 minutes or longer. Stir occasionally.

In a large saucepan bring 2–3 quarts of water to boil. Add the pasta. Add a little oil to prevent the noodles from sticking. Boil to the desired tenderness, stirring occasionally.

For a lower-calorie meal, use 7-percent-fat meat and serve the sauce over rice, not pasta.

Serve the pasta and sauce in separate serving bowls. Or you can serve the pasta and sauce on individual plates. Serve Parmesan cheese on the side.

For leftovers, opinions vary. The sauce will keep in the refrigerator for a few days and may improve as flavors blend. Noodles can be combined with sauce to keep for leftovers, but some prefer fresh-cooked noodles.

Variations:

↳ If desired, add 2 teaspoons dried oregano and/or more garlic and onion. For other seasonings, veggies, and variations, see Fast Spaghetti with Meat, page 152.

Yield: 3 servings

HAMBURGER HASH PLUS

1	pound frozen hash brown potatoes (2 cups or half of a 30-oz. bag), thawed
1	pound ground beef
1	Tablespoon cooking oil, to taste
¼	teaspoon corn-free salt (optional, to taste)
⅛	teaspoon pepper (optional, to taste)

Thaw the potatoes in a microwave oven or a skillet (see box below).

In a large skillet on medium-high heat crumble-fry the hamburger (see the box on the opposite page). When the meat is lightly brown, push it to the sides of the pan. In the center, add the oil, salt, pepper, and the thawed potatoes. Cover the pan and turn up the heat to brown the potatoes lightly. Turn the potatoes to brown them on both sides.

Stir the hamburger and potatoes together. Brown the mixture lightly.

To thaw potatoes in a microwave: Spread the potatoes on a microwaveable plate. Pour hot water over the potatoes and drain, leaving some water with the potatoes. Microwave on high until the potatoes are thawed and soft, about 5–10 minutes. Add more water and heat longer for softer potatoes.

To thaw potatoes in the pan: Heat water and potatoes in a skillet on medium heat until potatoes are thawed and soft. Add more water and heat longer for softer potatoes.

Variations:

ᔰ Add green or red vegetables (such as peas, green beans, diced tomatoes).

ᔰ Add one of the seasonings below (or your own favorites):

  ᔰ ½ teaspoon powdered onion and/or ⅛ teaspoon garlic

  ᔰ 1 teaspoon dried oregano and/or dried basil with diced tomato

  ᔰ 1 teaspoon cilantro with diced tomato

  ᔰ 1 teaspoon dried parsley or tarragon

  ᔰ 1 teaspoon chili powder or curry powder or Cajun/Creole seasoning mix.

Yield: 4 servings

For a lower-calorie meal, use 7-percent-fat meat and
serve the sauce over rice, not pasta.

❧ ❧ ❧

To crumble-fry hamburger: Place the hamburger in a large, hot frying pan
and turn the heat down to medium. As the meat browns, cut it into smaller
pieces with a spatula. Scrape the browned meat from the bottom of the pan
and turn it to brown it evenly. Cover the pan with a spatter screen. If you are
using meat with a high fat content, you may want to drain off the fat.

SLOPPY SHAWNS

1	pound ground beef
¼	cup diced yellow onion (optional, to taste)
2	6-oz. cans tomato paste, to taste
½–¾	cup water (or substitute 1 14.5-oz. can tomato sauce for tomato paste and water)
¼	cup ketchup (to taste; for corn-free ketchup, see page 77)
1	cup Sweet Pickle Relish (optional, to taste; see page 76)
4–6	oz. shredded cheddar cheese (optional)
1	teaspoon mustard powder (optional)
1	6.5-oz. can mushrooms (optional)

If you need to make corn-free pickle relish, make it the day before or weeks before.

In a large skillet crumble-fry the ground beef, stirring occasionally (see page 98). Dice the onion and add it. When the meat is cooked through, drain it to remove excess fat.

Turn the heat to medium-low and stir in all the other ingredients. Continue heating, stirring occasionally, until the mixture is hot and the cheese is melted.

Taste and adjust the flavor, as desired. Try new ingredients such as okra or garlic. Sloppy Shawns are never the same twice.

Serve hot on corn-free hamburger buns or bread.

Mustard, catsup and sweet relish all contain corn in the form of vinegar made from corn and corn syrup. Instead, this recipe uses mustard powder and the ketchup and relish recipes (pages 76– 77) made with sugar and apple cider vinegar.

Variations:

↪ Serve the mixture over cooked rice, pasta, or couscous. Or serve it over mashed potatoes, mashed yams, or cooked cauliflower. Try salad greens on the side.

↪ Add diced tomatoes and/or bell peppers, to taste.

↪ For mild spice, add chili powder, black pepper, and/or red pepper.

↪ For more spice, add diced jalapeño (or hotter) pepper. For pepper preparation, see Salsa, page 42.

Yield: 4 servings

CHICKEN CHUNKS IN CLEAR SAUCE

2   6-oz. cans chicken chunks (or 1½ cups cooked, diced chicken)
2   cups chicken broth (or cold water or a mixture of both)
4   Tablespoons arrowroot powder (or flour, which makes a
       cream instead of clear sauce)
4   teaspoons cooking oil (or butter—optional, to taste)
½   teaspoon corn-free salt (optional, to taste)
¼   teaspoon pepper (optional, to taste)
½   cup cooked vegetable pieces, such as peas, carrots, onions or
       other favorites
1   teaspoon sugar (optional, to taste)

Drain the liquid from canned chicken into a measuring cup. Add enough cold water to make 2 cups. (Use chicken broth instead of water, if preferred.)

Mix the cold water, arrowroot powder, oil, salt, and pepper in a medium-size skillet. Heat to a boil on medium while stirring frequently. The white mixture will turn clear just before it boils. Stir constantly and continue simmering for a few minutes.

Add the chicken and vegetables, as desired. A touch of sugar may help bring out flavors. Simmer lightly for 2 minutes. The mixture can simmer long enough to prepare cooked rice or pasta on the side for serving.

Serve warm over cooked rice, pasta, or warm bread.

Variations:
   ᕦ Add ½ teaspoon lemon pepper or other favorite poultry seasoning mix.
   ᕦ Add 1 teaspoon dried, cut-up rosemary and/or 1 teaspoon thyme.
   ᕦ Add ⅓ cup cooked, diced bell peppers.
   ᕦ Instead of rice or pasta, serve over cooked potatoes or biscuits.
   ᕦ Substitute canned tuna or salmon for canned chicken.

Yield: 2 servings

For lower calories, use skinless chicken and fat-free broth
or skim milk. Read ingredients! Canned meats and meat broths
may contain corn products.

WHITE SAUCE
(also called Cream Sauce)

1	cup cold milk (or water)
2	Tablespoons flour
2	teaspoons cooking oil (or butter)
¼	teaspoon plain salt (optional, to taste)
⅛	teaspoon pepper (optional, to taste)
	Seasonings (optional, to taste)

In a skillet stir the flour into *cold* milk or water. Heat the mixture to a boil, stirring frequently. Boil and stir constantly until the mixture thickens into sauce. Stir in the oil, salt, pepper, and any seasonings desired. Add any meat, fish, and/or vegetables desired (see variations below) and simmer for 5 minutes to blend the flavors.

Variations:
Meat: Add ½ pound of crumble-fried hamburger (see page 98), plus seasonings.
Fish: Add 1 6-oz. can tuna fish, plus seasonings.
Vegetables: Add ½ cup cooked potato chunks or slices or other cooked vegetables, plus seasonings. Try adding cheese, too.

Yield: "creams" about 2 servings of meat, fish, potatoes, vegetables, or cream soups

---

For thin White Sauce, reduce the amount of flour to 1 tablespoon or less. For thick sauce, increase the flour to 3–4 tablespoons.

◦ ◦ ◦

Just like bread or noodles, white sauce contains grain (flour). You can use white sauce to replace bread or noodles in a meal. You can also use white sauce with meat, fish, or veggies over noodles, bread, or potatoes.

CLEAR SAUCE

Follow the White Sauce recipe on the opposite page, but use water not milk. Substitute arrowroot powder (or potato starch or cream of tarter) for the flour. Stir and boil as above. The white mixture will turn clear just before boiling. Continue heating and simmer the mixture for a few minutes. Stir in the oil, salt, pepper, and any seasonings desired. Clear Sauce is good with poultry, eggs, fish, and fruit cobblers or pies.

Variation:
Poultry: Add 1 5-oz. can chicken pieces, plus seasonings.

Yield: "creams" about 2 servings of cooked poultry, fish, or clear soups

---

See the Spice Chart Appendix on page 257 for seasoning ideas. Look up the food you want to cream and find seasonings that go with it. You can season cream sauces with mild herbs or give them spice with black pepper. Hot chili peppers do better with tomato sauces.

Lumps? Adding flour or arrowroot powder to hot or boiling water causes lumps. It takes time to smooth a lumpy sauce in a blender; be sure to start with COLD water.

FISH PATTIES

2	cups soft bread crumbs (about 1 slice) or crackers
1	6-oz. can tuna (or flaked salmon)
1	Tablespoon cooking oil (to taste)
¼	teaspoon corn-free salt (optional, to taste)
⅛	teaspoon pepper (optional, to taste)
1	beaten egg (or egg white)
½	cup water

Coat or spray a medium-size nonstick skillet with cooking oil.

Measure the bread crumbs or cracker pieces. If using crackers, mash them into crumbs with a potato masher after measuring pieces.

Combine the fish, bread crumbs, oil, salt, and pepper. Stir.

Beat the egg. For fluffier patties, whip the egg. Add the water and beaten egg to the bread and fish mixture. Stir.

Shape the mixture into 4 patties. Fry on medium heat, turning occasionally, until the patty is golden brown and the center is cooked through. Serve hot.

Variations:

Loaf: Shape the mixture into a loaf and bake in a loaf pan at 350° for 35–45 minutes.

Tomatoes: Add ¼–½ cup diced tomatoes when adding water and egg.

Onion: Add half of a small onion, diced.

Seasonings: Add ⅛ teaspoon lemon pepper or ¼ teaspoon dill weed or ¼ teaspoon dried tarragon flakes or ¼ teaspoon dried rosemary.

↪ Serve with cooked rice and garnish with orange slices.

↪ Serve with lemon and/or corn-free tartar sauce made with mayo, apple cider vinegar, and dill seed with a pinch of sugar, if desired.

Yield: 4 servings

FRIED RICE WITH EGG

2	cups drained, cooked rice (white or brown)
2	eggs
1	Tablespoon water
2	Tablespoons cooking oil, to taste
¼	teaspoon corn-free salt
3–4	Tablespoons frozen peas (optional)
3–4	Tablespoons diced frozen carrots (optional)
3–4	Tablespoons diced frozen onions (optional)
Dash	pepper (optional, to taste)
2	Tablespoons soy sauce (optional, to taste)

Cook the rice according to package directions. Drain if needed. (One cup of instant rice or ⅔ cup of dry rice makes about 2 cups of cooked rice.)

Break the eggs into a cup and stir briskly with a fork until the yolks and whites are thoroughly mixed, and a few small bubbles form. Stir the water into the eggs.

Heat the oil in a medium-size skillet or wok. (The oil should be very hot but not browning or smoking.) Add the salt.

Add the cooked rice and pour the egg-and-water mixture over it, stirring thoroughly. Brown the rice, turning occasionally. Add the frozen peas, carrots, and/or onions, if desired. Heat long enough to warm the veggies. Stir in pepper and other seasonings, if desired.

Serve hot with a side of fruit slices or fruit juice.

Variations:

↪ Add 6 ounces (¾ cup) of canned, diced chicken chunks or leftover diced, cooked chicken.

↪ Add or replace other veggies with 3–4 tablespoons of diced, cooked bell peppers or broccoli.

↪ Add or replace other veggies with cooked pieces of oriental favorites like bok choy, water chestnuts, bamboo shoots, and/or bean sprouts.

Yield: 2 servings

Frozen vegetable pieces may be misted with cornstarch to prevent sticking. If you are extremely sensitive, try rinsing frozen veggies thoroughly before cooking.

CHILI

1	pound ground beef
¼	onion, diced (or 1½ teaspoons powdered onion—optional, to taste)
2	cans kidney beans (or pinto beans or 1 can of each), drained and rinsed
3	6-oz. cans tomato paste
2	cups water (adjust to desired sauce thickness)
¼	teaspoon corn-free salt (optional, to taste)
¼	teaspoon sugar (optional)
⅛	teaspoon garlic powder (optional, to taste)
⅛	teaspoon pepper (optional, to taste)
½	teaspoon chili powder (to taste)

In a large skillet crumble-fry the ground beef with onion, if desired, (see page 98). Drain the beans and rinse them well and set aside.

Crock-pot method: Dump all the ingredients except the pepper and chili powder into a crock pot. Stir well. Set the pot to low heat and go play for the day. (Check your crock pot directions for time ranges.)

Stove-top method: If you don't have a crock pot, keep the meat in the skillet. Add the tomato paste. Stir in the water a little at a time until the tomato sauce is smooth. Use more water if you want a thinner sauce. Stir in the salt, sugar, and garlic powder. Turn down the temperature when the sauce starts to bubble. Add the beans. Simmer long enough to heat the beans and blend flavors, from 20 minutes to several hours.

Add the pepper and chili powder about 10 minutes before serving. (Some seasonings dissipate or turn bitter with long cooking times.) Stir. Serve hot with bread or crackers.

Chili will keep, covered, in the refrigerator for a few days.

Variations:
↪ After simmering the chili, add grated cheddar cheese for a topping.
↪ For a stronger tomato flavor, add a half to a whole tomato, diced.
↪ For spicy chili, add red pepper or jalapeño or stronger peppers.

Yield: 4 servings

SAVORY MEAT LOAF
Preheat oven to 350° • Cooking time: 50–60 minutes

1	egg (or egg white)
1	pound ground beef (or ground chuck)
⅓	cup rolled oats
¼	teaspoon corn-free salt (optional, to taste)
¼	teaspoon pepper (optional, to taste)

Preheat the oven to 350°.

In a medium mixing bowl beat the egg. Add the ground beef, oats, salt, and pepper. (See variations below for more seasoning choices.) Mix well.

Place the mixture into a loaf pan or baking dish.

Bake at 350° for 50–60 minutes.

Variations:
Add one of the following options:
↪ ¼ teaspoon tarragon and ¼ teaspoon oregano
↪ ½ teaspoon parsley flakes and ¼ teaspoon celery seed
↪ 1 teaspoon onion powder and ¼ teaspoon garlic powder
↪ ½ cup diced tomatoes and ½ cup sliced mushrooms

Yield: 4 servings

For fewer calories, use meat with 7 percent fat.

SWEET MEAT LOAF

Preheat oven to 300° • Total cooking time: 2 hours 15 minutes

1	egg
1	cup bread crumbs
¼	teaspoon corn-free salt, to taste
¼	teaspoon pepper (optional)
1	pound hamburger (or other ground meat)

Tomato topping (optional):

¾	cup tomato sauce (or tomato paste mixed half-and-half with water)
⅓	cup sugar (brown or white) (or ¼ cup molasses)

Break and stir the egg. Mix in the bread crumbs, salt, and pepper. Mix in a vegetable option, if desired (see variations below). Add the meat and stir well.

Coat or spray a baking dish or pan with cooking oil. In this pan, form the meat loaf mixture into a loaf. Make a depression in the loaf by pressing the back of a spoon along the center lengthwise.

Mix the tomato sauce and sugar. Pour the tomato topping over the meat loaf. The tomato topping can be mixed into the meat mixture, if preferred.

Bake the loaf in a loaf pan or dish or a cake or pie pan at 300° for 2 hours. Turn the oven up slightly (about 305°) and bake the loaf for another 15 minutes, just hot enough and long enough to caramelize the topping, not enough to burn it.

Cool the loaf for several minutes before serving. Serve with applesauce or fruit slices.

Variations:
Add one of the following options:

> ½ cup canned spinach (half of a small 7.75-oz. can)

> ⅔ cup diced bell peppers and/or 1 teaspoon onion powder

> ½ cup diced tomatoes and/or ¼ teaspoon dried oregano flakes and/or 1 teaspoon dried basil

> ½ cup diced tomatoes and/or ½ cup sliced mushrooms and/or 1 teaspoon dried basil flakes

> Pinch of dried parsley flakes and/or celery seed and/or dry chervil flakes

Yield: 2–3 servings

STIR-FRY VEGGIES

1	cup (8–10 ounces) per person your choice of veggies
4–5	Tablespoons peanut oil (or cooking oil that will cook hot without burning)
	Salt to taste; see more seasoning choices under Stir-Fry with Meat, page 168

Vegetable Choices:

1	can sliced water chestnuts
½	carrot or celery stick, thinly sliced
½	cup cut-up cauliflower and/or broccoli florets
¼	onion, diced (to taste)
1	garlic clove, sliced (to taste)
1	can bean sprouts
½	cup shredded cabbage and/or pieces of bok choy and/or fresh spinach

Choose several favorite vegetables. Open and drain the canned veggies that you plan to use. Cut up the raw veggies that you plan to use. Keep the various kinds of vegetables separate since they will start cooking at different times.

Coat or spray a wok or large skillet with cooking oil. Heat the wok on medium or medium high. You want the oil hot enough to cook the veggies quickly without burning. Veggies can absorb too much oil if the heat is too low. Peanut oil is a frequent choice for stir-fry cooking.

Begin with the hardest veggies first, such as water chestnuts or carrots. Add the cut-up vegetables to the hot wok. Stir frequently. As these become partly cooked, add the next hardest veggies.

Add the softest veggies last. Stir frequently. If you want, add cooked, well-drained, small noodles or rice after all the veggies are nearly done.

If you need more oil or water, add only one teaspoon or tablespoon at a time. Add oil or water in a swirling motion around the outside of the wok, so that it can heat up before reaching the vegetables. Vegetables are done when soft and brightly colored—avoid overcooking.

Serve hot with black pepper, if desired, noodles or rice and fresh fruit pieces on the side.

Other veggie choices include:

✎ Bamboo shoots, sliced bell peppers, chopped brussels sprouts, green beans, shredded lettuce, sliced mushrooms, peas, and snow peas

Yield: 3–4 servings

STIR-FRY VEGGIES with MEAT

1   pound shaved meat slices (very thin—4–6 oz. per person)
5–6   Tablespoons peanut oil (or cooking oil that will cook hot
        without burning)
8   ounces very thin pasta, such as angel hair or capallini
        Salt to taste; see more seasoning choices below

Choose one or several favorite meats (beef, chicken, etc). Ask your butcher to shave or slice the meat very thin.

Coat or spray a wok or large skillet with cooking oil. Heat the wok on medium or medium high. You want the wok hot enough to cook the veggies quickly, avoid absorbing the oil, and avoid burning the oil or meat. Peanut oil is a frequent choice for the very hot temperature of stir-fry cooking.

Cook the noodles in boiling water according to package directions. Use a few drops of oil to prevent sticking. You may want to set a timer to notice when to stop boiling and drain the noodles.

Choose and prepare several favorite vegetables; see the Stir-Fry Veggies, page 167, for more details.

Add the meat and seasonings to the hot wok. Stir frequently. As the meat becomes partly cooked, add the veggie pieces, starting with the hardest ones first, softest last. Stir frequently.

Add the cooked, well-drained noodles after all the veggies are nearly done.

If you need more oil or water, add only 1 teaspoon or tablespoon at a time. Add oil or water in a swirling motion around the outside of the wok so that it can heat up before reaching the meat, veggies, or pasta.

Serve hot. If desired, serve with black pepper and fresh fruit pieces on the side.

Variations:
➢ For a sweet flavor, add pineapple chunks with the softest veggies.
Meat Choices: Beef, chicken, pork, lamb, turkey, or shrimp
Seasoning Choices: Sesame seeds, pineapple juice, and ginger powder in water, soy sauce, and cooking sherry; cinnamon, cumin, and Oriental seasoning mix; curry mix; hot chili peppers, such as cayenne (red) pepper, jalapeño, habanero, Chinese or Thai peppers

Yield: 3–4 servings

RICE with MEAT and VEGGIES

¾   cup instant rice, white or brown (or ½ cup dry rice)
1   pound ground beef (or diced chicken or canned chicken pieces)
1   Tablespoon cooking oil (or butter or corn-free margarine)
½   cup sliced carrots (⅛″ circles)
1   cup sliced celery (⅛″ crescents)
1   cup broccoli florets
1   zucchini, sliced
1   cup shredded cabbage
¼   teaspoon corn-free salt (optional, to taste)
¼   teaspoon pepper (optional, to taste)
       Additional seasonings as desired (see variations below)

In a medium saucepan start the rice boiling according to package directions.

In a medium skillet start the hamburger or chicken pieces crumble-frying on medium heat. Cut and stir the meat as it cooks.

In a large skillet add the oil and hardest vegetables, such as carrots and celery. Cover and sauté on medium heat, stirring often.

When the hard vegetables are nearly as soft as desired, add the next vegetables. Cover and sauté, stirring often. When these are nearly as soft as desired, add the softest vegetables, such as shredded cabbage.

When the vegetables are as soft as desired, add the salt and pepper and any other seasonings, the cooked rice, and meat. Cover and allow the mixture to steam on very low heat for about 20 minutes.

Seasoning Variations:
Southwestern: Cilantro, lemon juice, black pepper, bell pepper, jalapeño pepper, onion, tomato
Italian: Onion, garlic, oregano, basil, tomato, dill weed, parsley, corn-free shredded cheese
Oriental: Soy sauce, ginger, sesame seed, cinnamon, and/or 5-spice powder

Yield: 3–5 servings, depending on the quantity of vegetables used

CABBAGE-MEAT CASSEROLE

1	pound crumble fried hamburger
1	10-oz. package shredded cabbage or about ¼ head of cabbage, shredded, divided
2	cups water
1	cup instant rice, uncooked
½	teaspoon corn-free salt (optional, to taste)
½	teaspoon paprika (optional, to taste)
Dash	garlic powder (optional, to taste)
Dash	onion powder (optional, to taste)
1	14.5-oz. can stewed tomatoes
	Cheese (optional)
	Fruit slices (optional)

Crumble-fry the hamburger (see page 98). Shred the cabbage, if you are not using preshredded.

In a crock pot or baking dish, add about half the cabbage, the water, and then the rice. Add the seasonings and stewed tomatoes. Then add the rest of the cabbage. (The water will not cover the cabbage.) Add the crumble-fried hamburger on top.

Heat the mixture in the crock-pot or 300° oven until the rice is tender, about 30–40 minutes. Stir the mixture to moisten all parts and add a few tablespoons of water, if needed. Cook for an additional 30 minutes to several hours, depending on temperature used.

Serve warm. If desired, garnish with cheese and/or fresh fruit slices.

Variations:

➷ Instead of hamburger, use pieces of chicken (precooked or canned) or precooked shrimp.

➷ Substitute mixed veggies for the cabbage or mix the two.

Green Chili: Add 1–2 small green chilies, diced, instead of or in addition to paprika. Canned green chili contains citric acid, usually derived from corn. To prepare fresh green chili (Anaheim peppers), broil the chilies on the top rack in the oven until they are blackened and then peel. Discard the stem, seeds, and membranes. Slice or dice the chilies. Do not touch the face or eyes while handling fresh chilies.

Yield: 4–6 servings

For fewer calories, use beef with 7 percent fat or skinless chicken.

✳ FAJITAS ⟶ *use chicken & salsa wraps seasoning (scrapbook)*

— guacamole?

1	recipe Fast Salsa (see page 44)
2	chicken breast pieces (boneless, skinless), or about ¾ pound of steak
1	Tablespoon oil
½	medium onion, sliced
2	bell peppers (green, red, yellow, or orange)
5–6	tortillas*

Prepare Fast Salsa as described on page 44. Refrigerate.

Cut the chicken breast or steak into strips. In a large skillet, heat the oil on medium-high heat. Add the meat slices to the hot skillet and brown, turning frequently.

While the meat is cooking, slice the onion and bell peppers. Add them to the skillet. Cook the meat, onion, and peppers, turning frequently, until the meat is browned. The onion will turn translucent when done. Keep this mixture warm.

Preheat the oven to 250° or heat the tortillas in the microwave.

To eat a fajita, build it like a burrito. Lay the warm tortilla flat on a plate and put the toppings (meat, veggies, salsa, and cheese, as desired) in the center. Fold the tortilla over the toppings, then fold in one side. Fold the top down, and you have made a fajita wrap.

*Note: Read ingredients. If the tortillas are not corn-free, make your own (see page 19).

Salsa without corn may not be available in the grocery store. If you make the cooked Salsa recipe (see page 42), allow plenty of time for the spices to blend.

Variation: Add cold side dishes such as diced tomatoes, shredded lettuce, grated cheese (Monterrey Jack or Colby Jack), guacamole, and sour cream. Make guacamole the same day (see page 41), and refrigerate it while preparing fajitas. Buy commercial sour cream, preferably from the organic foods section. Read ingredients!

Yield: 2 servings

BURRITOS

Preheat oven to 400° • Cooking time: about 5 minutes

2	ounces Monterrey jack cheese, shredded (optional)
2	ounces cheddar cheese, shredded (optional)
¼	cup diced or sliced onion (optional, to taste)
1	can pinto beans (or refried beans)
4	7- to 10-inch tortillas
1	tomato, diced (optional)

Shred the cheese and set it aside.

If you are using onion, discard the onion stem and skin, and dice or slice the onion. Sauté the pieces in a small skillet.

Preheat the oven to 400°.

While the onions are cooking, in a medium-size saucepan heat the pinto beans. If they are not already refried, stir in a little water, a little oil, and salt to taste. Mash the beans.

To build a burrito, lay the tortilla flat on a plate and put the toppings (beans, onions, cheese, etc. as desired) in the center. Fold the bottom of the tortilla over the toppings, then fold in one side. Fold the top down (one end is still open), and you have made a wrap that can be eaten with your fingers like a sandwich.

Lightly coat or spray a baking sheet with oil. Place the burritos on the baking sheet and warm them in the preheated oven until the cheese inside is melted.

If desired, serve with salsa or diced tomatoes.

Variations:

◌ Add crumble-fried hamburger or diced chicken on top of the beans. Fried beef or chicken strips work, too.

◌ Add chili powder, cayenne (red) pepper, garlic powder, and/or jalapeño pepper, to taste.

◌ Smother the burritos with mild or hot salsa. A smothered burrito needs a fork; it is not eaten as finger food.

◌ Substitute refried black beans for the refried pinto beans.

Yield: 4 servings

A burrito is a wrap, or sandwich, usually with beans, cheese, and South-western seasonings. Meat, onions, hot chili peppers, and even rice can be added. Garnish may include salsa, guacamole, sour cream, and/or veggies.

TOSTADA

1	can pinto beans (low-salt pinto beans may be corn-free)
1	Tablespoon cooking oil
½	teaspoon corn-free salt (optional, to taste)
2–3	small tortillas (read ingredients)
1	recipe Fast Salsa (see page 44)*

Drain the pinto beans and rinse them thoroughly. Heat the beans in a saucepan with a few tablespoons of water, the oil, and salt. Stir occasionally.

When the beans are hot, mash them with a potato masher. Keep the beans warm while preparing other toppings, as desired.

If you are using meat, crumble-fry the hamburger or fry the diced chicken pieces (or canned chicken). Keep the meat warm while preparing the tostada and other toppings desired.

Brush the tortillas with oil on both sides.

Coat or spray a baking sheet with cooking oil. Spread the tortillas on the baking sheet. Bake at 350° about 10 minutes, turning once. When the tortilla is lightly brown and crisp, it can be used as a tostada shell.

Lay the tostada shell on a plate. Spread it with beans. Serve with beans only or sprinkle on other toppings, as desired (see variation below). Serve warm with salsa on the side.

*Note: Fast Salsa (see page 44) can be made just before the tostada recipe. A cooked Salsa (see page 42) needs more time to make.

Variation:

➣ Top with ⅓ pound crumble-fried hamburger (see page 98) or bite-sized chicken pieces, shredded lettuce, diced tomato, and/or corn-free shredded cheese.

Yield: 2 servings

POT PIES

Preheat oven to 400° • Cooking time: 15–20 minutes

1   recipe Pie Crust (see page 198)
1   recipe Chicken Chunks in Clear Sauce (see page 159)

Line two individual baking dishes with pie crust. If you do not have small baking dishes, make two dishes of aluminum foil and fit them into a bread pan or baking dish.

Make the Chicken Chunks in Clear Sauce. Instead of simmering in the pan, pour the filling into the pie dishes. Cover with a top pie crust, if desired. Bake at 400° until the crust is golden brown and crisp, 15–20 minutes.

Variations:

Tuna Pot Pie: Instead of chicken, make 1 recipe Creamed Tuna (see page 114) for the filling. Proceed as above.

Meat Pot Pie: Instead of chicken, make a double recipe of Cream Sauce (see page 160). Stir in about ½ pound of hamburger, crumble-fried, or cooked stewing beef, or other cooked meat. Add cooked veggies and/or potato chunks, as desired. Proceed as above.

Yield: 2 servings

CHAPTER 8: SOUPS

The symbol ▼ marks healthier recipe choices.

CHICKEN SOUP FOR THE TUMMY

2–3   cups chicken broth (or water)

1½–2   cups flat, broken egg noodles (regular noodles or fettuccini)
       (or use ½ cup tiny soup noodles like riso, stelline, orzo,
       or alphabet noodles)

1   cup cold water

2   Tablespoons arrowroot powder

½   teaspoon corn-free salt, to taste

2   Tablespoons cooking oil

1   10-oz. can chicken chunks, white meat (or white and dark,
       if preferred)

In a medium-size saucepan boil the chicken broth. Break longer noodles, measure, and add them to the boiling liquid. Boil the noodles until they are soft. *Do not drain.*

In a medium-size frying pan add the cold water, arrowroot powder, and salt. Stir frequently with a spatula while heating the mixture to a boil. The mixture will turn clear as it heats just before it boils. Simmer for about a minute.

Take the mixture off the heat. Stir in the oil and chicken chunks. Break up the canned chicken chunks with the spatula. Add the cooked noodles and chicken broth.

If you have time, allow the soup to stand on very low heat for 5–10 minutes to blend the flavors. Serve warm or hot.

Note: This soup can be kept, refrigerated, for a day or two. It can be reheated. It can also be kept warm in a thermos for lunches. Flavors blend well when the soup is kept, refrigerated, overnight.

Variation: Add ⅛ teaspoon black pepper (more, if desired) to the soup while thickening. Allow the soup to stand and blend flavors. Other seasoning ideas: onion powder, garlic powder, and dried parsley flakes.

Yield: 2–3 servings

Read ingredients! Canned chicken or chicken broth may contain corn products. Look for a short ingredients list, such as "ingredients: chicken, water and salt." If you cannot find safe canned chicken, use cooked, diced chicken pieces. If you cannot find safe store-bought chicken broth, make your own (see next page).

CHICKEN BROTH

1	pound chicken wings, thighs, and/or drumsticks
5	cups water
1	teaspoon corn-free salt
½	teaspoon pepper
¼	cup diced onion
1	clove minced garlic
	Other spices: basil, dill, oregano, parsley, sage, thyme, rosemary, tarragon, or poultry seasoning, as desired

Clean the chicken of extra fat, dark spots, and any sweet meats. Remove the skin for less fat, if desired.

Place the chicken pieces in a large saucepan or crock pot. Cover the meat with water and add salt. Cover the pan tightly and simmer for 3–4 hours.* If the pan lid does not seal tightly, you will need to add more water.

Add pepper, onion, garlic, and other seasonings, as desired, about 20 minutes before taking the broth off the heat. The broth is done when the chicken meat is white with no pink and the meat falls off the bones.

Strain the bones and meat out of the broth. Chill for the broth to form a fat skim on top. Remove the fat, if desired.

Variation: Most of the meat flavor will simmer into the broth. If you serve pieces of the meat, use a strong-flavored sauce, such as a tomato sauce or hot sauce.

*Note: Simmer means just barely boiling.

Yield: 1 quart

→ double, slow cooker

✗

VEGETABLE SOUP (MINESTRONE)

1½	quarts water (or meat or vegetable broth)
1	cup cubed potatoes *(or sweet potato)*
1	cup cross-sliced carrots
1	cup diced celery
1	cup chopped onion (optional)
1	cup shredded cabbage
2½	cups diced tomatoes
¼	teaspoon corn-free salt (optional)
1	small bay leaf (optional)
⅛	teaspoon pepper (optional)
¼	teaspoon dried thyme (optional)
¼	teaspoon dried basil (optional)
¼	teaspoon dried parsley (or 1 teaspoon chopped fresh parsley)

Measure the water into a large saucepan and heat on medium. Prepare the vegetables. Start with the toughest first, as vegetables like potatoes and carrots require more cooking time. Add each vegetable to the water as it is ready. Add the salt and bay leaf, if desired.

Bring the mixture to a boil. Simmer for about 1 hour. Add more water as needed.

Add pepper and other seasonings about 10–15 minutes before the soup is done. Flavors may improve if the soup is refrigerated overnight, but do not overheat or overcook pepper and most herbs, as they can turn bitter.

Remove bay leaf before serving. Serve warm.

Variations:
↪ Add about 1 pound of hamburger, crumble-fried, after the vegetables.
↪ Add diced cooked chicken or other poultry.
Minestrone: Add ½ cup of vermicelli or small soup noodles and use the herb seasonings.

Yield: 5 servings

If you like to use fresh seasonings, try bouquet garni. The stalks of the seasonings are tied together, hung in the soup, and removed before serving. Alternatively, you can place the fresh seasonings in a cheesecloth bag to hang in the soup and remove before serving.

TOMATO CREAM SOUP

1	6-oz. can unseasoned tomato paste
2¼	cans water (14 oz.) (or 1 can milk + 1¼ can water)
½	teaspoon arrowroot powder (optional)
1	Tablespoon cooking oil
2	Tablespoons sugar
¼	teaspoon corn-free salt, to taste

Warm the tomato paste in a saucepan. Stir the arrowroot powder into the water. Stir in the water a little at a time.

Continue heating. If you are using milk, stir it in next. Stir in the oil. Stir in the sugar and salt, to taste. Heat to taste, stirring frequently. Serve warm or hot.

Variations:

◔ Boil about ¼ cup of soup pasta in plain water. Add the pasta to the Tomato Cream Soup, along with a little extra oil and salt. Tiny soup noodles come in a variety of shapes: alphabet noodles, stellini (stars), rizo (rice shape), and many others.

◔ Add any or all of these seasonings:

   ¼ teaspoon paprika
   dash onion powder or flakes
   dash garlic powder or flakes

◔ Add ¼ teaspoon of any dried herb that goes well with tomato—for example, basil, chives, oregano, and thyme.

◔ Instead of plain water, dilute the tomato paste with potato water reserved after boiling potatoes.

Yield: 2–3 servings

POTATO CREAM SOUP

2   large (or 3 medium) potatoes (about 1 pound)

The white sauce:

3   Tablespoons flour
2   cups milk (or corn-free cream or potato-water)
½   teaspoon corn-free salt (optional, to taste)
¼   teaspoon pepper (optional, to taste)
½   teaspoon parsley flakes (or 1½ teaspoons minced
           fresh parsley—optional, to taste)
¼   teaspoon celery seeds (or celery salt or ⅛ cup finely diced
           celery—optional, to taste)
¼   teaspoon onion powder or flakes (optional, to taste)
4   teaspoons cooking oil (or butter or corn-free margarine)

Peel the potatoes and cut out the eyes and any bad spots. Dice them into bite-sized chunks. Boil the potatoes chunks until they are soft but not falling apart.

In a medium skillet stir the flour into cool milk or water. Stir in seasonings, as desired. Heat the mixture to a boil, stirring frequently until the mixture thickens into sauce. Stir in the oil.

When potatoes are done, drain and add them to the white sauce. Barely simmer the soup for a few minutes to blend the flavors.

Serve warm. If desired, garnish with sprigs of parsley, tarragon, or rosemary.

Potato soup can be stored, covered, in the refrigerator for a few days. It can be reheated and served as is or used as a stock-base for other soups.

Variations:
Onion Lovers: Add ¼ cup diced onions, leeks, chives, green onions, or shallots. Before making the white sauce, sauté the chopped onion. Continue making white sauce in the skillet with the onions.

Garlic Lovers: Add 2 cloves of garlic, minced. Before making the white sauce, sauté the garlic. Continue making white sauce in the same skillet with the garlic.

Carrots: Add 1–2 tablespoons finely shredded carrots to the white sauce.

Soup Stock: Potato soup can be used for a soup base. Add pieces or chunks of cooked vegetables, meat, or fish. Or combine potato soup with another soup mixture, such as vegetable soup.

Yield: 5–6 servings

MUSHROOM CREAM SOUP

2   cups milk (or cold water)
¼   cup flour
2   Tablespoons cooking oil
½   teaspoon corn-free salt (optional, to taste)
⅛   teaspoon pepper (optional, to taste)
¼   teaspoon powdered onion (optional, to taste)
1   4-oz. can sliced mushrooms, drained (or fresh mushroom
         pieces, cooked)

Pour the *cold* milk or water into a medium-size skillet and stir in the flour. Heat the mixture to a boil, stirring constantly while heating. Boil until the mixture thickens into sauce.

Stir in the oil and any seasonings desired.

Drain the mushrooms and add them to the soup. Simmer to blend the flavors, about 5 minutes.

Yield: 2 servings

SPLIT-PEA SOUP

8	cups water
2	cups dried split peas (1 16-oz. bag)
1	teaspoon corn-free salt (optional, to taste)

Optional flavorings:

1	cup diced ham (or diced, cooked chicken)
½	cup diced carrots (or dried carrot bits and/or celery)
1	medium-size potato, cubed into 1-inch squares
⅛	teaspoon pepper
¼	teaspoon onion powder (or ¼ onion, finely chopped)
¼	teaspoon garlic powder (or 1 clove garlic, minced)

In a large saucepan combine the water, peas, and salt. Simmer gently until the peas are soft and soupy (about 5 hours).

If you are using precooked meat or vegetable bits, add these during the last 20–30 minutes of cooking time. Add any seasonings during the last 10 minutes.

Serve warm.

Variations:

↪ Instead of some of the water, use potato stock, the water reserved after boiling potatoes.

Crock-pot method: Use only 6 cups of water instead of 8. Cook the peas on high for 3½ hours and then on low for about 6½ hours. Keep the temperature on low after adding pepper.

Yield: 6 servings

A crock-pot cooks soups and stew-meats very easily. It also uses less electricity than an oven. It heats the food without heating the whole house, more useful than an oven in summer or warm climates. Many kitchen gadgets sit in the cupboard unused, taking up space, but if you like soups or stews, a crock pot can be very useful.

BROCCOLI CREAM SOUP

2	cups diced broccoli (or broccoli spears)
½	cup nonfat dry milk
2	Tablespoons corn-free margarine (or butter or cooking oil)
¼	teaspoon corn-free salt (optional, to taste)
⅛	teaspoon pepper (optional, to taste)
⅛	teaspoon onion powder (optional, to taste)

Wash, trim, and dice the broccoli. In a medium saucepan, barely cover the broccoli with water and simmer until the broccoli is very tender, 25–45 minutes.

Pour the broccoli with its cooking water into a blender. Blend until the mixture is smooth. Add powdered milk, margarine, salt, pepper, and onion powder. Blend to mix.

Serve warm.

Variation: Use the broccoli florets as a cooked vegetable or raw in salads. Use the remainder of the stalks blended into broccoli soup.

Yield: 2 servings

For fewer calories, use half the oil.

LENTIL SOUP

1	cup dry lentils (about 2 cups, cooked)
½	carrot, finely diced
¼	cup finely diced celery (optional)
1	Tablespoon cooking oil (or butter)
	Corn-free salt (to taste)
	Pepper (optional, to taste)
1	Tablespoon dry minced onion (or onion powder or about ½ onion, diced—optional, to taste)

Drain and rinse the dry lentils in cold water. Cull the bad ones and discard.

Cover the lentils with fresh water and bring to a boil. Simmer for about 30 minutes. Meanwhile, dice the carrot and celery, if desired.

Add the oil. Stir in the salt, pepper, onion, carrot, and celery. If you are using fresh onion, sauté the diced onion and add it to the soup. Simmer for about 10 minutes on the stove top or in a crock pot.

Variations:

↪ Instead of dry lentils, use 1 15-oz. can plain cooked lentils (15 oz., about 2 cups)

↪ Cook, cool, and crumble about 4 slices of corn-free bacon and add as the soup simmers.

↪ Add a few diced broccoli and/or cauliflower florets.

↪ Use chicken broth instead of water for thinning the soup.

↪ Add half a can of tomato paste and about ⅓ cup water. Season with oregano, garlic, and red pepper, if desired.

↪ Add 1 potato, peeled and diced. Use this for the potato-lentil flavor or for a soup that has acquired too much salt or other seasonings.

Yield: 2 servings

For fewer calories, use half the oil.

POT SOUP

1   pot leftover soup
      Other leftovers (veggies, meats, rice casserole, spaghetti sauce,
          etc.—optional)
      Favorite vegetables (optional)
      Another kind of soup (optional)

Start by refrigerating leftover soup for a base. Potato soup, lentil soup, vegetable soup, cream soups, and broths can all start a delicious pot soup.

Noodles will disintegrate if left in pot soup and repeatedly reheated. That's okay; they simply add to the thickening.

Use the pot soup every 3–4 days. If you do not use it, be sure to simmer the pot soup for at least 5 minutes (longer at high altitude) every 3–4 days.

To use pot soup, add more water and other soup ingredients, such as favorite vegetables, seasonings, or another kind of soup. Simmer for 10 minutes (longer at high altitudes), stirring occasionally. Serve hot. Refrigerate the leftover.

Variations:

⤵ To recover a soup that has become too flavorful, add potatoes or a cream soup.

⤵ Seasonings dissipate over time. To revive a pot soup that has become too mild, add more seasoning or try a dash of sugar or oil. Another possibility is to include strong-flavored veggies, such as broccoli, tomatoes, etc.

⤵ Try adding to pot soup: favorite veggies such as diced carrots, tomatoes, onions, zucchini, broccoli or cauliflower florets, peas, chopped green beans, or shredded cabbage. Harder veggies, such as diced potatoes, yams, squash, or beets may need to be precooked.

⤵ Consider what is in your soup base and flavors that you and your family like. Try adding meat, chicken, fish, beans, cheese, and/or rice.

If you like to have soup frequently, pot soup can make an endless variety of meals. When there is not enough left over, simply start a new pot soup with any base.

EGG DROP SOUP

3   cups chicken broth
     Seasonings: salt, sugar, celery salt, onion powder, pepper
       and/or ginger (optional—to taste)
1   egg
1   teaspoon water
1   scallion, minced

In a medium saucepan boil the chicken broth. Taste test; add seasonings as needed.

In a separate cup or bowl stir the egg with a teaspoon of water.

Lower the heat under the broth. While stirring, pour the egg very slowly into the broth. Stir fast for fine pieces of egg drop; stir more slowly for larger egg drops.

Mince the scallion and add.

Simmer for about 5 minutes to blend the flavors. Serve hot.

Variations:

↳ For a creamier soup, add arrowroot powder. Mix 5 tablespoons arrowroot powder with 3 tablespoons cold water. While stirring, pour this thickener slowly into the boiling chicken broth (before adding the egg). Simmer for a minute or so, stirring constantly, until the broth becomes a translucent, light-syrup consistency.

↳ Add cooked, shredded bamboo shoots; cooked, minced celery; cooked carrots; and/or peas.

↳ Add 2 tablespoons finely shredded, canned, or leftover cooked chicken.

Yield: 4 servings

The broth makes the soup. Flavors in the broth can include salt, sugar, celery salt, onion powder, garlic, pepper, and/or ginger, to name a few. Make sure the broth you use is corn-free. Then taste and adjust the seasonings to your preference before adding egg.

CHAPTER 9: DESSERTS / SWEETS / NUTS

Cookies

Cakes and Frosting

Cobblers and Pies

Nuts

CHOCOLATE-CHIP COOKIES
Preheat oven to 375° • Baking time: 9–11 minutes

1	cup butter (or corn-free margarine or ⅞ cup cooking oil)
¾	cup sugar
¾	cup dark brown sugar
1	teaspoon corn-free vanilla (optional)
2	eggs
2¼	cups flour
½	teaspoon baking soda
½	teaspoon corn-free salt
12	ounces corn-free semisweet chocolate chips

Preheat the oven to 375°.

In a large bowl mix the butter with the sugar, brown sugar, and vanilla. Stir until smooth.

Add the eggs to the side of the bowl, stir them, and then stir them into the mixture. If you prefer, beat the eggs to a light froth before adding them.

In a separate bowl mix the flour, soda, and salt.

Add the flour mixture to the sugar mixture a little at a time, mixing thoroughly with each addition. Add chocolate chips and/or other variations. Stir.

Drop the cookie dough by teaspoonfuls onto an ungreased baking sheet. Bake at 375° for 9–11 minutes.

Variations:
No-Chip Cookies: Make as above except omit the chocolate chips.

↳ With or without the chocolate chips, add 1 cup quick-cooking oats or other dry cereal.

↳ With or without the chocolate chips, add 1 cup peanut butter or chopped walnuts.

↳ With or without the chocolate chips, add 1 cup raisins.

Yield: 4 dozen cookies

OATMEAL COOKIES

Preheat oven to 375° • Baking time: 8–12 minutes

1	cup brown cane sugar
½	cup white cane sugar
¾	cup cooking oil (or 1 cup butter or corn-free lard)
2	eggs
1	teaspoon vanilla
2¼	cups unbleached white flour (or mix white and whole wheat plus 2 teaspoons water), divided
½	teaspoon baking soda
½	teaspoon corn-free salt
1–2	cups rolled oats

Preheat the oven to 375°.

In a large mixing bowl combine the brown and white sugar and oil. Beat the mixture until smooth. Blend in the eggs and vanilla.

Measure out 1 cup of the flour, add the baking soda and salt to it. Stir or sift this into the sugar mixture. Stir or sift in the remainder of the flour. Stir in the oats.

Drop the cookie dough by teaspoonfuls onto an ungreased baking sheet. Bake at 375° for 8–12 minutes.

Variations:

If desired, stir in any or all of the following ingredients before baking:

4–5	tablespoons oat bran (for higher fiber)
6–8	oz. chocolate chips (check ingredients!)
½	cup chopped walnuts
¾	cup raisins

Yield: 4 dozen cookies

Oat bran is one source of soluble fiber, recommended for intestinal difficulties, as sometimes experienced in food reactions.
See Chapter 15, "Allergy or Intolerance."

GRANDMA'S MOLASSES COOKIES

Preheat oven to 375° • Baking time: 10–12 minutes

1	cup brown sugar (or white sugar or mix brown and white)
½	cup cooking oil (or butter or corn-free margarine)
1–2	eggs
1	cup molasses (dark or light)
4	cups flour (or 3 cups white flour + 1 cup whole wheat flour)
1	teaspoon cinnamon
½	teaspoon corn-free salt
½	teaspoon ground ginger
⅔	cup hot water
1	teaspoon baking soda

Preheat the oven to 375°.

In a large bowl combine the sugar, oil, egg(s), and molasses. Mix well.

In a separate large bowl combine the flour, cinnamon, salt, and ginger. Stir gently.

In a cup measure combine the hot water and baking soda. Stir until the soda dissolves.

To the sugar mixture, alternately add part of the flour mix and part of the soda water. The final dough will be thick.

Drop the cookie dough by teaspoonfuls onto an ungreased baking sheet. Bake at 375° for 10–12 minutes. The cookies will be soft if not over-baked.

Note: To store Grandma's Molasses Cookies, refrigerate or freeze the cookies by first placing them side by side on plates in layers separated by waxed paper, plastic, or aluminum foil. If stacked together, molasses cookies will stick together!

Yield: 4 dozen cookies

A holiday favorite from the 1800s. Notice the method of using baking soda, which makes the cookies "rise" without baking powder. How is the baking soda prevented from clumping? With hot water, not cornstarch!

POWDERED SUGAR FROSTING

2½   cups corn-free confectioner's sugar
½   cup butter (or corn-free margarine)
¾   teaspoon vanilla
1½   Tablespoons milk (or hot water)

Press lumps out of the powdered sugar with the back of a spoon.

Warm the butter or margarine. Mix in the sugar. Add the vanilla and milk or water. Beat the mixture until smooth. An electric mixer on high works well for beating the frosting.

If the frosting is too dry and crumbly to spread, add hot water, 1 teaspoon at a time, until the mixture is creamy enough to spread. You can also melt the frosting in a microwave for about 15 seconds. (Do not overheat, as the oils may separate, requiring you to refrigerate and remix.)

Variations:
Double quantity, for frosting layer cakes:
5   cups corn-free confectioner's sugar
1   cup butter (or corn-free margarine)
1½ teaspoons vanilla
3   Tablespoons milk (or water)

Sweet Chocolate Frosting: Add ¼ cup cocoa to the dry ingredients, single recipe. Increase the butter by about 1 teaspoon. Increase the hot water by 2 teaspoons. Press out any lumps of powdered sugar with the back of a spoon.

Dark Chocolate Frosting: Heat 4 ounces unsweetened baking chocolate on medium-low until it is melted and hot. Make the powdered sugar frosting, single recipe, but leave out the vanilla. After the frosting is made, stir in the hot, melted baking chocolate. Press out any lumps of powdered sugar with the back of a spoon.

Yield: frosting for 1 cake

CAUTION—Confectioner's sugar, or icing sugar, has a large amount of cornstarch. It can be difficult to find corn-free confectioner's sugar. One source is allergygrocery.com, a mail-order firm for some allergen-free foods.

COOKED SUGAR FROSTING

½   cup cooking oil (or butter or corn-free margarine)
2   cups sugar
3   oz. unsweetened baking chocolate
⅔   cup milk (or water)
½   teaspoon corn-free salt, to taste

In a medium-size saucepan mix all the ingredients. Heat to boiling, stirring frequently. Boil for about a minute.

Cool the mixture quickly by placing the saucepan in a larger bowl of ice and cold water. Beat the frosting until it is smooth and thick enough to spread.

Variation:
Vanilla Frosting: Leave out the chocolate and stir in 2 teaspoons vanilla.

Yield: frosting for 1 cake

PINEAPPLE UPSIDE DOWN CAKE
Preheat oven to 350° • Baking time: 35–40 minutes

½	cup cooking oil (or melted margarine or butter)
1	cup brown cane sugar
1	16- to 20-oz. can corn-free pineapple (crushed or slices)
2⅓	cups flour
1½	cups sugar
1¼	cups pineapple juice
½	cup cooking oil (or melted margarine or butter)
3	teaspoons corn-free baking powder (see page 11)
1	Tablespoon warm water
¾	teaspoon corn-free salt
2	eggs
¼	teaspoon vanilla (optional, to taste)
¼–½	teaspoon lemon juice (optional, to taste)

Preheat the oven to 350°. In a 9 x 13-inch cake pan add the oil. Stir the brown sugar into the oil with a spatula and spread the mixture evenly. Drain pineapple and reserve the liquid for part of the pineapple juice ingredient. Coat the sugar evenly with crushed pineapple or arrange pineapple slices on top of the sugar mixture.

In a large mixing bowl stir the flour and sugar together thoroughly. Add the pineapple juice and stir until the mixture reaches a smooth consistency. Add the oil and stir until smooth.

Stir the baking powder into the warm water. Stir in the salt. Add this mix to the batter and beat until smooth. (The water mix helps the baking soda stir in evenly.)

For a fluffier cake, use a separate bowl and whisk the eggs to a froth. Then fold the eggs into the batter. For a faster job, break the eggs into the same bowl on one side of the mixture. Then break the yolk and stir the eggs alone. Stir the eggs into the mixture until smooth.

Stir in vanilla, if desired. Stir in lemon juice, if desired.

Pour the batter into the baking pan on top of the pineapple mixture. Bake at 350° for 35–40 minutes. The cake is done when a fork inserted in the center comes out clean. Serve the cake pieces upside down with the pineapple on top.

Yield: 15 servings

YELLOW FLUFFY CAKE

Preheat oven to 350° • Baking time: 25–30 minutes

2⅓	cups flour
1½	cups sugar
1¼	cups milk (or cold water)
½	cup cooking oil (or melted margarine or butter)
3	teaspoons corn-free baking powder (see page 11)
1	Tablespoon warm water
¾	teaspoon corn-free salt
2	eggs
½ –1	teaspoon vanilla (optional, to taste)

Preheat the oven to 350°. Oil a 9 x 13-inch cake pan and sprinkle it with flour.

In a large mixing bowl stir the flour and sugar together thoroughly. Add the milk and stir until the mixture reaches a smooth consistency. Add the oil; stir until smooth.

Stir the baking powder into warm water. Stir in the salt. Add this mix to the batter and beat until smooth. (The water mix helps the baking soda stir in evenly.)

For a fluffier cake, use a separate bowl and whisk the eggs to a froth. Then fold the eggs into the batter. For a faster job, break the eggs into the same bowl on one side of the mixture. Then break the yolk and stir the eggs alone. Stir the eggs into the mixture until smooth.

Stir in vanilla, if desired.

Pour the batter into the baking pan. Bake at 350° for 25–30 minutes. The cake is done when a fork inserted into the center comes out clean. Cool before frosting.

Variations:

Cranberry Cake: Substitute cranberry juice or cranapple juice for the milk or water.

White Cake: Use 3 egg whites instead of 2 whole eggs. For a lighter cake, beat the egg whites separately into stiff peaks and then fold them into the batter last.

Spice Cake: Add 1 teaspoon ground cinnamon, ¼ teaspoon ground cloves, and ¼ teaspoon allspice to the flour mixture.

Yield: 15 servings

ANGEL FOOD CAKE

Preheat oven to 350° • Baking time: 35–40 minutes
This recipe requires time and special materials.
A sifter and an angel food cake pan are essential.

1¼	cups sifted cake flour
½	cup sifted sugar
1½	cups (12) egg whites (room temperature)*
¼	teaspoon corn-free salt
1¼	teaspoons cream of tartar
1	teaspoon vanilla
¼	teaspoon almond extract (optional)
1⅓	cups granulated sugar

*Note: Use room temperature eggs. Leave a dozen eggs out of the refrigerator, just long enough to warm.

Sift the flour and sugar once before measuring. Measure the sifted flour and sugar and combine. Sift the mixture 4 more times, back and forth between 2 mixing bowls. Set the mixture aside.

In a separate large metal or glass bowl combine the egg whites, salt, cream of tartar, vanilla, and almond extract, if desired.

With an electric beater, beat the egg-white mixture to soft peaks.

Measure the 1⅓ cups of sugar. Sift it 4 times, and blend it into the egg white mixture.

Sift the flour-sugar mixture again and fold gently into the egg whites.

Pour gently into an ungreased angel food cake pan. Bake at 350° for 35–40 minutes. Turn the cake upside down to stand on the pan-prongs for cooling.

Serve angel food cake plain or with a fruit sauce or glaze, or a sugar syrup or glaze. Traditionally, angel food cakes are not frosted.

Yield: about 8 servings

An angel food cake is fat-free. Never allow oil or fat to contact the interior of an angel food cake pan. If even a tiny spot of oil remains, it will create large dents in the angel food cake where the cake pulls away from the side of the pan.

APPLE CRISP

Preheat oven to 375° • *Baking time: 45 minutes*

4	cups cubed apples (about 6 medium Jonathan or Winesap)*
½	cup brown sugar
½	cup white sugar
¾	cup flour
⅓	cup cooking oil (or corn-free margarine or butter)
¼	teaspoon ground nutmeg
½	teaspoon ground cinnamon (optional)

Preheat oven to 375°.

Coat a medium-size baking dish with cooking oil, corn-free margarine, or butter. Put the chopped apples into the baking dish.

In a mixing bowl combine the brown sugar, white sugar, and flour. Cut in the oil, stirring until crumbly. Add the nutmeg and cinnamon, if desired. Sprinkle the mixture over the apples.

Bake at 375° for about 45 minutes.

*Note: The apples may be peeled or not, your choice.

Yield: 8–10 servings

CHERRY COBBLER
Preheat oven to 400° • Baking time: 25–35 minutes

2	14.5-oz. cans red tart (sour) pitted cherries, drained, liquid reserved
¾–1	cup sugar
2	Tablespoons arrowroot powder
1½	cups flour
1½	Tablespoons sugar
1½	teaspoons corn-free baking powder
½	teaspoon corn-free salt
¾	cup water (or milk)
4½	Tablespoons cooking oil (or corn-free margarine or butter)

Drain the liquid from 2 cans of cherries into a large skillet. In a measuring cup combine the sugar and arrowroot powder and stir to blend. Stir the sugar mixture into the cherry liquid a little at a time.

Over medium heat, bring the mixture to a boil, stirring frequently. The mixture will turn translucent as it heats. Stir constantly while it boils until the mixture is slightly thick.

To test the thickness, lift the spatula. The mixture dripping back into the pan will show the thickness. When the syrup has thickened, remove it from the heat.

Pour the cherries into a 9x13-inch cake pan or 9-inch pie pan and add the syrup mixture. Set aside.

Preheat the oven to 400°.

In a separate bowl mix the flour, sugar, baking powder, and salt. Add the water and mix well. Stir in the cooking oil.

Drop the batter by spoonfuls onto the warm fruit mixture in the baking dish. For a crisp cobbler, bake as it is. For a more moist cobbler, press the batter down until the cherry juice flows over it.

Bake at 400° for 25–30 minutes. Cool before serving.

Yield: 8–10 servings

RHUBARB CRISP

Preheat oven to 350° • Baking time: 40–50 minutes

4	cups chopped rhubarb
½	teaspoon corn-free salt
1⅓–2	cups sugar
¾	cup flour
1	heaping teaspoon cinnamon
⅓	cup margarine (or ½ cup cooking oil)
	Cream (or milk)

Put the rhubarb in an ungreased 9x13-inch cake pan or 9-inch pie dish. Sprinkle it with the salt.

In a medium mixing bowl blend the sugar, flour, cinnamon, and margarine. Sprinkle this mixture on top of the rhubarb.

Bake at 350° for 40–50 minutes.

Serve warm with light cream or milk.

Yield: 6 servings

SINGLE PIE CRUST

(For an 8-inch or 9-inch single crust)

1½	cups flour
½	heaping teaspoon corn-free salt
⅓	cup + 1 Tablespoon cooking oil
3	Tablespoons + 1 teaspoon very cold water

Clear a countertop surface for rolling the dough. Lay out a pastry cloth and cover the rolling pin. Sprinkle flour to cover the rolling pin and surface evenly. Keep extra flour on hand to use while rolling the dough.

In a large mixing bowl mix the flour and salt. Add the oil. Stir well, scraping the sides of the bowl and breaking any clumps. The mixture will form pea-size particles. Add cold water, about 1 tablespoon at a time. Stir well. (The dough cleans the surface of the mixing bowl.)

Quickly press the dough into a ball. (Handle the dough as little as possible to keep it cool.) Flatten the ball and set it on the floured surface for rolling.

Roll the dough to size, about 1 inch extra all around than the pie pan. Roll from the center out, keeping the thickness even. For a thinner crust, roll it out even wider.

When the dough is rolled to size, place the pie pan upside down over it. Turn over the pastry cloth and pie pan together. Slowly remove the pastry cloth, and gently press the dough down to line the bottom of the pie pan. The excess dough will hang over the edges all around.

Fill the crust with the pie filling (unless the recipe calls for crust to be baked before filling). Use a sharp knife to trim off the excess dough. For a pretty edge, lift the dough all around and then pinch it repeatedly, all around the edge, to form a ruffle.

To bake with filling, see recipe. Otherwise, bake the crust alone at 450° for 10–12 minutes.

2-CRUST PIE CRUST

3	cups flour
¾	teaspoon corn-free salt
¾	cup cooking oil
6	Tablespoons + 2 teaspoons very cold water

Mix the dough as outlined in the Single Pie Crust recipe. Before rolling, press the dough into two balls. Roll each crust separately from one of the dough balls.

It's easier to roll if you handle the dough as little as possible and keep it cool. If the dough gets too warm to roll, you can refrigerate it for up to an hour to cool it.

APPLE PIE

Preheat oven to 400° • Baking time: 40–50 minutes

1	recipe 2-Crust Pie Crust (see page 199)
5–6	cups thinly sliced, tart apples (4–5 apples)
½	cup sugar (or brown sugar, to taste)
2	Tablespoons flour
½	teaspoon nutmeg
½	teaspoon cinnamon (optional)
Dash	lemon juice (optional)

Follow instructions for the 2-Crust Pie Crust on page 199. Set aside.

Peel and core the apples and slice them very thinly. Preheat the oven to 400°.

In a large mixing bowl combine the apple slices, sugar, flour, nutmeg, and cinnamon, if desired. For more tart apples, sprinkle with lemon juice. Stir.

Spoon the apple mixture into the pastry-lined pie pan. Cover with the top crust.

Cut several slits for steam to escape.

Trim away excess pie crust around the edge. Seal the edge firmly to prevent leaking: wipe a thin layer of water on the bottom crust edge and press the top crust down to seal all around.

You may want to place the pie on a large baking sheet for baking. Sometimes pies will run over during baking; the baking sheet can prevent the need to clean up the oven.

Bake at 400° for 40–50 minutes or until the crust browns and juice begins to bubble through the crust-slits.

Variations:

◔ Add ½ cup raisins to the pie filling mixture.

◔ Cover the crust-edge with aluminum foil to prevent overcooking. Remove the foil for the last 10–15 minutes of baking.

◔ Instead of the top crust, cover the pie with a crumb topping: ½ cup oil, ½ cup brown sugar, and 1 cup flour, mixed. After the pie is baked, drizzle lines of frosting glaze over the top.

Yield: One 8-inch or 9-inch pie

> **Granny Smith is a popular choice for apple pie. Other frequent, available choices of pie apples include: Braeburn, Fuji, Jonathan, golden delicious, Rome beauty, and winesap.**

CHERRY PIE

Preheat oven to 450° • Total baking time: 35–40 minutes

1	recipe 2-Crust Pie Crust (see page 199)
2	14.5-oz. cans red tart (sour) pitted cherries, drained, liquid reserved
¼	cup arrowroot powder
½–1	cup sugar
⅛	teaspoon corn-free salt
2	Tablespoons cooking oil (corn-free margarine or butter)
⅛	teaspoon almond extract (optional)
⅛	teaspoon cinnamon (optional)

Follow instructions for the 2-Crust Pie Crust on page 199. Set aside. Preheat the oven to 450°.

Drain the liquid from 2 cans of cherries into a medium skillet. Add the arrowroot powder and stir until smooth. Heat the mixture to a low simmer, stirring constantly, until the mixture thickens and turns translucent. Simmer, still stirring, for about 1 more minute.

Remove the mixture from the heat and add the sugar, salt, and oil. Stir well. Stir in the cherries. Stir in the almond extract and cinnamon, if desired.

Pour the warm cherry mixture into a pie-crust-lined baking dish. Cover with a top crust or lattice (woven strips of crust) or other decorative pieces of top crust. Bake at 450° for 10 minutes. Then lower the oven temperature to 350° and continue to bake for another 25–30 minutes.

Yield: 6–8 servings

For a woven lattice crust, roll the second half of the pie crust dough and cut out 16 strips. Lay 8 strips evenly spaced across the pie. At the center, fold back every other strip. Lay the next strip in the opposite direction, across the four unfolded strips. Then lay the 4 folded strips back in place. Continue folding back every other strip and laying a new one across, weaving the strips alternately as you go.

For fun decorations, use cookie cutters, such as heart shapes or circles, on the rolled pie crust dough. Lay the cut-out shapes on top of the cherry pie to decorate.

PUMPKIN PIE

Preheat oven to 375° • Baking time: 40–45 minutes

1	recipe Single Pie Crust (see page 198)
2	cups mashed, cooked pumpkin (about 15 ounces)
1½	cups water
1	cup sugar
2	eggs
1½	Tablespoons cooking oil
¾	teaspoon corn-free salt
¼	teaspoon nutmeg (optional)
½–1	teaspoon cinnamon (optional)
½	teaspoon ginger (optional)
½	teaspoon allspice powder (optional)

Follow instructions for the Single Pie Crust on page 198. Set aside. Preheat the oven to 375°.

In a large mixing bowl combine the pumpkin, water, sugar, eggs, oil, salt, and desired spices and stir until smooth.

Pour the filling mixture into the pastry-lined pie pan. To prevent the pie crust edges from burning, cover the edges with aluminum foil. Remove the foil for the last 10 minutes of baking.

Bake in a preheated oven at 375° for 40–50 minutes. The liquid filling bakes to a soft solid. When the pumpkin pie is done, a fork or toothpick inserted into the center will come out clean. Cool for a few minutes before serving.

Variation: For a spicy pumpkin pie, add all of the above spices plus ⅛ teaspoon ground cloves.

Yield: 6 servings

If you use canned, mashed pumpkin, be sure to check ingredients for corn derivatives. A can of "pumpkin pie filling" will likely contain corn sweeteners and other corn-based additives.

TOASTED ALMONDS

Preheat oven to 350° • Total baking time: 7 minutes

1   6-oz. package almond slivers

Preheat the oven to 350°.

Spread the raw almond slivers on a cookie sheet. Bake at 350° for about 4 minutes. Stir, and continue baking until the almonds are lightly browned. The hot nuts will continue to cook slightly as they cool.

Yield: 5 servings

SUGARED NUTS

1   6-oz. package raw sliced almonds
⅓   cup sugar

Put the nuts and sugar in a skillet. Heat on low to medium, stirring constantly, until the sugar melts and coats the nuts. Spread the nuts on a baking sheet or pan to cool.

Sugared nuts will keep in an airtight container in the refrigerator.

Yield: 5 servings

MERINGUE

2	egg whites
¼	teaspoon cream of tartar
¼	cup sugar

In a metal, ceramic, or glass mixing bowl whip the egg whites and cream of tartar to a fine froth with an electric beater. Keep beating as you add the sugar, a little at a time.

The mix becomes finer froth, then turns to white liquid. Next the mix stands in soft, rounded hills if you pull it up with the beater. Then the mix forms stiff peaks. Keep beating until the peaks are much more stiff.

Pile the meringue on top of a pie, such as pumpkin, lemon, or key lime, or on candied yams. Pull up points or swirl for decoration. Bake the pie as directed in the pie recipe.

Yield: topping for 1 pie

MERINGUE COOKIES/MERINGUE MALLOWS
Preheat oven to 350° • Baking time: 8–12 minutes

Cover a cookie sheet with aluminum foil. Oil lightly.

Make meringue, as above. Instead of putting it on a pie, drop balls of meringue on the foil-covered cookie sheet.

Bake at 350° until the balls are solid, about 8–12 minutes. Brown them for cookies or leave them white to replace marshmallows.

Yield: 20 Meringue Cookies or Meringue Mallows

Variations:

ↄ Drop the meringue into smaller bits. Bake for about 5 minutes, until solid but not brown.

S'mores: Make Oatmeal Cookies (see page 189) in thin flattened squares. Place a warm Meringue Mallow and a slice of chocolate between two thin squares of oatmeal cookie (or corn-free graham crackers).

ↄ Use Meringue Mallows like marshmallows to roast over a campfire or garnish hot cocoa, sweet potatoes, desserts, or sweet salads (especially apple salad).

BUCKEYE BALLS

1½	cups creamy peanut butter
1	pound corn-free confectioner's sugar
½	cup butter (or corn-free margarine)
1	teaspoon vanilla (optional)
6	oz. corn-free chocolate chips
¼	block paraffin (or 2 Tablespoons corn-free margarine or shortening)

Line baking sheets with waxed paper.

In a large mixing bowl mix the peanut butter, powdered sugar, butter, and vanilla, if desired. At first, fold in the powdered sugar, or cut it in using a pastry blender. The mixture will form crumbles. Use your hands to knead it into a more solid ball.

Shape the mixture into 1-inch balls, placing each ball on the waxed-paper-lined baking sheet. If the mixture is too dry to hold the balls, knead in more peanut butter.

Refrigerate the sheets of peanut-butter balls.

In the top of a double boiler (or a small bowl in a pan of hot water) melt the chocolate and stir in the paraffin.

Insert a toothpick into the top of a peanut-butter ball and then dip the ball about three-fourths down into the melted chocolate, leaving an "eye" of peanut butter showing on top.

Place the buckeye ball back on the waxed paper, chocolate side down. After dipping the balls, cool them in the freezer until the chocolate is firm. Or for fun, set them outside on the snow to cool. (Watch out for squirrels!)

After the buckeye balls are cool, remove the toothpicks and cover the hole by pressing it with the fingertips. Then refrigerate.

Store Buckeye Balls, refrigerated, with waxed paper or aluminum foil between layers of balls. (If you have any left uneaten!)

Yield: 5 dozen buckeye balls

The horse chestnut tree is the state tree of Ohio. Children love to play with its dark-brown, glossy, inedible fruit. These candies look like buckeyes.

CAUTION—Confectioner's sugar has a large amount of cornstarch. It can be difficult to find corn-free confectioner's sugar. One source is allergygrocery.com, a mail-order firm for some allergen-free foods.

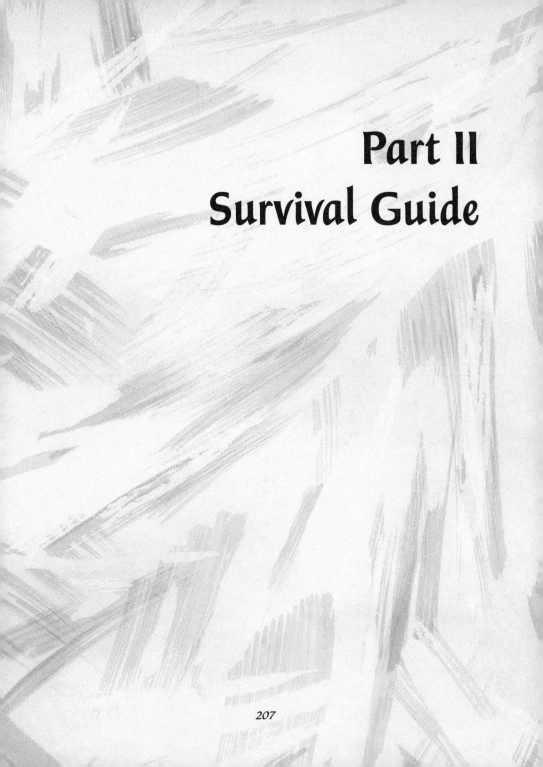

Part II
Survival Guide

CHAPTER 10: ALWAYS READ INGREDIENTS!

Your doctor said, "No corn." You drive home, depressed, munching chocolate. Did you know that most candy contains corn products (dextrose, corn syrup, etc.)?

You throw out the chocolate bar. You want to stop for fast food, but you've heard that those delicious French fries might be cooked in corn oil. You can't eat the cheeseburger either because it has a bun made with corn syrup. Instead, you go to the grocery store. Bravely, you bypass the cookies and get yogurt instead. You wind up in the ER. How were you to know that yogurt can contain forms of corn? *What can you eat?* Just bread and water? No, the bread might contain bits of corn. . . .

Read Ingredients!

Begin with reading *short* ingredients lists. For example, a can of food might list beans and water as its only two ingredients. Short labels are faster to read, but more important, such packages are less likely to contain a corn derivative.

Long lists of ingredients frequently include corn products. Worse, the labels usually don't clearly state "corn." Derivatives of the dangerous yellow stuff can masquerade under several dozen other names. For example, corn parts may lurk within iodized salt, baking powder, powdered sugar, dextrose, glucose, polysorbate, syrup, condiments, spices, and dozens of other additives (see Back Insert II: Words for Corn Derivatives). Ketchup, mustard, and relish all have vinegar, made from corn. There are also maize, hominy, grits, polenta, etc. Do you have to memorize all those weird words before you're safe?

No, you wouldn't want to. The list is several pages long. That's why this book contains tear-out back inserts that show lists of words for corn and corn parts and products that contain them. Take these lists with you to the grocery store and to restaurants and keep a copy in your kitchen.

Many Products Other Than Food Contain Corn Derivatives

Prescription pills may include corn derivatives. Over-the-counter painkillers or herbal remedies may contain corn parts. Even shampoo or hand cream may have corn in it! (Yes, if you are allergic, corn on your skin can cause a reaction.)

Of course, many delicious food products are laced with corn, such as cake and cookie mixes, baked goods, stuffing and breading mixes, frozen vegetables, frozen meals, fruit juices, salsa sauces, and more. Even "made-from-scratch" takes on a new meaning. The iodized salt in your cupboard contains dextrose, which is usually made from corn. Baking powder has cornstarch. Margarine may be made of corn oil or contain corn products.

Does that mean you have to read ingredients for *everything*? Yes, for everything you ingest or put on your skin. What does that include? See Back Insert I: Products with Corn Derivatives for a long list of products that commonly contain corn in its myriad forms. *Be warned, however, that these lists of corn-containing products are not complete.* Such lists can never be complete. New ingredients appear constantly, and so do the names for them as well as the chemicals that go into them. In addition, every day someone introduces a new food to the market, and it may well contain a bit of corn. When in doubt, check it out. Call the manufacturer.

Labels on medicines, herbal remedies, cosmetics, skin creams, and shampoos all need careful reading. Anything you ingest or put on your skin can cause reactions if you react to the allergen it contains.

Read the Label *Every* Time

Ingredients change. Don't assume that the product you bought last week, which was corn-free then, is still corn-free. Check every time. Ingredients change constantly. How can you read all those long chemical lists every time? Never fear: if a food has a very long list of ingredients, it probably won't be on your grocery list.

Read ingredients when you shop *every* time. Read ingredients again at home before you eat the food *every* time. What if someone else bought the can that you found in the pantry? What if you missed a word while at the store? A second (or third) reading could prevent a reaction.

Check It Out or Don't Consume It

When you come across a word you don't know, find out what it is. Call the company that produced the food or use a dictionary, another reference book, or maybe the Internet. You can also check the appendixes, glossary, and bibliography at the back of this book.

Warning! Not All Ingredients Are Always Listed on the Label

When in doubt, ask the people who made the product. The manufacturer's toll-free phone number is often listed on labels, along with website address and mailing address. If you find conflicting or inconsistent information, check another source. If you have a reaction and you cannot find the corn factor, consider eliminating that product from your food anyway.

Ingredients lists use many words for whole corn. Maize, or maiz, is Spanish for corn, from the Caribbean *mahiz*. (In Europe, maiz can mean any grain.) Polenta is cornmeal that is more coarsely ground. Masa harina is a kind of finely ground corn used to make corn tortillas.

CHAPTER 11: DEFENSIVE SHOPPING

Okay, from the previous chapter you know that you need to read ingredients. You have your list of dangerous words clutched in your hand (Back Insert II), and you know about suspect products (Back Insert I). But you only have a half hour to buy groceries. Is this possible?

Yes. Here's how:

↬ Start with fresh, raw, unprocessed foods.

↬ Look for *single* ingredients in canned, boxed, bagged, or frozen foods.

↬ After single ingredients, look for very short ingredients lists. Long lists of ingredients are almost sure to contain corn derivatives.

↬ Notice bold labels that say no salt, low salt, or low sodium. The low-salt versions may also leave out many seasonings and chemicals that include corn. (You can always add your own corn-free salt.)

↬ If you don't know where to find an item, ask a clerk for help.

Buy for Balanced Meals

You'll need food from *all* of the USDA Food Pyramid categories (see Chapter 12, "Meal Planning"). Here are some ideas for each of the groups—grains, veggies, fruits, meat, milk, fats, and sweets.

1. Grains can make fast meals: try quick rice, oatmeal, and/or pasta (such as flat noodles, spaghetti, or macaroni). Find the baking aisle for flour to make muffins, pancakes, biscuits, cakes, cookies, etc. While you're there, get some baking soda and arrowroot powder to make your own baking powder, or purchase baking powder made with potato starch. (Regular baking powder contains cornstarch.) For baking, remember to get sugar and cooking oil—but *not* corn oil! Also, do you have your favorite seasonings? Non-iodized salt and pepper? Onion? Garlic? Oregano? Hot seasonings? Lemon? Celery?

Try basic French or Italian bread fresh from the bakery. Be sure to read the ingredients, however, as baked goods often contain corn.

2. Vegetables can be found in the fresh produce section, the freezer section, or in the canned goods aisle. You may already know where to find the ones you like, such as carrots, tomatoes, peas, green beans, broccoli, spinach, asparagus, etc. In dry and frozen potato products, look for a single ingredient: potatoes. Mashed or sliced potatoes often contain corn products. Canned tomato paste can be found with one ingredient, tomatoes. Canned tomato juice can be found with just tomatoes and salt, but it may contain citric acid, ascorbic acid (vitamin C), MSG, and corn syrup—all corn-derived additives. Tomato sauce and whole tomatoes may include seasonings. Read carefully.

Be aware that frozen vegetables may have a fine coating of cornstarch to prevent the pieces from sticking together. In addition, the processing line may not have been washed thoroughly after handling corn when your peas and carrots were being packaged. Contact the manufacturer for details. Canned vegetables may be safer.

3. Fruits can also be found in the fresh produce section in cans or in the freezer. They're fast to fix. Apples, applesauce, berries, cherries, grapes, oranges, grapefruit, peaches, pears, and a host of other fruit all come *au naturel*. Be sure to avoid corn syrup in packaged fruit.

4. Meat, poultry, fish, beans, and **eggs** are all available raw. Fish, hamburger, poultry pieces, and eggs cook quickly. Beware of poultry processing. For frozen poultry, read the ingredients carefully. Plain dried beans may have no additives, but if you want less cooking time, look for canned beans that list beans and water as the only ingredients. Be persistent; beans are also canned with corn starch, modified food starch, corn syrup, corn flour, corn protein, MSG, maltodextrin, dextrose, and other corn-based additives. In addition, soybeans may be harvested with corn, getting cross-contaminated even before the packaging process. If you are severely allergic, check with manufacturers before risking even small amounts of corn.

5. When buying **milk, cream, cheese, yogurt,** etc., look for single ingredients. Plastic or glass milk bottles may be safer than paper cartons as the paper coatings can have corn products in the carton. Get blocks of cheese, not sliced or grated cheese. The grated and sliced varieties can be dusted with cornstarch to prevent sticking.

6. You need some **fat,** in spite of its bad reputation! Check margarine for corn-based ingredients. Get a bland cooking oil, such as canola or safflower, *not* corn oil! If you like, also get a flavorful oil (olive, sesame, almond, etc.) for variety in cold dishes.

7. Satisfy your **sweet** tooth with jams, jellies, and syrups since the bakery offerings probably won't be safe. Try pure maple syrup. Maple-flavored syrup has corn syrup. Look for a brand of jelly made with sugar, not corn syrup. Remember to beware of fructose, which is normally made from corn now instead of extracted from fruit. If the store has a "natural foods" section, check it for products with cane sugar instead of corn syrup or other sweet additives.

Read Longer Lists of Ingredients

Shopping gets faster as you get familiar with safe brands and their locations in your store. Then you'll have time to read those longer lists of ingredients. Try finding just one or two new items per shopping trip.

Another way to find an elusive item is via the website allergygrocery.com. This resource does more than show you ingredients lists; it can search for the exact type of food you want in a corn-free version. It can eliminate other ingredients, too, if you have more than one concern. You can find brand names and even order online if you choose.

If you travel, you may want to locate products with national brands wherever possible. Keep notes on the safe brands you find. Your familiarity with name brands will mean quick food shopping anywhere, as name brands are often available across the U.S. and sometimes in Canada (see Chapter 18, "Food for Travel").

For even faster shopping, take along your grocery list but don't wait until shopping day to start making the list! Keep paper and pencil handy in the kitchen and jot down an item any time you notice something running low. Don't wait until you run out either. Keep backups on hand: an extra bag of flour, a box of rice, dry pasta, oatmeal, canned or frozen favorites, and frozen meat. Also remember household cleaning supplies. Add these items to your grocery list any time you open the last package.

Cornstarch is used to separate plastics (cheese slices, meat wrap), grated cheese, frozen vegetables, or bits of fruit. Cornstarch also keeps powders (powdered sugar, etc.) from clumping.

CHAPTER 12: MEAL PLANNING WITHOUT CORN

Caution: *Ask your nutritionist or health care provider about the foods you need. The following information is not intended to replace medical advice.*

Food Cravings

Do you still feel hungry after a meal, even when you're stuffed and have consumed plenty of calories? Especially since you've been avoiding corn? Food cravings could mean that you didn't get a well-balanced meal. Your body knows when it's missing vitamins or minerals, grains or meat, or other kinds of food. Your head may not know, but your body knows and demands what it needs.

Think about craving a cookie or a beer. What's in both of those foods? Grains. Such a craving probably means that your body wants grains. Unfortunately, that cookie or beer might contain corn. Such a craving might be a nuisance if you are trying to lose weight, but if a food craving urges you to eat food containing corn, it's more than a nuisance—it's dangerous. This book can be a useful tool to help you plan balanced meals and avoid food cravings.

Food Pyramids

The original U.S. Department of Agriculture (USDA) Food Pyramid provides a useful tool for meal planning. The USDA recommends eating a variety of foods from each of six food groups every day. If you have corn intolerance, eating a wide variety of foods is especially important. People with food intolerances often tend to eat the same things too frequently or in large quantities. This can lead to sensitivities to additional foods. Avoiding corn is difficult enough; you don't want to have to avoid even more foods.

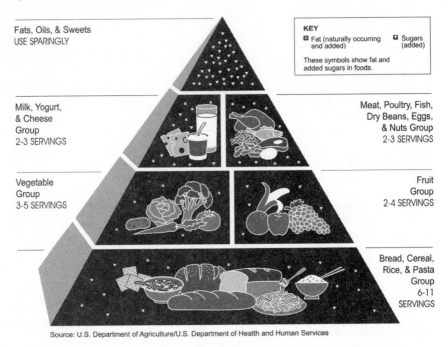

Fats, Oils, & Sweets
USE SPARINGLY

KEY
◼ Fat (naturally occurring and added)   ▽ Sugars (added)
These symbols show fat and added sugars in foods.

Milk, Yogurt, & Cheese Group
2-3 SERVINGS

Meat, Poultry, Fish, Dry Beans, Eggs, & Nuts Group
2-3 SERVINGS

Vegetable Group
3-5 SERVINGS

Fruit Group
2-4 SERVINGS

Bread, Cereal, Rice, & Pasta Group
6-11 SERVINGS

Source: U.S. Department of Agriculture/U.S. Department of Health and Human Services

Some might prefer to use a vegetarian pyramid which leaves off meat, poultry, and fish. Other suggested pyramids add exercise or emphasize omega-3 fatty acids. While experts argue about the details, the bottom line remains the same: grains. We need more grains than any other food group. The ideal choice is whole grains. See Chapter 2, "Bread and Grains," for many grain recipes without corn. In addition, Chapter 7, "Casseroles and Combinations," includes dishes that contain grains along with many other items.

Food Groups

The original USDA pyramid, shown above, divides food into six groups: grains, vegetables, fruits, meat-fish-bean proteins, milk-cheese proteins, and fats and sweets.

Grains form the foundation of a healthy meal. Wheat, oats, rice, barley, and rye are some of the many choices. For variety, try millet, amaranth, quinoa, and other grains. All whole grains are low in fat (about 6 to 8 percent), high in vitamins (especially B vitamins), and high in certain proteins.

Serve grains with milk, beans (dried beans, peas, or lentils), or seeds for more complete proteins.[1]

Vegetables appear in a smaller box on the next layer of the pyramid. These include the vitamin-rich dark green and red vegetables such as spinach, broccoli, green beans, tomatoes, carrots, and beets. Leafy vegetables include spinach, many kinds of lettuce and cabbage. Cruciferous vegetables, which may help reduce cancer risks, include broccoli, Brussels sprouts, cabbage, and cauliflower.

Vegetables also include potatoes, a high-carbohydrate food. Potatoes get a bad rep, but they do not equate to eating sugar. They include nutrients missing in refined sugar. More important, potatoes contain fiber, which helps to moderate blood sugar spikes and drops. Both white and sweet potatoes are recommended in *Recipes for a Healthy Heart* and *Recipes for Weight Loss*.[2] Potatoes are also recommended in *Potatoes, Not Prozac* for help with sugar or alcohol cravings.[3] If you have difficulty resisting sweets, sweet baked goods, or alcohol, even though you know the product might contain corn, consider adding baked potatoes to your meals.

Fruits are on the same food pyramid level with veggies. Fresh whole fruits provide vitamin C, essential to life. They also add other nutrients and fiber. Those yummy fruit pies and cobblers don't have quite the same benefits because heat (as in baking) destroys vitamin C.

Canned fruits and fruit juices may contain corn syrup. Think first of fresh fruits such as berries, grapes, or fruits that have to be peeled— oranges, grapefruit, melons, etc. Make sure that your fruit *juice* has a label with only one ingredient: fruit. Many fruit drinks actually list corn syrup as one of the first ingredients!

Milk and milk products come on the next layer of the pyramid. Milk is an excellent source of protein and calcium. In addition, vitamins A and D are added to milk in the U.S. Cheese and butter also contain protein, calcium, and a lot of high-cholesterol fat.

Meats, poultry, fish, dry beans, eggs, and nuts appear in the box beside milk on the USDA food pyramid. Be sure to choose a variety of proteins, such as different kinds of fish, seafood, lamb, pork, turkey and various beans, as well as beef, chicken, and eggs. Fish—especially mackerel, lake trout, herring, sardines, tuna, and salmon—are high in omega-3 fatty acids, which may reduce the risk of coronary heart disease.[4]

What about beans? You might think of beans (soy, mung, peas, lentils, limas, pinto, kidney, black, and other beans) as a half-protein. To form a more complete protein, beans need to be eaten with grains or seeds at the same meal.

Fats are on the small tip of the pyramid to indicate that you need fewer of these than other foods. Some fat is still essential; if you cut back too far on fat, you will be left feeling hungry even after a full meal. Meat, poultry (especially the skin and dark meat), cheese, and egg yolks all contain animal fat with cholesterol. Cooking and salad oils, such as canola oil, peanut oil, safflower oil, sunflower oil, soy oil, olive oil, sesame oil, and almond oil, all have less of the "bad" cholesterol.

Meal Planning

See the USDA website (www.usda.gov) for detailed information about the exact quantities of food needed from each group. The following suggestions are intended to give you a varied diet. As a person who is food-intolerant or allergic, your diet may have been somewhat limited. It is safer to eat a wide variety of foods, especially if you are food-intolerant. Just make sure that your new choices don't contain corn!

In planning complete meals, choose one or more foods from each of the five food groups in the base of the pyramid (see chapters 2 through 6). You won't need to be concerned with the tip of the pyramid. Fat occurs in sufficient quantities in almost any main dish, and sweets are not essential at all. Casseroles and combination dishes may contain meat, grain, cheese (milk group), several kinds of vegetables, and fat. These combinations usually require a fruit choice be added to the meal for balance. Soup might include very few food groups and need items from the rest to make a more balanced meal.

In this book, chapters 2 through 6 follow the pyramid groups to help with meal planning. Recipes are listed by major food group. You can pick foods from each chapter, or you can use combination dishes and plan what needs to be added to complete the meal.

Meal Plan Examples

1. Hamburger   protein (meat), fat
    cheese   protein (milk)
    bun   grain
    lettuce, tomato, salad   veggies
    grapes or apples slices   fruit

2. Creamed tuna   protein (fish), protein (milk),
                                      grain, fats

    biscuits   grain, fat
    peas, green beans   veggies
    berries   fruit

3. Tofu and stir-fry veggies   protein (beans), veggies, fat
    rice   grain
    cherries   fruit

4. Chicken chunks   protein (poultry), grain, fat
    peas, carrots, onions, etc.   veggies
    rice   grain
    cottage cheese   protein (milk)
    apple   fruit

5. Broiled salmon   protein (fish), fat
    cottage cheese   protein (milk)
    rice with veggies   grain
    (broccoli, carrots, tomatoes, etc.)   veggies
    orange   fruit

6. Ground beef   protein (meat), fat
    spaghetti sauce with cheese   veggies, protein (milk), fat
    spaghetti   grain
    Roman salad   veggies, fat in dressing
    peach   fruit

7. Nacho chips, bean dip   proteins (meat, beans, cheese),
                                     grain, fat

    diced tomatoes   veggies
    banana-pineapple salad   fruit

Cultures all around the world have ethnic dishes that combine beans and grains, for example Mexican corn tacos with pinto beans or Chinese dishes with rice and soy.

Three Types of Food

Planning a balanced meal from five of the six USDA food groups will include three types of food: carbohydrates, proteins, and fats.

Carbohydrates include grains, fruits, and also vegetables such as potatoes and peas. Sugar and alcoholic beverages contain highly refined carbohydrates which provide calories with little else in terms of nutrition or fiber.

Proteins come from many sources: milk, all kinds of meat, fish, nuts, and beans plus grains. Major sources of protein are in the "meat, poultry, dried beans, fish, and nuts" box of the USDA food pyramid and also in the "milk" box.

Fats have twice as many calories per gram as proteins or carbohydrates. In general, fats from animal sources contain higher cholesterol, and fats from plants contain little or no cholesterol, with the exception of palm oil and coconut oil.

CHAPTER 13: CUSTOMIZING RECIPES

Now that you're more comfortable with corn-free cooking, you can alter other recipes.
Here are some ideas for substitutions:

Instead of	Try
Baking powder	1. Corn-free baking powder (see recipe, page 11) 2. Baking soda, ⅓ the quantity needed, melted in a little hot water 3. Commercial baking powder with potato starch
Ketchup	Mix tomato paste, sugar, and apple vinegar (see recipe, page 77)
Corn oil	canola, safflower, peanut, soy, or other cooking oils
Cornstarch	1. Arrowroot powder 2. Tapioca starch 3. Potato starch 4. Cream of tartar 5. A mixture of the above
Corn syrup, Karo syrup	1. Simple syrup (boil to mix 3 parts sugar to 2 parts water) 2. Clear Sauce (see recipe, page 161) plus sugar (for pies, cobbler)
Cornmeal	Flour under pizza crust to prevent sticking

Powdered sugar	1. simple syrup (see above)
	2. corn-free confectioner's sugar (available at www.allergygrocery.com)
Corn	Other grains, other vegetables
Dijon mustard paste	Mustard powder or mustard seed with a bit of European red wine
Iodized salt	Plain salt, non-iodized
Mustard paste	Mustard powder or mustard seed
Sweet pickle relish	See corn-free recipe, page 76
White vinegar	Apple cider vinegar
Xanthan gum	Tapioca starch

Will substitutions always work? No! Apple fritters do not equal corn fritters. Besides, some of your experiments may end up edible only for the dog. Then again, other changes you make may have people begging for more. Before you choose a substitute, ask what job it needs to do. Does it need to replace the chemical action during cooking? Replace a texture or consistency? Is it for nutrition? Is it for flavor?

Replacing Chemical Action

The easiest change to make in a recipe is to replace a chemical action. Cornstarch thickens a soup or sauce; it also keeps powders from clumping. Arrowroot powder is even better than cornstarch for thickening. Cream of tartar and potato starch also work, but they may add flavors of their own.

Corn oil may be useful to prevent sticking, but peanut oil and canola oil actually do a better job of preserving the flavors of other foods. Expensive restaurants often use them. Peanut oil can cook at higher temperatures, making it the first choice for stir-frying in a wok. Soy oil adds the flavor of cheap fast foods since most fast food chains use soy oil.

Corn syrup saves time. You don't have to boil and stir to make simple syrup from sugar and water. However, without soda pop or corn syrup flavored fruit drinks, you may soon get spoiled to the richer flavor of the sugar.

Dough conditioners often contain corn. In breads, try lemon juice for a lighter texture. One teaspoon of lemon juice per 2 cups of flour helps with higher rising without changing the bread's flavor.

Replacing Food Components

Corn additives, so often a form of sweetener, do not need to be replaced. Corn as a whole grain can be replaced with other whole grains, such as whole oats, whole wheat, or brown rice.

Corn tacos with pinto beans are a staple of Southwestern food. The grain plus beans equals a whole protein. You can replace this nutrition by using a wheat tortilla instead of a corn taco. It won't look or taste the same, but it will taste delicious and offer the same nutrition.

Corn cereal? Exchange this with oat, rice, or wheat cereals with no corn additives. Granola bars? You may prefer to make your own granola (see recipe, page 26).

Approximating Corn Product Flavors

Which do you want first, the good news or the bad news? Here's the bad news: You probably won't find a real replacement for cornmeal muffins, a fresh ear of roasted corn, corn flakes, corn chips, or a corn taco. The good news? Without corn additives, you will discover a whole world of wonderful fresh flavors. Muffins, chips, and cereals come in dozens of flavors. A variety of meals can nestle on wheat tortillas, pita bread, or rice egg roll wrappers instead of corn tacos. Rice comes in many flavors and textures. Oats can range from creamy to crunchy. Food manufacturers have spent millions of dollars researching food chemistry. They now offer so many products with corn additives that it is difficult to find any processed food without corn. Even many fresh foods are often packaged with corn in the packaging materials!

Unfortunately, all this corn adds a mild but pervasive flavor to all those foods. On your corn-free diet, you may get spoiled; your fare will taste like the real foods! In addition, you may discover new favorite herbs and spices when their flavors are not diluted with corn (see Chapter 14, "Seasonings").

Experiment

Can you change a recipe? You bet! The more you practice, the more you learn about how ingredients cook and what changes will work. What makes the pieces stick together? What makes them rise? Can you alter an old favorite to leave out those unsafe ingredients? Of course! Here are some basic tips for experimenting with food.

1. Change *one* thing at a time. Sometimes you have several ideas about what went wrong. If you change everything and it works, great! But if it doesn't work, you're back to square one. Change one thing at a time, and you'll know if that particular change helped.

2. Write the changes down. What if you create the world's most wonderful new concoction, and then you can't repeat it? What if you didn't measure? What if you don't remember what you put in it? Save yourself frustration by writing down your changes.

3. Make up a theory and test it. Theory: eggs make the batter rise enough to leave out baking powder. Test: add eggs and leave out baking powder. How did it work?

4. Keep notes about your results. Who liked the food, everybody or only you? Keep both recipes! Other people may have lots more food choices than you do. Sometimes you'll need a dish just for you. When everybody wants more, even though they do not need to avoid corn, you know you've got a winner!

Experimental Cooking 101

This is a true story. In the 1930s a young woman went to college to study geology. The school did not allow her to enroll in geology "because women do not have inquiring scientific minds." Instead, the school placed her in experimental cooking (i.e., chemistry).

One day, while the coeds whipped up some pancakes, the teacher left the room. Some students delicately turned their half-cooked batter with a spatula. Others tried flipping the pancakes. This quickly turned into a contest. Who could flip a pancake the highest?

The winner's pancake hit the ceiling. It stuck, dripping, for a few moments before it fell. A new experiment promptly followed. Who can make the pancake batter stick to the ceiling the longest? What ingredients make a batter sticky? The coeds altered batches of batter, and they flipped every new experiment onto the ceiling. You've got to test it! When the teacher returned, she found the entire ceiling coated with half-cooked pancakes and dripping ultra-sticky batter all over the floor.

You too can customize recipes. Test and record your results, but most of all have fun!

CHAPTER 14: SEASONINGS

Try some new taste sensations! Beyond salt and pepper, hundreds of flavors await you. Herbs, spices, syrups, extracts, vegetables, fruits, and an infinite variety of flavors can spice up your meals. There is no "right" way to season food. Some like it hot, some do *not!* That goes for any flavoring you might use. What do *you* like?

Fresh or Dried?

To chop or not to chop? Fresh seasonings need extra time, but many people think they're worth the trouble. It's your choice, based on the flavors you like and the time your schedule allows. In this book, seasonings are usually given in dry amounts because people often have limited time for cooking. If you prefer fresh seasonings, these conversions may help. Amounts shown here are general guides, not hard-and-fast rules.

Dried	*Fresh*

Most herbs: 1 part dried herbs = 3 parts fresh, finely chopped

Onion: 1 tablespoon powdered onion = 1 medium onion (½ cup chopped onion)

Garlic: ⅛ teaspoon powdered garlic = 1 small clove, minced (Pressed garlic is much stronger than minced.)

Gingerroot: ⅛ teaspoon powdered gingerroot = 1 tablespoon raw, finely chopped

> Dried herbs are stronger than fresh. If the recipe specifies
> dried seasonings and you want to use the milder fresh seasonings,
> increase the quantity. If the recipe calls for fresh and you want
> to use dried seasonings, reduce the amount.

Storage

Keep dried herbs and spices away from heat, sunlight, and moisture. Even with care, dried herbs and spices do not last forever. Over time, the flavors fade. Leafy herbs may keep for one to three years, ground spices two to three years, and whole spices (e.g., peppercorns, nutmeg, cinnamon sticks, cloves) up to four years. To test for freshness, crush the herbs in your hand or shake the spice in the jar then sniff for fragrance. If there is none, throw it out. With spice, a faint scent means you can still use it, but increase the amount. For more specifics, see websites about herbs and spices or Dr. Richter's *Fresh Produce Guide*.

Trying New Tastes

After salt and pepper come an endless variety of other flavors. People all around the world add onion, garlic, and hot chilies, but those are only the beginning. Do you like rosemary? Tarragon? Cilantro? Cumin? Fennel? Do you know?

You may want to test a new flavor before you make a whole recipe with it. You can try out unfamiliar seasonings—just a pinch—with a mild-flavored food such as bread, rice, potatoes, lettuce, tofu, eggs, or chicken. For the test, use a food that the herb or spice complements. See the Spice Chart Appendix on page 257 or check other spice charts or the label on the spice jar for ideas. Some seasonings go well with many foods; others are more limited.

Some flavors may only taste good in small doses. If you like the flavor, you may want to try more. Maybe you'll find a new favorite that you love—or a seasoning you *never* want to use again! Are you sure? Maybe it goes with a different food? You may also want to try out combinations. Flavors can change completely in a blend.

Combinations

Blue and yellow combine to produce a very different color, green. Likewise, combining two seasonings can make a very different flavor. For example, cilantro (a mint) and black pepper (a peppercorn) combine to make a third, quite different, flavor. We see millions of colors, all combined from only *three* primary colors. We can taste *four* primary flavors—sweet, sour, bitter, and salt. In addition, nerves react to the "hot" in peppercorns and chilies to produce pleasing endorphins. There are dozens, if not hundreds, of plant families that yield seasonings, each with its own distinctive flavor. Classic seasoning combinations all have many variations in flavor and hotness. Here are just a few to try.

Bouquet garni: Parsley, thyme, and a bay leaf are tied in cheesecloth (or simply tied together with a string) and hung in a soup or stew while cooking for the last 20–40 minutes. The herbs are removed before serving. Other flavors may be added, such as peppercorns, dried orange peel, celery leaves, basil, chervil, rosemary, or tarragon. Every European country has a different popular variation, and every cook may have yet another preference. The same combinations of herbs can soak in oil and/or vinegar to make a vinaigrette (oil and vinegar) salad dressing.

Chili Powders: Used in Southwestern and Mexican dishes, chili powder is a mixture of chili pepper, cumin, oregano, and sometimes salt, garlic, and other spices. The chili in the powder may be mild paprika or a much stronger variety.

Chinese Five-Spice Powder: Finely ground pepper, star anise, cinnamon, fennel seed, and cloves form the basic five-spice powder. Variations add other spices.

Curry Powders: These are mixtures invented by the British in India to imitate the local flavors. Curry powders usually begin with cumin, but they vary immensely in taste and hotness and may include coriander, black pepper, cayenne pepper, cardamom, cinnamon, ginger, mace, fenugreek, bay leaves, mustard seed, and turmeric or saffron.

Fines Herbs: Traditionally, parsley, chervil, tarragon, and chives are chopped finely and used with mild foods such as eggs, poultry, fish, and cheese. The delicate flavors are lost if cooked too long. Variations add other herbs such as burnet, savory, marjoram, and basil.

Garam Masala: May include fresh ground cardamom seeds, cinnamon sticks, coriander seeds, peppercorns, and cloves. In India, where every family has its own version of this combination, dishes often contain garam masala.

Onion and garlic: Most people like onion and garlic, which are used in breads and savory dishes around the world. Some consider that a savory dish without onion and garlic is not seasoned at all! (Others have intolerance issues and avoid onion and/or garlic.) Used in combination with other seasonings, onion and/or garlic color the other flavors strongly.

Poultry seasoning: This seasoning can include herbs—sage, thyme, rosemary, savory, marjoram, parsley—and spices—ground pepper, nutmeg, allspice, ginger, cloves. It is used for many kinds of poultry (chicken, turkey, duck, goose, etc.) and poultry stuffing.

Quatre Epices: The name is French for "four spices": finely ground black (or white) pepper, nutmeg, cloves, and ginger. *Quatre epices* may contain additions such as allspice and cinnamon.

Sauces: Many sauces contain multiple flavors, including mayonnaise, ketchup, tomato sauces (including spaghetti, pizza sauces, and salsa), barbeque sauces, steak sauces, Worcestershire sauce, Hoisen sauce, master sauces, teriyaki, plum sauce, soy sauces, emulsion sauces (like béarnaise and hollandaise), and many, many more. Since many sauces contain corn or corn derivatives, you may want to learn to use the seasonings directly.

Some Like It Hot

People from hotter climates tend to prefer hotter flavors. Over time, perhaps the preservative power of spices conveyed survival value. In northern climates, the cold helped to keep food safe and the milder seasonings of herbs were more available.

Hot seasonings include cinnamon, ginger, mustards, horseradish (also called wasabi), black pepper (peppercorn), and of course, chili peppers. The hotness of a chili can be measured in Scoville units, often used to compare the hotness of different chilies, from the hottest varieties (Chinese and Habanero, 200,000–300,000 Scoville units), to Thai (100,000 Scoville units), jalapeño (below 5,000 Scoville units), green chili, paprika, and even the very mild bell pepper (usually called a green pepper, from 0–100 Scoville units). Fifteen Scoville units equals 1 part per million of capsaicin, the plant chemical that creates the distinctive flavor of the hot chili. For more information on Scoville ratings, see websites like grindhot.com or www.uni-graz.at/~katzer/engl/index.html. In spite of their oriental names, all chili peppers originated on the American continents.

Peppercorns—black, white, and green pepper—are all from the same plant's peppercorn berry, picked at different times and processed differently. Pepper rose (pink pepper) is a different plant with a mild, sweet berry. That flavor is lost if mixed with black, white, or green pepper. Red pepper comes from a chili, not a peppercorn.

Herb or Spice

The chart below lists just a few of the spices once shipped by merchant camel caravans on the Silk Road. Mariners who sought pepper risked their lives crossing uncharted oceans, hoping not to fall off the edge of a flat Earth. Nowadays, all these spices—plus herbs and chilies from the New World—are available at your local grocery store.

Herbs	Spices
arugula	allspice
baby dill (weed)	anise/aniseed
basil	caraway seed
bay leaf	celery seed
chervil	cinnamon/cassia
chives	cloves
cilantro (coriander leaf)	coriander seed
dill weed	cumin
fennel (leaves)	dill seed
fenugreek	fennel seed
Italian parsley	garlic
lemongrass (Thai dishes)	ginger
marjoram	horseradish (wasabi)
mint (spearmint,	mace
peppermint)	mustard seed
oregano	nutmeg
parsley	onion
rosemary	peppercorns (black
sage	peppers)
savory	pepper (chilies)
tarragon	poppy seed
thyme	saffron
turmeric	sesame seed
	star-anise
	sunflower seed

In general, an herb comes from plant leaves and a spice from seeds, bark, or root. Chili peppers are neither herb nor spice, but a vegetable. Zest is neither herb nor spice; it is the grated skin (colorful part only) of a citrus fruit, such as lemon zest or orange zest. It can have a stronger flavor than other parts of the fruit. Salt is neither herb nor spice but an essential mineral. We like the taste of salt in many dishes as well as pepper—a true spice—from the peppercorn seed.

Sugar is very common in American foods. Sweeteners such as cane sugar (sucrose), beet sugar (also called sucrose), molasses, corn syrup, lactose, and fructose are often used in packaged foods. A tiny amount of sugar can help bring out the flavor of a savory (non-sweet) dish.

Onion and garlic, both from roots of the same plant family, are so common around the world that their flavors show up in almost any savory dish or salad. Onion, chives, scallions, shallot, and leeks all have a similar taste.

Savory means non-sweet; it is also the name of an herb with a flavor similar to thyme.

Dill weed is an herb flavoring very different from dill pickles; dill seed, a spice from the same plant, flavors dill pickles.

While we're comparing, marjoram, Mexican oregano, and Italian or Mediterranean Oregano have slightly different flavors. Flat-leaf parsley (the common variety) and curly leaf parsley have slightly different flavors. Cilantro looks similar to parsley, but tastes different. Licorice root, anise/aniseed, star-anise, and fennel root have similar flavors. Turmeric does *not* substitute for the costly taste of saffron; it only imparts the same yellow color.

Balsamic is not even a flavoring. Balsamic vinegar has a unique taste that comes from a specific grape aged in wooden casks. A technical process imitates aged balsamic vinegar at a much lower cost. Other vinegars are commonly made from apples, grapes, corn, barley (malt vinegar), and rice. Many more flavors can be added by steeping herbs and/or spices in the vinegar.

There are far more flavors than those listed above: capers, chamomile, ginseng, hyssop, juniper berries, lavender, lemon balm, lemon verbena, rose hips, sassafras, and sorrel, to name just a few. As you experiment, be aware that people can react to seasonings as well as to foods. Some of the most common seasonings that cause reactions are nuts, peanuts, onion, garlic, cinnamon, chocolate, mints, and hot peppers. Migraines can result from raisins, papaya, passion fruit, avocado, red plums, and canned figs, as well as from vaso-active amines, alcohol, chili peppers, and MSG.

With all those warnings, why try new flavors? For adventure, but also for safety. Eating a wide variety of foods and flavors can help those with a food intolerance. Eating the same foods over and over every day, or in large quantities, may result in developing reactions to more foods. Just be aware of how you respond to new dishes.

References

Books and websites abound with information about herbs, spices, and other seasonings. Richter's *Fresh Produce Guide* tells about many herbs and spices in addition to fruits and vegetables. This book is sold in many grocery produce sections, near the fresh herbs. In a library, some of the most complete and informative books about seasonings can be found in the reference section. See the bibliography and resource appendix in the back of this book for more information.

CHAPTER 15: ALLERGY OR INTOLERANCE?

Comparisons

Allergy (involves the immune system)

Intolerance (biochemistry as yet unknown)

• Symptoms usually occur immediately.

• Symptoms often occur a day or two later.

• Reactions can become life-threatening quickly, within seconds.

• Reactions often begin mildly and increase gradually. Health declines over years.

• Tiny amounts, even just a touch or smell, can cause a reaction.

• Reactions normally occur after a whole bite or whole serving.[1]

• Anaphylaxis (an allergic reaction) to foods causes an estimated 120 deaths each year.[2]

• Over years, intolerance may lead to frequent, sometimes serious, illnesses.[3, 4, 5]

• A single food may be the only allergen, even if it is rarely eaten. Or one person may be allergic to several foods.

• One or many frequently eaten foods can cause symptoms.[6, 7] More foods often become involved if the diet lacks variety.[8]

• In adults, food allergies usually last for life.

• In some people, avoiding the food for months or years can reduce intolerance.[9]

Similarities

Avoidance. Both the food-allergic and the food-intolerant must avoid one or several foods. Currently, there are no shots and no reliable cures for food allergy or intolerance. If you have either, you should avoid the offending foods.

Differences

Amount. For some of the food-allergic, a tiny taste can kill. Some people react to the touch or smell of the allergen, for example the touch or smell of peanuts, fish oil, or popping corn. If you have a food allergy, you must avoid the offending allergens. Sometimes, allergic people "take a chance" and eat a known allergen. Sometimes they "get away with it;" sometimes they don't. There's a name for that game. It's called Russian roulette.

For the food-intolerant, a tiny taste won't kill. The touch or smell probably won't cause a reaction. Food intolerance is sneakier than that. Just one bite might make the body less able to fight off disease. It might lead to one bite more or a whole serving. In time, the offending food causes a painful reaction. Eating problem foods for months or years adds up to ill health. Sometimes, food-intolerant people "take a chance" and eat a known problem snack, but they do not "get away with it." True, just this once, they may still be able to go to the show, the game, the business meeting, or the holiday party. Over time, though, frequent illness results. How often can you miss meetings at work or call in sick before it costs you your job?

Symptoms of food allergy can include but are not limited to:

anaphylactic shock	itchy, runny eyes or itchy, runny nose
angioedema (swelling)	mental confusion
asthma	nausea
diarrhea	passing out
difficulty breathing	rapid heart rate
difficulty swallowing	redness
dread (a sense of impending doom)	rash
eczema	shortness of breath
flushing	swelling of the skin, lips, mouth, tongue, and/or throat
hives (urticaria)	turning blue
intolerance symptoms (see below)	wheezing
itching	vomiting (right after eating the food)

Symptoms of food intolerance can include but are not limited to:

aching muscles	headache	vomiting
anxiety	indigestion	Crohn's disease
bloating	joint pains and aches	IBS (irritable bowel syndrome)
constipation	mental confusion	rheumatoid arthritis
depression	migraine	diarrhea
nausea	edema (water retention)	tiredness (excessive)
chronic fatigue	flatulence (gas)	ulcers (duodenal or stomach)
ulcers (recurrent in mouth)		

Food intolerance may begin with gradually increasing symptoms that are usually ignored, such as headaches, excessive tiredness, or frequent indigestion, diarrhea, cramps, gas, or constipation. On the other hand, food intolerance may suddenly follow a bad bout of flu or a course of antibiotics. Signs and symptoms vary widely.

Diagnosis

Diagnosis can be difficult for the food-allergic, and the difficulties lead to controversy in the medical community. Skin tests, R.A.S.T. blood tests, or the newer ImmunoCAP may identify the culprit. (Or they may not: these tests can be falsely negative or falsely positive.) A medical doctor specializing in allergies can interpret these tests. Keeping a food diary can help with food allergy diagnosis. Objective proof comes from a double-blind, placebo-controlled (DBPC) oral food challenge. The danger of serious reactions, however, often prohibits such a challenge.

Diagnosis can be even more formidable for the food-intolerant. Currently, no medical tests can identify the offending food(s). The condition has no standard signs or symptoms. Keeping a food diary can help with food intolerance diagnosis. Objective proof comes from multiple-food elimination-diet tests. Some medical doctors know how to administer and interpret these tests.

To complicate diagnosis even more, food intolerance reactions mimic many illnesses which can have other causes. They include, but are not limited to, irritable bowel syndrome (IBS, also called chronic diarrhea, irritable colon or spastic colon),[10] migraine,[11] psychosomatic illness (hypochondria),[12] Crohn's disease,[13, 14, 15] inflammatory bowel disease (IBD),[16] rheumatoid arthritis,[17] celiac disease (celiac sprue),[18] and adrenal fatigue.[19, 20] Some of these conditions can have clinically observable signs, even entire patterns of signs and symptoms. Others are diagnosed "by exclusion." Diagnosis by exclusion is not a positive test but rather an elimination of other possibilities. Patterns of signs and symptoms may have a name but no known cause. In either case, food intolerance is one of the possibilities that needs to be checked. Unfortunately, some doctors frequently make these diagnoses without first performing multiple-food elimination tests to rule out food intolerance.

When all your tests come out negative, and you have a fat medical file proving that you are not sick, what's next? When the doctor says "it's all in your head" or makes a diagnosis by exclusion without testing for food intolerance, what do you do? If you suspect food culprits, it's your job to find a qualified medical doctor who keeps up with new information and has experience dealing with food intolerance. Check the Internet. Ask your relatives. Ask at your health food store. Depending on the nature of your symptoms, you may need to look for a general practitioner, a nutritionist, a gastroenterologist, a neurologist, or an allergy specialist.

Make some phone calls. Ask about a doctor's interest in food intolerance before you make an appointment. Ask if the doctor can direct multiple-food elimination-diet tests. The doctor may work with a nutritionist or a dietician in order to prevent nutritional deficiencies during testing. For more details about such testing, see Chapter 14 in Jonathan Brostoff's *Food Allergy and Food Intolerance*. A qualified doctor will test for food intolerance by directing multiple-food elimination-diet tests, not just single-food elimination tests. Be aware of several facts about food-elimination testing:

1. Elimination of only *one* food at a time may fail to find the culprit(s). Food-intolerant people often react to *several* different items. When two or more foods are involved, the combination is normally unique to the patient.

2. Elimination of many foods can cause serious vitamin and protein deficiencies. Such diets, especially for children, must be planned by a qualified nutritionist.

3. Elimination diets must be followed only for short testing periods (weeks, not months).

4. Long-term avoidance diets, unlike elimination-diet tests, avoid only one or a few foods, those which have been proven to cause you problems.

5. Results can be negative. The conditions diagnosed by exclusion are not always caused by food intolerance.

Treatment

Treatments do not currently prevent or cure food intolerance or allergy. Treatments help with *symptoms*. People who are severely allergic may need to carry an Epi-Pen(r), which might temporarily alleviate the life-threatening symptoms of anaphylaxis. This can buy time to reach an emergency room. Additional treatments may include antihistamines, bronchodilators, and/or steroids administered by shots, pills, or inhalants. New studies for new treatments are encouraging, but still there is no cure. Anti-IgE treatment *may* increase the tolerance to an offending food; however, it is not yet fully studied.

Treatments for food intolerance vary as widely as intolerance symptoms. For example, your doctor may suggest caffeine for a migraine or administer IV fluids for dehydration from diarrhea or vomiting. Your doctor may recommend soluble fiber, such as mucilage, pectins, gums, psyllium seed, beans, potatoes, oat bran, and other sources. Your doctor may prescribe an avoidance diet, with partial or complete avoidance of corn and possibly other culprit foods indicated by your multiple-food elimination-diet test. Food addictions are common among the food intolerant, who often crave the very foods causing their reactions. Overeating a food in terms of quantity or frequency seems to contribute to food intolerance. The doctor or dietician may recommend a more varied diet or a strict rotation diet.

Recovery
For adults, food allergies are generally considered lifelong. Childhood food allergies may continue for life, or they may disappear as children grow up and may reappear in adulthood.

Food intolerance, in some people, may improve after avoiding the offending food for many months or even a year. After this time, eating a small amount of the food occasionally *might* not cause symptoms (hence the myth that food intolerance does not exist). Eating the culprit food every day or in large quantities will usually make intolerance symptoms reappear.

Cause
Any food can potentially cause an allergic or intolerance reaction. Foods causing allergy include but are not limited to:

corn	peas	sesame seed	tomatoes
eggs	peanuts	shellfish	tree nuts
fish	poppy seed	soy	wheat
milk	potatoes		

Classic allergic reactions are defined as an immune system response. With a food allergy, the immune system reacts to the food proteins, or even to a specific part of a food protein. Exact details are not yet known about corn allergy, first demonstrated by medical testing only recently.[21] Corn proteins are believed to cause corn allergy reactions such as anaphylaxis, eczema, asthma, etc. Even a trace amount of protein found in derivatives of corn or in foods contaminated with corn can cause such reactions.

Foods commonly causing intolerance include but are not limited to:

alcohol	eggs	rice	sugar
caffeine	fish	shellfish	tree nuts
cheese	grapefruit	soy	wheat
chocolate	milk	strawberries	yeast
corn	peanuts		

Food intolerance can be caused by other parts of the food, not just the protein. For example, milk intolerance is caused by the inability to digest a milk sugar. Corn intolerance symptoms may be caused by corn proteins or other parts of the corn; science does not yet know.

Commonly eaten foods are usually the cause of intolerance. For example, in the U.S. intolerance is frequent to corn, wheat, and milk, all staple foods. In Taiwan, where corn, wheat, and milk are seldom eaten, the common foods rice and soy are normal causes of intolerance.[22]

Science

Medical science knows a great deal about classic allergic reactions, much about other types of allergic reactions, and very little about food intolerance. Classic allergic reactions can be dramatic. History describes deaths from such reactions even thousands of years ago. Modern science has studied food allergies for nearly a hundred years and today doctors often save lives with modern treatments for anaphylactic shock. Modern medicine defines a classic *allergic* reaction as an immune system response. This often involves IgE antibodies, mast cells, which the antibodies affect, and chemicals which the mast cells release (including histamine). However, IgE is only one of several types of immune system reactions. Doctors vary in their particular definitions of *allergy*. Since the 1920s, the definition has narrowed to mean only immune system (not intolerance) responses. Many doctors define "allergy" even more narrowly to mean only IgE-mediated immune system reactions.

Biochemically, a classic IgE-mediated allergic reaction involves IgE antibodies and mast cells. Your body builds many kinds of antibodies to recognize many kinds of invaders: viruses, bacteria, even parasites. When IgE antibodies attach to an "invader," this signals mast cells to release chemicals, including histamine. The histamine causes allergic symptoms, such as hives, itching, swelling, difficulty breathing, etc.

What if your body mistakenly builds an IgE antibody to recognize a certain food protein as an invader? You eat that food, and all over your body, these microscopic, confused antibodies signal to their mast cells, "Invader! Invader!" The mast cells then release their chemicals, including histamine—lots of histamine. Anyone with classic allergies can guess what happens next: redness, swelling, itching, hives, breathing difficulties, etc. Too much histamine causes any or all of these allergy symptoms and many more. Hence the name of a common allergy medicine—*anti*histamine, since antihistamine blocks histamine.

Food intolerance symptoms do not respond to allergy treatments such as antihistamines because the immune system, IgE antibodies, and histamines are not involved in the reaction. "Intolerance" is a broad term used for many different reactions, most of them not yet understood by medical science. For the past century, studies of intolerance reactions gave such anomalous results that many doctors do not "believe in" food intolerance.

However, science is a matter of fact, not faith. About twenty years ago, modern science devised studies that proved food intolerance certainly does exist. In the 1980s, studies showed improvement, even cures, for 66 percent to 93 percent of patients who were seriously ill, some hospitalized, with conditions like rheumatoid arthritis, irritable bowel syndrome, and migraine.[23] The difference? Unlike earlier research, these studies involved eliminating *many* foods from the patients' diets, all at the same time, not just *one*. Typically, the food intolerance patient reacts to two or more foods. Eliminating only one at a time can cause misleading results.

Note that the studies above did *not* cure or improve *all* of the patients, only a statistically significant number of them. All of the conditions mentioned can have causes which are not related to food. Food intolerance symptoms can mimic illness with other causes, and this stubborn fact makes intolerance even harder to study.

Modern science can explain a few types of adverse food reactions which are not classic allergic reactions, such as milk (lactose) intolerance, food poisoning, and reactions to chemicals like caffeine or additives like MSG. These well-known reactions only scratch the surface of intolerance issues. Many adverse reactions can disappear when a patient avoids one or several foods, and medical science has yet to unravel the biochemical details. The vast variety of reactions and causes makes food intolerance extremely difficult to study. If *some* patients with a certain symptom respond to avoiding certain foods, why not *all* of them? And why don't they *all* react the *same* way to the *same* food? Undoubtedly, food intolerance covers many biochemically different conditions.

References
For more detailed information about food allergies, resources abound. Food intolerance sources are fewer. The above information and many more details are clearly organized and indexed in F*ood Allergy and Food Intolerance* by Brostoff, M.D., and Gamlin. See the Bibliography and Resource Appendix for a few of the many books and websites dealing with classic food allergies and intolerances. Since medical science is constantly researching and discovering more information, be sure to check your sources for recent dates.

CHAPTER 16: SOCIAL EVENTS

Awkward social situations can arise from avoiding a food as common as corn. How do you prevent difficulties? One approach is to plan and think ahead. Imagine some of the many social events involving food.

Situations

You're invited to Thanksgiving at Grandma's. She has no clue how to roast a turkey without corn. She'll be insulted if you refuse the invitation or the food. It's your birthday, and your co-workers "surprise" you with cake and ice cream. Your church or club holds a potluck dinner where everyone expects you to try their special dish. "You just have to try this!" You and your pals go to a movie or sports event. Surely you'll share the popcorn they get for everyone?

Solutions

When problems surface, how do you deal with them? If you arrive hungry, do you let people talk you into eating something with corn? Let's think about this. How will you handle an acute reaction during one of these social events after making a bad decision? Maybe you'd rather plan ahead to avoid bad decisions! Eat before going to the event. Take along your own safe snacks and drinks. These tactics may be helpful, but they won't resolve every issue.

You have many choices. Only you can decide which is best for you. One obvious possibility is to say, "No, thank you" to the invitation. That's not always a realistic choice. You can always attend and say, "No, thank you" to the food. That might not go over very well at Grandma's for Thanksgiving or with the co-workers who just bought you a birthday cake full of corn products.

You may need to deal with such situations ahead of time. Maybe tell Grandma you'll bring a dish or two and bring enough to share. You can make combination dishes which contain enough food groups to keep you from getting hungry. Or you can make a certain dish that you know you'll have trouble resisting. You might choose to eat before attending the holiday meal to make sure you won't want everything in sight! You might even ask Grandma to make a recipe that you know she can make without corn additives, if you can think of one.

As for the co-workers, you may want to tell them about your corn sensitivity and suggest alternatives. Who knows? Someone might have fun making the corn-free pineapple upside-down cake recipe from this book. From the store, angel food cake might work, with some fresh berries on the side, or that one brand and flavor of ice cream you know is safe.

At the potluck or the movie, saying, "No, thank you" might not work if someone insists again and again. How can you respond when someone gets pushy? You might try changing the subject. "No, thank you, and how was your weekend?" If that doesn't work, another choice is to step away from the situation. Silence works for some people; being blunt works for others. Some would rather tell a white lie, "Oh, that corn stuff makes me break out." Or you could always accept a little bit of corny food and stash it in the trash when no one's looking!

Some people will ask you about your allergy or intolerance. What are the symptoms? This could be a sign that they are very critical or very caring. Either way, it may not be a question you want to answer at dinner. You can be blunt: "I don't want to talk about it right now." You may decide to tell only those who have a need to know. If you are allergic and you carry emergency medications, perhaps you want to let people know who are around you frequently. If you have a reaction, they'd want to know how to help. Your family members who share meals with you probably need to know about your intolerance or allergy. Many people really like to help. Do they have ideas for you? Do they have family, friends, or acquaintances who have dealt with allergies or food intolerance? If so, how do these people deal with it? Discussions with such people can be really helpful.

Unfortunately, some people have attitudes about food allergies or intolerances, such as, "It's all in your head," or "There's no such thing as a food intolerance," or "It's not an allergy; it's *only* an intolerance." How do you deal with these attitudes? If they come from your doctor, you may need to find a different doctor. If it's a friend, family member, or co-worker, how do you act or react? Ignore it and change the subject? Tell them how insulting that is? Step away from the situation? Most people would not make fun of a person with a disability. Unfortunately, that courtesy may not always be extended to a person with a food intolerance or allergy. You may need to plan in advance how you will respond.

Emotions

If you're newly diagnosed and new at dealing with food intolerance or allergy, keep in mind that you've just suffered a loss. Maybe you've always been able to eat whatever you want, and you've lost that freedom. Perhaps you like to be spontaneous, and now you're faced with the need to plan ahead for every meal and snack. Almost certainly, you've lost some favorite foods. Your frustrated feelings may well surface at social events. After any loss, it's common to go through a grief cycle. Typically, this starts with denial and/or blame. Next come depression and/or anger. In time, you come to understanding, acceptance, and growth.

Maybe at that office party you think, *That frosting isn't really a problem . . . today.* Or at the movies, *The popcorn surely won't bother me . . . this time.* Denial? (And a rude awakening at the ER?)

Do you get depressed trying to deal with the difficulties of avoiding corn? Are you angry watching everyone else eat that yummy stuff with no worries? Do you think, *It isn't fair! Why me?* If you're having trouble with any of these emotions, you are not alone! Your friends, family, and co-workers have also suffered a loss. Their friend can no longer share that carefree holiday dinner, that birthday cake, or that popcorn and soda pop. Your friends may deny that your problem exists; they may even blame you. They may become angry and difficult to be around. Be patient. Give them time. They'll learn to adjust, too.

Acceptance and growth will come. Obviously, you've already started to learn some of the skills you need (growth); you're reading this book, after all! Your friends will learn, too, and the social events will get easier.

Meanwhile, plan ahead. Find out who is a useful part of your support system. Take food along to the event. If that's not an option, eat before you go.

Millions of people have successfully adjusted to food intolerance or allergy. You don't have to wing it alone. You can find a support group, possibly among friends and family. You can also check websites such as www.cornallergens.com, http://forums.delphiforums.com/AvoidingCorn (the Avoiding Corn Forum), www.vishniac.com/ephraim/corn.html, or others. The Internet has lots of information from other corn-sensitive people. You may want to find a counselor who has worked with people learning to cope with a chronic illness. Professional help could make your transition easier and faster.

CHAPTER 17: EATING OUT—DON'T!

Well, okay, never eating out is not a practical solution. Graduations, weddings, professional meetings, and many other occasions practically demand that you visit a restaurant. Several strategies may contribute to your safety at such times.

Strategy 1: Call the restaurant ahead of time. Speak to the owner or manager. Explain that you must avoid corn, corn syrup, cornstarch, etc. Ask if they have suggestions from their menu. You might get a positive response. For other types of answers, listen between the lines. Is the owner or manager friendly and helpful? You may be able to find safe food at that establishment, even if you have to explain that baking powder contains corn! If the response is bored, rushed, belligerent, or haughty, then you know that your choices will be limited or nonexistent. You may not wish to trust the answers, even if they eventually assure you of safety. Find a different restaurant, if you have a choice. If you don't, eat in advance or take along your own food.

Strategy 2: Eat a balanced meal before you go, with foods from all six food groups (see Chapter 12, "Meal Planning"). You can still order a partial meal or just a beverage and not end up craving something dangerous.

Strategy 3: Take along corn-free versions of foods that are difficult to find at restaurants—for example, a slice of bread. Your family and friends will understand, but this may not be the best choice at a professional meeting.

Strategy 4: If you're choosing the restaurant, think about the types of meals restaurants can easily prepare without corn. Real Italian, salad bars, steak places, and some mom-and-pop restaurants may be your best hope. Pizza can work, but pizza may be coated with cornmeal on the bottom. Fancier restaurants with knowledgeable chefs are often a good choice.

Strategy 5: When you order, don't even consider foods that most people make with corn. *You* can cook soup safely, but at a restaurant, it will often contain corn. Anything may be cooked with corn-oil margarine. Baked goods, including bread, often contain corn products. Stick with simple foods. Avoid highly processed foods and meals with elaborate sauces. At every visit, ask your server to check with the cook. Can this selection can be made with no corn, cornstarch, or corn syrup today? You never know whether, if they ran out of some ingredient, they made substitutions. Remember, ingredients change all the time.

Strategy 6: Fast food restaurants usually have printed ingredients lists. Get these to read ahead, but also verify the details before you order. Make sure they didn't substitute an ingredient containing corn. Be aware that not all locations have identical ingredients, especially if the franchise is allowed to vary the menu. Sometimes things vary, even if it's "not allowed." Remember that the more processed a food is the more likely it is to contain corn products. A fresh salad is always a good choice.

CHAPTER 18: FOOD FOR TRAVEL

Day Trips—Plan Ahead for Safety

1. Take along fruit juice and soft drinks. Unless you like diet soda pop, you may not find a corn-syrup-free drink at the gas station. Use a cooler and ice packs if you like those drinks cold.

2. Bring a picnic lunch. Try putting foods in small, square plastic boxes that pack easily, make dishes at mealtime, and also hold the leftovers afterwards. A rectangular, soft-sided cooler bag holds ice packs as well as plates and spoons. Plastic grocery bags double for trash bags. If friends stop to eat out, you can have your own food at their restaurant. In summer, your outdoor picnic site may be more attractive! You may want to bring extras to share. Your homemade food will likely become popular.

3. Remember to include something from all the food groups (grains, proteins, fruits, vegetables, and fat) to prevent hazardous cravings. (See Chapter 12, "Meal Planning.")

4. Mayonnaise (with salad or sandwiches) can be difficult to keep safely cold. Surround mayo dishes with several ice packs to keep them *cold*, not just cool. Or take along a small, unopened jar of mayo and toss it after use.

5. Check the index for ideas and recipe page numbers. Thoughts for day trips include:

   ↩ Oatmeal cookies—whole grain and high fiber help prevent the munchies.

   ↩ Canned chicken, tuna, etc., for sandwich toppings.

   ↩ Hard-boiled eggs—be sure to use ice packs and eat eggs before the ice melts.

   ↩ PBJ—peanut butter and bread (nuts + grains) equals a whole protein.

   ↩ Salad finger-food—carrot sticks, celery sticks, broccoli or cauliflower branches, cherry tomatoes, bell pepper slices, etc.

   ↩ Fruit—apples and oranges travel well, but oranges can be sticky to eat.

ↄ Oil—in place of sandwich butter or mayo. Mix with canned meats before spreading.

ↄ Nuts—an alternative to oil. (Remember: those French fries cooked in corn oil may prove irresistible if you aren't getting enough fat in your diet.)

Weekend Trips

With planning, you may be able to take enough cold food for a weekend trip; see "Day Trips"above for suggestions. If you prefer hot meals, see below under "Longer Travel."

Running low on supplies? The grocery store is your safe shopping place. Nationally known brands may be available, if you know where to look. For example, Safeway stores are usually called Safeway, but a Kroger store can be called Kroger, King Soopers, City Market, QFC, Fred Meyer, Food4Less, Ralphs, Dillon Store, Kwik Shop—and the list goes on. You might want to check with your local grocer or the Internet if you'll need to look for your usual brands in a faraway place. Sports stores with backpacking equipment often carry dry, lightweight convenience meals. From your regular grocery, try dry foods such as instant potatoes, pasta, or nuts.

Longer Travel

Longer travel requires more thorough planning. If you keep a list, you can reuse the ideas for another trip, maybe with changes and improvements.

If you're gone for a week or longer, you may want some hot meals. If you can stay at a condo or cabin that has a kitchen, great! Some motel rooms include a refrigerator, which can be very useful. A microwave (also available at some gas-station convenience stores) helps. If no kitchen appliances come with the room, you can still reheat meals or cook them with your own electric skillet (frying pan). If you're camping or picnicking, consider a camp stove; it's faster and cleaner than a campfire for regular meals. Take along some seasonings: salt and pepper, onion, garlic powder, and a few herbs. Maybe a hot chili powder and other favorites.

Electric Skillets

One electric frying pan can easily reheat a whole balanced meal from recipes that combine grains, vegetables, and proteins into a single dish. Prepare some in your home kitchen, others on the road. Be sure to unplug and clean up after cooking—you want the motel to welcome you again!

Recipes that reheat easily include:

1. Any "creamed" dish—see the white sauce recipes. Add veggies for balance.

2. Soups, casseroles, and cobblers—mix ahead in your own kitchen, and take along bowls.

3. Pizza—also good cold.

4. Spaghetti—stir sauce into the noodles, then pack. Hey, yours is better than canned!

Foods that cook quickly include:

↩ Noodles/pasta couscous. (Good for grains when you can't find corn-free bread.)

↩ Hamburger, especially crumble-fried, and canned meats such as chicken or tuna.

↩ Dry instant potatoes.

Camp Stoves

A camp stove has the disadvantage of needing reasonable weather. It also has advantages over an electric skillet: it has more than one burner, no electricity is required, and it is compact for packing. Greater variety is possible with two cooking surfaces. Setup takes a minute, but the gas burners heat up instantly. Cleanup is easier, too. Be sure to pack pans for use on the camp stove.

Almost any recipe in this book that does not need an oven can be made in a camp kitchen. You'll need to carry along ingredients, mixing bowls, measuring equipment, cooking pans, a spatula, etc. You may want to avoid cutting to keep from packing sharp knives. In primitive campsites, you may find countertop space at a minimum, so select accordingly. Picnic tables can accommodate more elaborate cooking plans. Bring finger foods, cold sandwiches, etc., for quick lunches—and more time for play—during the daylight. If you cook meals in the evening, it's easier to begin preparation before dark.

In bear and mountain lion country, ask park rangers where to store food and cooking equipment. Unless you're at the campsite, you'll need to pack away all food-stuff, including ice chests, canned goods, utensils, water coolers, and the camp stove. If the park has no bear boxes, and food goes inside the car, toss other gear over the ice chest, to mask its outline and help conceal the scent. You don't want a bear deciding to break into your car. Yes, over the decades, we've trained wild bears. They know what an ice chest looks like. They break windows easily. They'll also happily chew holes through your good plastic plates, even the clean ones. Hmm, maybe go for the motel-and-skillet in bear country?

Bed and Breakfasts
Call ahead and explain your needs. From the response, you'll recognize a host/hostess who's willing to prepare a corn-free breakfast. If not, you'll need to bring your own.

Foreign Travel
Can you read the language? A dictionary, not just a phrase book, may be necessary for reading ingredients. A bilingual local friend can help a lot. Keep in mind that other countries don't have FDA labeling regulations, but don't despair. They often use old-fashioned, less-processed foods, which means fewer hidden corn derivatives. Also, keep in mind that all electricity is not created equal. An electric appliance may need a converter or transformer to work abroad. Ask your hotel or travel agent before you lug along the electric skillet.

Cruise Ships, Campers, and Sailboats
Commercial cruises *may* be able to offer you safe eating. Call ahead to make sure the line you're booking can handle your needs. Take along a variety of snacks as well (see Chapter 17, "Eating Out").

A private camper or sailboat often has its own kitchen. On a sailing venture, limited space and port facilities may dictate some of your choices. See the "Electric Skillets" section above for recipe ideas. Heating elements take a lot of power; make sure this quantity is available onboard. If not, consider a camp stove instead.

CHAPTER 19: DIETING FOR WEIGHT LOSS

CAUTION: Ask your nutritionist or health care provider about the foods you need. The following information is not intended to replace medical advice.

If you begin a corn-free way of eating, you have a great opportunity to lose weight. A diet that has failed you before could work now. Why? You will be avoiding corn-based food additives. These include high-fructose corn syrup (HFCS), which may be a major cause of obesity. Around 1970, HFCS became the leading sweetener in soda pop and many other foods. The consumption of HFCS rose by over 1000 percent! The current obesity epidemic parallels this 1000 percent rise in the consumption of HFCS.[1,2] Science also knows that HFCS can also raise your risk for diabetes.[3] In addition, obesity contributes to other diseases, too many to list here. With all this, you may have some friends joining you in your corn-free cooking.

Is there any *proof* that simply eliminating corn syrup from your eating habits will make you lose weight? No. But what if it does?

To Lose Weight
Eat less, exercise more, and drink *lots of water*. You can get started now.
   1. High-fructose corn syrup: Eliminate HFCS from *all* of your food.
   2. Water: Drink lots of water, 8 glasses (64 ounces) per day or more.
   3. Exercise: Begin an extra aerobic exercise program, such as a gentle walk for 12 minutes every day. Work up to longer, more strenuous exercise as needed.
   4. Food: Eliminate or cut down on *refined* carbohydrates. Limit your fat intake. Skip dessert! When a recipe calls for a little sugar or fat, leave out the sugar and cut down on the fat.

Water

Water helps your body to metabolize fat into energy. A weight loss program works best when you drink a lot of water, at least 8 glasses (64 ounces) of water daily, or more. If you live in a very dry climate, or exercise heavily, you need even more water. Milk, coffee, tea and sweet drinks (including fruit juice) are no substitute for water—they add calories and/or caffeine, a diuretic. When you think you're hungry, drink water before eating anything. It's likely that you're actually thirsty. It's common to snack instead of drinking enough water. Drinking water can help you reduce the number of calories you eat.

Exercise

You burn calories when you exercise, but you also raise your metabolism. That means you continue to burn more calories for a whole day *after* the workout. That's right, the *whole* day, including while you're sitting at a desk, watching TV, and even sleeping! Regular exercise can also lower your body's "set point," which is the weight your body automatically tries to retain.

Exercise that gets the heart and lungs to work out is called aerobic exercise. The more aerobics you do, the more calories you will burn and the more weight you are likely to lose. Aerobic exercise normally works large muscles (thighs and buttocks). Walking, climbing stairs, running, biking, and swimming all can be aerobic. What's aerobic for you depends on your current fitness. Different people need different amounts and intensity of workouts. If you can't keep it up for 12 minutes, then the workout activity is too intense *for you*. Active people may need to add a brisk walk or run to their routine, 20 minutes or more, six days a week, in order to lose weight. Athletic people may need to add even more strenuous workouts of an hour or more. You can increase the workout by adding a longer or more intense activity every other day.

Be sure to check with your health care provider before starting or changing your exercise program. If you are sedentary, starting from scratch, you might need to begin with a short stroll, six days a week. By the next month, you may be able to do even longer and faster walks. It's safer to start out easy. Remember, no pain, *more* gain. (Besides, the tortoise won the race, not the rabbit.) Strength training also builds muscles that burn extra calories. If you like, add strength training (lifting weights, using exercise machines, doing sit-ups, push-ups, gymnastics, etc.) to your exercise program.

Eating fewer calories than you burn is still the bottom line. Your body must fuel its energy needs. Without enough fuel from food, your body takes that fuel from your fat. After you work up an appetite by exercising, you need to exercise caution with your snacks and meals.

Food

Healthy diets all include lots of vegetables (whole carbohydrates). Successful diets lower carbohydrate and/or fat intake. Either approach can work. This leaves proteins. A healthy, successful diet will include lots of low-fat proteins and lots of vegetables.

The symbol ▼ next to a recipe name in the chapter opener pages denotes healthier recipe choices. Be sure to use the variations with green or red vegetables and low-fat proteins. Use less fat in any recipe. Fat has twice as many calories per ounce as other foods. If you use wheat flour, try whole wheat. Be sure to keep your diet balanced (see Chapter 12, "Meal planning"). You can eliminate refined sugars entirely, but do not try to eliminate any food group. Eating some carbs and fats daily is essential to good health.

No-fat Proteins Include:
↪ Skim milk

↪ Egg whites (boiled, poached, or in other recipes)

Low-fat proteins include:
↪ Low-fat (7 percent or less) red meat

↪ Low-fat chicken (skinless)

↪ Fish (especially healthy are tuna, salmon, mackerel, lake trout, herring, and sardines)

Two chapters in this cookbook contain protein recipes. You can vary these recipes by using skim milk instead of 2 percent or whole milk. You can vary them by using egg whites instead of whole eggs. (Use two or three egg whites in place of one or two whole eggs.) You can use low-fat meat and skinless (low-fat) chicken.

If a processed food is advertised as "low fat," read the ingredients! Sometimes the "low fat" just means that the manufacturer added more refined carbohydrates, such as sugars or even HFCS. Such foods will *not* help you to lose weight.

To lower carbohydrates, eliminate or cut down on refined carbohydrates, such as HFCS, sugar, honey, processed sweeteners, fruit juice, other sweeteners, and white flour. Go easy on the grains. Eat lots of vegetables instead. For example, have green beans instead of noodles. Try a salad tray (with bean dip instead of high-fat salad dressings). Munch on broccoli, snow peas, or carrots instead of cookies. When you do eat grains, remember that highly refined wheat (white flour) is a "bad guy" carb, just like HFCS and sugar. Try for whole grains, such as oats, oatmeal, brown rice, wild rice, whole wheat, etc.

If you want a more formal diet, take a look at the USDA recommendations (www.usda.gov) or select any healthy diet plan. Use Chapter 13, "Customizing Recipes," to help keep you safe from corn while trying other diet recipes.

Setting a Goal

Be realistic. If you're built like a St. Bernard, no amount of dieting or exercise will make you look like a skinny greyhound. Think about other issues you may need to deal with if you want to get serious about weight loss. Are you a Type A personality, always rushing, stressed out to the max, and grabbing munchies instead of meals? Do you need to shed more than 20 percent of your current weight? Are you diabetic or prediabetic? Do you have other medical issues? If so, you may need to seek professional help.

Food Diary

If you keep a food diary, even for just a week or two, it can help in many ways. To start a food diary, you can buy a calendar or make your own. The easiest way to record the information is to have a whole page for each day. On one page, write the date, and list the hours of the day in a column, 6:00, 7:00, 8:00, etc. Beside the date and time, write down every morsel of food that you eat and every drop of any beverage that you drink. Record the quantity and how you feel.

A quick review of several days can tell you a lot about yourself. Did you feel hungry shortly after eating sugar, white flour, or meals without vegetables? Did you overeat when you were tired, when you didn't get enough water, when you were stressed-out or rushing, or when you were traveling or visiting with friends? Even more important, did you feel awful or get a headache or some other symptom a day or two after eating a certain food? If you react to corn (and/or other foods), your food diary can help you trace the source of the problem. It can also help you track habits that interfere with weight loss.

If you have a reaction, you can search your food diary and find the culprit. Of course, you *do* read ingredients now, so you don't have reactions or visit emergency rooms anymore, right? If your symptoms are not under control, your doctor may ask you to keep a food diary.

Yoga

A recent study showed that overweight adults who did yoga, for at least 30 minutes per week for four years lost weight instead of gaining.[4] If you want to try yoga, take a reputable hatha yoga class. Books or videos can help you continue, but it's difficult to learn the fundamentals without a good trainer or teacher. If your food diary shows that stress or excessive tiredness contribute to overeating, you might try yoga.

Refined Carbohydrates

White sugar and white flour have long been known as refined carbohydrates, the archenemies of anyone trying to lose weight. High-fructose corn syrup (HFCS) is an even more highly refined carbohydrate. Refined carbs have lots of calories with no redeeming nutritional value. Even worse, they can create an insulin and blood sugar roller coaster.

If you have trouble saying *no* to HFCS, sugar, and white flour, try a baked potato.[5] Add some green veggies for toppings, and soon you'll be wanting more vegetables. Later, you can gradually replace potatoes with more green veggies and whole grains. When you use potatoes and/or yams to replace refined sugar calories, the fiber helps your body handle the carbohydrates more safely. In addition, your tastes may change. As you start eating healthier food, you also start to crave healthy food instead of sugar. Real, whole food *tastes* better that sugar, corn syrup, and HFCS! Once your body remembers the flavor of healthy, whole food, you probably won't settle for anything less. And you can keep those pounds off.

Check with Your Doctor

One word of caution: corn syrup is not the *only* reason for obesity. Weight gain can be caused by various medical conditions, some of them serious. Be sure to check with your health care provider before starting this or any new diet or exercise program.

APPENDIX A: EQUIVALENCES AND CONVERSIONS

Halving and Doubling Recipes:

Half	Original Recipe	Double
¼ cup	½ cup	1 cup
¼ cup + 2 tablespoons	¾ cup	1½ cups
½ cup	1 cup	2 cups
2 tablespoons + 2 tsp.	⅓ cup	⅔ cup
⅓ cup	⅔ cup	1⅓ cups

Equivalences:

3 teaspoons = 1 tablespoon

Tablespoons, teaspoons, cups, pints, quarts, gallons, milliliters, and liters are all measurements of volume. Ounces, pounds, and grams are measurements of weight. An ounce of water is ⅛ cup (or 2 tablespoons) in volume; moist food is approximately the same.

Volume	Weight
⅛ cup = 2 tablespoons	= 1 oz. of water or moist food
¼ cup = 4 tablespoons	= 2 oz.
⅓ cup = 5 tablespoons +1 teaspoon	
½ cup = 8 tablespoons	= 4 oz.
⅔ cup = 10 tablespoons + 2 teaspoons	
¾ cup = 12 tablespoons	= 6 oz.
1 cup = 16 tablespoons = ½ pint	= 8 oz.
2 cups	= 1 pint
4 cups = 2 pints	= 1 quart = 32 oz.
16 cups = 8 pints	= 4 quarts = 1 gallon

1 quart is almost 1 liter.
1 gallon is about 3.8 liters.

Metrics:

1 ounce = 28.35 grams   1 gram = 0.035 ounces
1 pound = 453.6 grams   1000 grams = 1 kg. = 2.2 pounds
1 quart = 946.4 milliliters   1 liter = 1.06 quarts
(or almost 1 liter)

1 teaspoon = 5 milliliters
1 tablespoon = 15 milliliters
⅛ cup = 30 milliliters
¼ cup = 60 milliliters
⅓ cup = 17 milliliters
½ cup = 120 milliliters
⅔ cup = 158 milliliters
¾ cup = 180 milliliters
1 cup = 237 milliliters

1000 ml. = 1 liter

Oven Temperatures:

Fahrenheit	Centigrade
200°F	95°C
250°F	120°C
300°F	150°C
325°F	165°C
350°F	175°C
375°F	190°C
400°F	200°C
425°F	220°C
450°F	230°C

Need More Info?

For further information, see www.onlineconversions.com or check your local library's references.

APPENDIX B: SPICE CHART

What flavors might spice up that hamburger or fish you plan to have for dinner? Use this spice chart to look up a food and find a new seasoning to try with it.

Grains
Bread: banana, basil, blueberry, caraway seed, cherry, cinnamon, dill weed, fruits, garlic, ginger, herbs, olive, onion, oregano, pecans, poppy seed, potato, pumpkin, saffron (sweet breads), sesame seed, sunflower seed, thyme, walnuts, zucchini

Noodles (pasta): arugla, basil, dill, garlic, oregano, parsley, poppy seed (with butter), rosemary, sesame seed, vegetables (especially tomatoes)

Rice: cinnamon, saffron, turmeric, vegetables

Oats: apple, cinnamon, maple syrup

Sweet breads: banana, cinnamon, coriander seed (in gingerbread), fruits, ginger (gingerbread), nutmeg, nuts, pumpkin, raisins, zucchini

White sauces: dill weed, garlic, mace, parsley

Vegetables
Artichoke: butter, garlic, hollandaise sauce, lemon juice, maltaise sauce, mayonnaise, vinaigrette

Asparagus: almonds, butter, cheese (Parmesan and others), hard-boiled egg yolk, hollandaise sauce, lemon, nutmeg, thyme

Beets: cabbage, carrots, lemon, onion, orange, pineapple, sour cream, sugar

Brussels sprouts: marjoram, summer savory

Cabbage: celery, celery seed, cumin (sauerkraut), dill seed (sauerkraut), summer savory

Carrots: anise/aniseed, basil, dill weed, mint, onion, raisins

Cauliflower: dill weed, mace, parsley, sage, summer savory

Celery: onion, peanut butter, raisins

Cole slaw: fennel seed, celery seed, dill seed

Cucumbers: allspice, basil, coriander seed, dill seed (pickles), dill weed (salads), garlic (pickles), sour cream, vinegar, yogurt

Eggplant: mint, olive oil, oregano, sesame seed, thyme

Green beans: basil, marjoram, poppy seed (with butter), thyme

Lettuce: baby dill, chervil, dill weed

Mushrooms: butter, cream, garlic, lemon balm, paprika, pepper, sour cream

Olives, olive oil: cream cheese, eggplant, fish, oregano, stuffing, tomato, zucchini

Onion (creamed): cloves, thyme

Peas: marjoram, mint (spearmint)

Potatoes: basil, celery, celery seed, cilantro, chives, dill weed, garlic, mace, mustard, nutmeg, paprika, parsley, tarragon

Potatoes, new: mint (spearmint)

Potato salad: fennel seed, celery seed, dill seed, winter savory

Pumpkin (a winter squash): allspice, cinnamon, ginger, nutmeg

Rhubarb: rosemary, sugar

Salad greens, salad dressings & salad dips: arugla, basil, chervil, chives, dill weed, garlic, ginger, lemon balm, marjoram, mint, onion, parsley, poppy seed, rosemary, sesame seed, tarragon

Spinach: butter, cream, bacon, basil, egg, garlic, nutmeg, mace, marjoram, onion

Squash, summer: basil, garlic, olive oil, onion, oregano, tomato

Squash, winter: allspice, cinnamon, cloves, honey, nutmeg

Sweet potatoes: allspice, cinnamon, ginger, nutmeg

Tomato dishes & tomato sauces: allspice, basil, bay leaf (remove before serving), celery, celery seed, chives, dill weed, dill seed, garlic, olive oil, onion, oregano, tarragon, thyme

Vegetables & vegetable sauces: ginger, lemon, lemon peel, marjoram (green veggies), nutmeg, onion, parsley, sesame seed, thyme

Vegetables, bland: celery, celery seed

Zucchini (a summer squash): mint, olive oil, oregano

Yams: allspice, cloves

Fruits

Avocado: black pepper, cilantro, fish, lemon, lime, mayonnaise, onion, red chili pepper, seafood, tomato

Banana: apple, breads, brown sugar, cake, chicken, cinnamon, cream, fritters, orange, pancakes

Apples: banana, cardamom, cinnamon, coriander seed, lemon, nutmeg

Cherries: cinnamon, mace

Cranberry: allspice, orange, walnuts
Fruit juice: mint, other fruit
Fruit salad: cardamom, cinnamon, mint, rosemary
Fruits: allspice, cinnamon, cloves, ginger, lemon peel, nutmeg, poppy seed
Oranges: banana, cloves, rosemary
Pears: arugla, coriander seed
Peaches: coriander seed
Tangerines, Clementines: cinnamon, lime zest, star anise, sugar, sweet wine, vanilla

Meats/ Fish/ Eggs/ Beans

Chinese dishes: five-spice powder (includes star-anise)
Clear soup: mace, parsley
Stews/soups: allspice, bay leaf (remove before serving), chives (soup), cloves, garlic, winter savory, onion, rosemary
Meats: cinnamon, cumin, garlic, lemon peel, marjoram, mustard, nutmeg, onion, oregano, paprika, thyme
Beef: allspice, anise/aniseed, bay leaf, cilantro, cinnamon, cumin, garlic, horseradish (with cream sauces), mustard, nutmeg, onion, oregano, paprika, thyme
Chicken, poultry: banana, basil, bay leaf, chervil (tender poultry), cilantro, dill, garlic, ginger, lemon balm, marjoram, mustard, onion, oregano, parsley, rosemary, sage, summer savory, tarragon, thyme, turmeric (adds yellow color)
Eggs: basil, bell pepper, celery, celery seed, chervil, chives, cumin, dill weed, mustard, nutmeg (especially eggnog), onion, paprika, parsley, rosemary, winter savory, tarragon, turmeric
Fish: allspice, almonds, anise/aniseed, basil, bay leaf, celery, celery seed, chervil (lean fish), chives, dill weed, fennel seed, fruits, garlic, ginger, lemon, mustard, olive oil, oregano, parsley, paprika, rosemary and thyme, tarragon (especially on salmon), sesame seed (Fish comes in many flavors, each best with certain seasonings.)
Ham: cinnamon (with ham glaze), cloves, sage
Lamb: basil, cardamom, celery, chervil, cinnamon, garlic, horseradish (with cream sauces), lemon balm, mint, onion, oregano, parsley, pepper, rosemary, thyme
Pork: basil, coriander seed, cumin, fennel seed, lemon balm, rosemary, sage
Sausage: allspice, aniseed, basil, bay leaves, caraway seeds, cayenne

(red pepper), cardamom, cassia (cinnamon), celery seed, chili peppers, chives, cloves, coriander seed, cumin, dill seed, dill weed, fennel seed, five-spice powder, garlic, ginger, mace, marjoram, mustard, nutmeg, onion, oregano, paprika, parsley, peppercorns, salt, summer savory, sugar, thyme

Seafood: anise/aniseed, celery, celery seed, cinnamon, dill weed, horse-radish (with tomato sauce), oregano, thyme, turmeric (adds yellow color)

Stock for cooking fish: rosemary

Turkey: celery, cranberry, current, onion, parsley, pepper, thyme

Beans (legumes): chili peppers, chili powder, fennel seed, garlic, lemon juice (navy beans), marjoram, onion, oregano, sage, sesame seed (especially garbanzo beans/chick peas), summer savory, tomato

Milk Products

Butter sauces: chives, garlic, poppy seed, rosemary, sesame seed, tarragon, thyme

Cheese dishes, including cottage cheese and cream cheese: banana, basil, celery, celery seed, chives, cumin, dill seed, dill weed, nutmeg, oregano, paprika, parsley, sage, thyme

Cream soups: chervil, chives, lemon balm, mace, thyme

Parmesan cheese: arugla

Milk: anise/aniseed

Pudding: cinnamon (rice pudding), coriander seed

Sour cream sauces: celery, celery seed, chives, dill weed, garlic

Sweet cream sauces: nutmeg, thyme, turmeric

Yogurt: chives, dill weed, fruit, vanilla

Oils

Mayonnaise: celery seed, chives, fennel seed, mustard, paprika

Oil and vinegar dressings: arugla, baby dill, basil, chives, cilantro, garlic, marjoram, mint, mustard, oregano (especially with basil), parsley, sesame seed, sage, tarragon, thyme, wine

Sweets & Nuts

Cakes: allspice, almond extract, banana, chocolate, cinnamon, lemon extract, nutmeg, pineapple, poppy seed, vanilla

Candy: mint, fruit extracts

Chocolate: allspice, cherry, cinnamon, mace, peppermint

Cookies: allspice, anise/aniseed, almond extract, chocolate, cinnamon, coriander seed, ginger (ginger snaps), mint, nutmeg, vanilla

Doughnuts: mace, sugar

Pastries: marzipan (almond paste), poppy seed
Pie: pecans
Pound cakes: mace, sugar
Sweets: allspice, anise/aniseed, licorice, cherry, chocolate, cinnamon, cloves, fruits, ginger, lemon, lime, nutmeg, orange, pineapple, strawberry, vanilla
Nuts: celery, celery seed
Peanut butter: celery, celery seed

APPENDIX C: GLOSSARY

almondine – French for "with almonds."

au gratin – French for "with cheese."

avgolemono – Greek for a soup with chicken stock, egg, and lemon.

baste – To drip a liquid over roasting meat or fish. The liquid may come from the meat drippings or a glaze or marinade sauce.

beat – To stir fast or to stir for a long time. A well-beaten mixture will have a smooth consistency. Beating adds many more bubbles, which lighten a batter. *See also* stir, fold, and blend.

blend – To mix very thoroughly. A well-blended mixture will have a very smooth consistency. *See also* beat, fold, and stir.

boil – To heat water (or other liquids) until it bubbles and starts turning to steam. When water is first heated, a fine stream of tiny bubbles may rise; this is not boiling. When a liquid boils, it has large, vigorous bubbles. *See also* simmer, rolling boil.

broil – An oven set on broil heats only the top elements and at a high temperature. To broil, raise the oven rack and place the food high, near the heat. Keep the oven door slightly open; a catch will hold the door in position for broiling. Foods being broiled can burn easily; watch them closely for the right time to remove them.

brown sugar – In this cookbook, refers to dark brown sugar, packed down well in measuring.

burrito – Southwestern dish made of a tortilla wrap around beans, meat, veggies, etc. A modern "wrap" can imitate a burrito, an egg roll, or a sandwich.

caramelize – To heat a sugar mixture until it browns slightly.

chop – Cut up, to no particular size. *See also* cube, dice, mince, shred, slice, and julienne.

cube – Cut into small cube-shaped pieces about ½ to 1 inch across.

dash – A small amount of seasoning—about two pinches—often sprinkled from a shaker. *See also* pinch.

dice – Cut into small pieces, smaller than cubed. *See also* chop, cube, mince, shred, slice, and julienne.

Florentine – French for "with spinach."

flour – In this cookbook, refers to unbleached flour or whole wheat flour.

fold – A folding motion goes straight down in the middle of the mixing bowl and across the bottom of the bowl. Then lift the batter gently and "fold" it over the top. Folding will gently mix ingredients in a very fluffy mix (such as whipped egg whites) without breaking bubbles and reducing the fluff. Folding will also mix powdery ingredients until they are wet enough to stir. A rubber spatula or wooden spoon works best for folding, though it can be done with a fork. *See also* stir, beat, and blend.

ghee – Clarified butter, made in India by boiling butter and skimming off the top bubbles and the particles on the bottom. The remaining clear liquid is then boiled and skimmed repeatedly. An easier way to clarify butter (but not as clearly), is to freeze pats of butter in a covered dish. In a few hours the butterfat (clarified butter) will separate from the other parts of the butter. Scrape away the thin foamy layer on top and the whitish liquid on the bottom. Clarified butter cooks at a higher temperature and does not go rancid as quickly, but it loses the "buttery" flavor.

glaze – A sweet sauce which may be basted over roasting meat or drizzled over baked goods.

gumbo – A Southern dish, a thick soup, usually containing okra.

julienne – To cut into matchstick-size pieces. *See also* chop, cube, dice, mince, shred, and slice.

knead – A dough-mixing method using bare hands instead of a spoon, fork, or mixer. Lift the dough on one side, fold it over and push down in the center with the heel of the hand. Turn the dough to lift another side and repeat the fold-push-down motions. Repeat until the mixture is smooth. Handle the dough as little as possible to keep it cool and light.

marinade – A mixture of herbs, spices, fruits, wine, or other seasoning, used for soaking meat, fish or other foods which can absorb the flavors.

marinate – To soak meat, fish, or other foods in a marinade.

mince – Cut into tiny pieces, smaller than diced. *See also* dice.

pinch – A small amount of seasoning, less than a dash, measured by pinching the powder between the finger and thumb. *See also* dash.

roll – To roll dough flat and evenly thin.

rolling boil – A very vigorous boil, using higher heat than a normal boil. *See also* boil and simmer.

sauté – To brown seasonings or vegetables lightly in a hot skillet in a very small amount of butter or cooking oil.

savory – Non-sweet flavors. Also a seasoning called savory.

sear – To brown meat on the outside only, in a very hot skillet. Done before roasting to help hold the juices inside the meat.

shred – Cut or use a grater to make small slivers of cheese, lettuce, cabbage, etc.

simmer – A very gentle boil, done with the lowest heat you can use and still keep the liquid boiling. *See also* boil and rolling boil.

slice – Cut into slabs, usually about ¼-inch thick. Thinly sliced might mean ⅛-inch and thick slices might mean ½-inch or larger.

stir – To use a fork or spoon in a circular motion, always in the same direction. Stirring creates bubbles in the mixture, which make it lighter. Changing direction breaks the bubbles. Be sure to scrape the sides and bottom of the mixing bowl while stirring. A well-stirred mixture may still be lumpy. *See also* beat, fold, and blend.

taco – A hard, round shell made of corn, used flat or folded, to hold fillings like beans, meat, tomato, sauces, etc. Also the name of the dish which uses taco shells.

tortilla – A soft, round wrap made of corn or wheat used to hold fillings like beans, meat, tomato, etc.

tostada – Southwestern dish made of a flat taco holding fillings like beans, meat, veggies, etc.

wrap – A thin, square, edible wrapper, something like a flour tortilla or egg-roll wrapper. A wrap can be made of various grains, soy, or even veggies and is used like bread, tortillas, or egg-roll wrappers to hold meat, bean, and/or vegetable fillings.

zest – A fruit flavoring made from the colored outer part of a citrus fruit skin, such as orange, lemon, or lime.

APPENDIX D: RESOURCE GUIDE

Corn Allergy and Intolerance Information
http://forums.delphiforums.com/AvoidingCorn. . . .The Avoiding Corn Forum
www.vishniac.com/ephraim/corn.html . . . . Site about corn allergy
www.texaschildrenshospital.org . . . . Site about corn allergy

Medical Professional Organizations
American Academy of Allergy, Asthma and Immunology
611 East Wells Street
Milwaukee, WI 53202
800-822-2762
www.aaaai.org

American College of Allergy, Asthma and Immunology
85 West Algonquin Road, Suite 550
Arlington Heights, IL 60005
800-842-7777
www.acaai.org

Foods and Cooking
www.onlineconversions.com . . . . Conversions for metric/U.S.
measurements
allergygrocery.com . . . . Mail-order source for corn-
free confectioner's sugar
and other allergen-free foods
ang.kfonigraz.ac.at/~katzer/engl/ . . . . .Gernot Katser's spice pages:
information and opinions
grindhot.com . . . . Information about scoville
units (pepper hotness ratings)
ochef.com . . . . Information about storing
herbs and spices

Evert-Fresh Corp . . . . Maker of vegetable/fruit storage bags
P.O. Box 540974
Houston, TX 77254-0974
713-529-4593
www.evertfresh.com

U.S. Department of Agriculture (USDA). . . . . . Producers of the food pyramid
Food and Nutrition Information Center
301-436-7725
www.mypyramid.gov
www.usda.gov

Survival Tools (air filters, bedding, etc.)
Allergy Free, Inc.
1502 Pine Drive
Dickinson, TX 77539
1-800-ALLERGY

National Allergy Supply, Inc.
1602 Satellite Boulevard, Suite D
P.O. Box 1658
Duluth, GA 30096
1-800-522-1448

For more recent information, you can try searching for "corn intolerance" or "corn allergy" in search engines like google.com and hotbot.com.

☙ ☙ ☙

You can bookmark your favorite sites by clicking on "Favorites" and then "Add to Favorites." Later, to return to the site, simply find it under "Favorites" instead of typing in long names or reworking a search.

NOTES

Chapter 12, "Meal Planning Without Corn"

1. Frances Moore Lappé, *Diet for a Small Planet* (New York: Ballantine Books, 1991), 178–82.

2. Simeon Margolis and Lora Brown Wilder, eds., *Recipes for a Healthy Heart* (New York : Rebus, 2003). Lawrence J. Cheskin and Lora Brown Wilder, eds., *Recipes for Weight Loss* (New York: Rebus, 2003). These cookbooks come from the Johns Hopkins Cookbook Library.

3. Kathleen DesMaisons. *Potatoes, Not Prozac* (New York: Simon & Schuster, 1998).

4. Margolis and Wilder, *Healthy Heart*, 7.

Chapter 15, "Allergy or Intolerance?"

1. Jonathan Brostoff and Linda Gamlin, *Food Allergies and Food Intolerances* (Rochester, VT: Healing Arts Press, 2000), 14.

2. Hugh A. Sampson, "New Treatments for Food Allergy: Anti-IgE Immunotherapy and the Future" (Session 58, American College of Allergy, Asthma & Immunology, Annual Meeting, Boston, November, 2004).

3. Brostoff, *Food Allergies*, 14.

4. Ibid., 144.

5. Ibid., 143–44.

6. Ibid., 14.

7. Ibid., 143. Brostoff says, "In food intolerance, it is almost always commonly eaten foods that are the source of the problem. In the United States, this means wheat, milk, and corn. . . ."

8. Ibid., 15.

9. Ibid., 15, 145.

10. Ibid., 157.

11. Ibid., 133. In discussing the 1982–83 study of migraine at England's Great Ormond Street Hospital, where patients were given elimination diets, Brostoff states, "The [positive] response . . . was 93 percent, a staggeringly high figure by any standards."

12. Ibid., 203. Brostoff says, ". . . doctors specializing in the treatment of food allergy and intolerance . . . see innumerable patients who have been told that their symptoms are psychosomatic, or all in their mind, by one doctor or another. Yet a high proportion of these patients respond to an elimination diet. They get better . . . and they stay better."

13. Ibid., 160.

14. James Scala, *The New Eating Right for a Bad Gut: The Complete Nutritional Guide to Ileitis, Colitis, Crohn's Disease, and Inflammatory Bowel Disease* (New York: Plume, 2000), 2–3.

15. Ibid., 3. Scala never uses the term "food intolerance." However, as his title *Eating Right . . .* implies, Scala argues that many forms of IBD respond to avoidance of certain foods.

16. Ibid., 30.

17. Brostoff, *Food Allergies*, 166.

18. Ibid., 106. "At present, the only treatment for celiac disease is to eliminate the foods that contain gluten, that is, any food containing wheat, rye, or barley. . . ." Currently the only known treatment for celiac is to avoid certain foods, yet the illness is not called a food intolerance. Many doctors do not consider celiac a food allergy, yet it "is an adverse food reaction" known to "involve the immune system."

19. James L. Wilson, *Adrenal Fatigue* (Petaluma, CA: Smart Publications, 2001), 178.

20. Ibid., 181–83. Wilson recommends keeping a food and reaction diary. He also suggests elimination diet testing, though he does not seem to be aware of the more accurate multiple-food elimination-diet tests.

21. Linda G. Tanaka, Samuel B. Lehrer, and Jane M. El-Dahl, "IGE Antibody Response in Corn Allergic Subjects"(Concurrent Session 58, American College of Allergy, Asthma & Immunology, Annual Meeting, Orlando, FL, November, 2001). The brief states: "There are few well-documented reports of corn-induced allergic reactions. Recently we challenged 17 subjects with a history of corn allergy and demonstrated several with positive reactions by Double-Blind Placebo-Controlled Food Challenge. . . . Results: Five of the 17 subjects had positive DBPCFC. The spectrum of symptoms ranged from rhinorrhea to anaphylaxis."

22. Brostoff, *Food Allergies*, 143.

23. Ibid., 126–36.

Chapter 19, "Dieting for Weight Loss"

1. George A. Bray, Samara Joy Nielsen, and Barry M. Popkin, "Consumption of High-Fructose Corn Syrup in Beverages May Play a Role in

the Epidemic of Obesity," *American Journal of Clinical Nutrition* (April 2004): 537–43.

2. George A. Bray, "The Epidemic of Obesity and Changes in Food Intake," *Physiological Behavior* (August 2004): 115–21.

3. Lee S. Gross, Li Li, Earl S. Ford, and Simin Liu, "Increased Consumption of Refined Carbohydrates and the Epidemic of Type 2 Diabetes," *American Journal of Clinical Nutrition* (May 2004): 711–12.

4. A. R. Kristal et al., "Yoga Practice Is Associated with Attenuated Weight Gain in Healthy, Middle-aged Men and Women," *Alternative Therapies in Health and Medicine* (July–August 2005): 28–33.

5. Kathleen DesMaisons. *Potatoes, Not Prozac* (New York: Simon & Schuster, 1998). This book lays out a proven plan for dealing with sugar addiction.

BIBLIOGRAPHY

Balch, Phyllis A., and James F. Balch. *Prescription for Nutritional Healing.* 3rd ed. New York: Avery, 2000. A reference to drug-free remedies using vitamins, minerals, herbs, and food supplements.

Brostoff, Jonathan, and Linda Gamlin. *Food Allergies and Food Intolerances: The Complete Guide to Their Identifications and Treatment.* Rochester, VT: Healing Arts Press, 2000. Clearly organized and indexed, this is one of the most accurate, complete, and up-to-date resources available about food intolerance.

Brostoff, Jonathan, and Stephen J. Challacombe, eds. *Food Allergy and Intolerance.* 2nd ed. Philadelphia: W. B. Saunders Co., 2002. A good resource for health care providers, this work provides detailed information about food allergy and intolerance.

Burks, A. Wesley Jr., and John M. James, eds. *Food Allergy: Current Knowledge and Future Directions* (Immunology and Allergy Clinics of North America). Philadelphia: W. B. Saunders Co., 1999.

Cheskin, Lawrence J., and L. B. Wilder, eds. *Recipes for Weight Loss.* New York: Rebus, 2003. From the Johns Hopkins Cookbook Library.

DesMaisons, Kathleen. *Potatoes, Not Prozac.* New York: Simon & Schuster, 1998. This book offers suggestions to help with sugar and alcohol sensitivity.

Frieri, Marianne, and Brett Kettelhut, eds. *Food Hypersensitivity and Adverse Reactions: A Practical Guide for Diagnosis and Management.* New York: Marcel Dekker, 1999.

Hamilton, Eva May Nunnelley, Eleanor Noss Whitney, and Frances Sienkiewicz Sizer. *Nutrition: Concepts and Controversies.* 5th ed. St. Paul, MN: West Publishing Co., 1991. A college textbook about nutrition, vitamins, minerals, etc.

Hillman, Howard. *The Cook's Book.* New York: Avon Books, 1981. A reference book about foods, herbs, and spices.Lappé, Frances Moore.

Diet for a Small Planet. 20th anniversary ed. New York: Ballantine Books, 1991.

Margolis, Simeon, and L. B. Wilder, eds. *Recipes for a Healthy Heart*. New York: Rebus, 2003. From the Johns Hopkins Cookbook Library.

Naguwa, Stanley, and M. Eric Gershwin. *Allergy and Immunology Secrets*. Philadelphia: Hanley and Belfus, 2001.

Rainville, Jerry. *The Migraine Gourmet*. Lincoln, NE: Writers Club Press, 2000. If you suffer from migraines, this little cookbook could save you a lot of pain.

Richter, Henry. *Dr. Richter's Fresh Produce Guide*. Apopka, FL: Try-Foods International, Inc., 2000. Ever wonder about that odd fruit in the grocery store? Or how to prepare or keep a vegetable fresh? This small but extensive guide to fruits and vegetables has a color picture for every entry. It is often available in grocery store produce sections or order online at www.tryfoods.com.

Scala, James. *The New Eating Right for a Bad Gut: The Complete Nutritional Guide to Ileitis, Colitis, Crohn's Disease and Inflammatory Bowel Disease*. Revised ed. New York: Plume, 2000.

Schroeder, Florence E. *Cooking Without Milk: Milk-Free and Lactose-Free Recipes*. Nashville, TN: Cumberland House Publishing, 2002. This cookbook contains more than 400 recipes for the milk-intolerant and allergic.

Shapter, Jennie. *The Ultimate Bread Machine Cookbook*. New York: Lorenz Books, 2000. Contains recipes using a bread machine for just about any kind of bread you can imagine.

Wilson, James L. *Adrenal Fatigue: The 21st Century Stress Syndrome*. Petaluma, CA: Smart Publications, 2001. According to the author, food reactions are one of many causes of this common affliction.

Winter, Ruth. *A Consumer's Dictionary of Food Additives: Descriptions in Plain English of More than 12,000 Ingredients Both Harmful and Desirable Found in Foods*. 6th ed. New York: Three Rivers Press, 1999. What are all those impossible-to-pronounce words in ingredients lists anyway? This book describes many additives, their sources, and some possible reactions to them.

RECIPE INDEX

Notes

Notes

_____   _____

_____   _____

_____   _____

_____   _____

_____   _____

_____   _____

_____   _____

_____   _____

_____   _____

_____   _____

_____   _____

_____   _____

_____   _____

_____   _____

_____   _____

Notes

Notes

BACK INSERT 1

PRODUCTS with CORN DERIVATIVES

These products may be available without corn. Check with the manufacturer for details.

alcoholic beverages (American wine)
ale
baby carrots (packaging)
baby formula
bacon
baked beans
baked goods
baking mixes
baking powder
batters, batter mixes
beer
bleached white flour
breaded food (cornmeal)
breads (containing corn ingredients or dusted with cornmeal or corn flour)
breath mints
buttermilk
candy
canned food
canned fruits, fruit juices, and fruit drinks
canned peas
canned soup
cake, cake mixes, commercial cakes
carbonated beverages (sweetened with corn syrup, dextrose, etc.)
catsup

cereals (corn sweeteners, corn flour, etc.)
cheese, cheese spreads
chewing gum
chicken (processed)
chili
chocolate candies, chocolate drinks, chocolate milk
chop suey
chow mein
coated foods (French fries, potatoes, rice)
coffee, instant
cold cuts
confections
confectioner's sugar (contains cornstarch)
cookies, cookie mixes, commercial cookie dough
corn chips, corn curls
corn fritters
corn oil, Mazola oil, vegetable oil (may be corn)
corn syrup, Karo syrup
corn tacos, corn tamales, corn tortillas
cottage cheese
crackers

crispy foods
cured meats
dates
diet soda (with caramel color)
distilled white vinegar
Doritos
dressings
eggnog
English muffins
fish sticks (check the breading ingredients)
flour (bleached)
French fries
fried foods (fried in corn or vegetable oil; coatings with corn)
fritters
Fritos
frozen foods
frozen French fries
frozen fruit (cornstarch to prevent sticking)
frozen potatoes (dextrose)
frozen vegetables (cornstarch to prevent sticking; contaminated with corn in the factory)
fresh fruit coated with wax
fresh vegetables coated with wax
fruit drinks (sweetened with corn syrup, fructose, etc.)
fruit juice (with corn-derived preservatives)
gelatin (if it contains glycerin, sweetened powders from corn, or other corn products)
gin
graham crackers
granola bars
gravy, gravy mixes
grits
gum

ham (may be found without corn; look for honey or sugar cured ham)
hard candies
Harvard beets
herbal teas
hominy
hot chocolate
hot dogs
ice cream
ices
iced teas with sweeteners
imitation cheeses
imitation seafood
iodized salt
jam
Jell-o
jelly
juice drinks
juices (may contain corn derivatives, especially corn syrup)
Karo® syrup
ketchup
lemonade
lunch meats
maize
margarine
marinades
marshmallows
marzipan
mayonnaise
milk in cardboard cartons (packaging contains corn)
milk shakes
muffins, muffin mixes
mustard
nut flavorings
pancakes, pancake mixes
pastries, pastry mixes
pies, pie mixes
pickles (vinegar)

pizza (cornmeal)
polenta
pop (soda)
pork
pork and beans
potato chips (coated or prepared in corn oil; can be contaminated with corn chips at the factory)
powdered drinks (corn sweeteners)
powdered sugar (contains cornstarch)
processed meats
puddings
Ricotta cheese
root beer flavorings
salad dressings
salt (iodized salt contains dextrose)
sauces
sausage
sherbet
shortening
shredded cheese (cornstarch to prevent sticking)
shredded salads (cornstarch to prevent sticking)
soda pop
soft drinks
sorbet
soups (canned, homemade, "clear," or creamed soups are often thickened with cornstarch)
sour cream
soy milk
spaghetti sauces (cornstarch is not always disclosed on the label—check with the manufacturer)
sports drinks
stuffing, stuffing mixes
succotash
sweet wines
tacos

tamales
tea, sweetened
tortillas
vanilla (corn syrup; made with alcohol, possibly corn)
vanillin
vegetable soup
vegetable (containing corn oil)
vinegar (distilled white vinegar; can be made with grain (corn) alcohol)
whiskey
wieners
wine (American—sweetened with corn)
yeast (fed corn)
yogurt (cornstarch, corn syrup)

Packaging

Bleached paper products, flour, etc.
Corn products keep meat bright red
Cornstarch keeps things from sticking together or clumping (frozen foods, shredded and sliced cheese, bread, powdered sugar, plastic bags, etc.)
Corn oil helps keep products from sticking to the packaging (toothpaste, etc.)
Paper cartons, plates, cups, etc. can contain cornstarch. They can be coated with corn oil.

Non-food products

adhesives (envelopes, stamps, stickers, labels, tapes—don't lick!)
baby powder
body powders
Bounce dryer sheets
breath sprays and candies
envelope adhesive

contact lens solutions
cosmetics
creams
dishwashing detergents
glue (envelopes, stamps, stickers, labels, tapes, meant to be licked)
label (adhesive)
laundry starch (on clothes or sprayed in the air)
lotion
medications (capsules and tablets often have cornstarch, liquids often have sorbitol)
paper cups (can be coated with corn oil, dusted with cornstarch)
paper plates (can be coated with corn oil, dusted with cornstarch)
paper boxes
plastic wrap (cornstarch)
shampoo, conditioner, hair sprays, gels, mousse

shaving cream, gel
stamp (adhesive)
sticker (adhesive)
sunscreen
suntan lotion
soaps (bar, liquids, etc.)
talcum powder
tape (adhesive)
tissue
toilet paper
toothpaste (often has corn products (starch or oil) not on the label—call the manufacturer)
vitamins (some can be made from corn and/or contain corn ingredients)

BACK INSERT II

WORDS for CORN DERIVATIVES

Asterisks (*) : may be available without corn. Check with the manufacturer for details.

acetic acid (vinegar)*
alcohol*
allomaleic acid
alpha tocopherol (vitamin E)*
annatto*
arlacel
armotan
artificial color*
artificial flavor*
artificial sweetener
ascorbates*
ascorbic acid (vitamin C)*
Aspartame
baking powder*
bleached flour
boletic acid
British gum
cake yeast
calcium stearoyl lactylate*
capmul
caramel
caramel color
caramel flavor
Cerelose
citnatin
citrate of potash*
citric acid*
citrosodine

Clintose
confectioner's sugar*
corn
corn "anything"
corn alcohol
corn chips
corn extract
corn flour
corn gluten
corn oil
corn sugar
corn sweetener
corn syrup
corn syrup solids
cornmeal
cornstarch
crill
crillets*
crystalline dextrose
crystalline fructose
cyclodextrin
cystosol
dextrates
dextrin
dextrose
dextrose anhydrous
dextrose monohydrate
d glucital
diglyceride

d-sorbital
Dyno
emsorb
enriched flour*
erythoric acid*
erythritol
ethanol
ethyl alcohol
flavorings*
flour (enriched)*
food starch
fructose*
fumeric acid
gluconate
gluconic acid
glucose
glucose syrup
gluten
glycerides
glycerin*
glycerol*
glycomul
golden syrup
Gommelin
grain alcohol
grain vinegar
grits
HFCS 42
HFCS 55

high-fructose corn

high-fructose corn syrup

hodag

hominy

honey*

hydrol

hydrolized corn

hydrolized corn syrup

hydrolyzed vegetable
    protein*

inositol

invert sugar

invert syrup

iodized salt

lactic acid

laundry starch

lecithin*

L-gulitol

linoleic acid*

liposorb

liquid invert sugar

lysine*

maize (corn)

maizena (cornstarch)

malt*

malt extract*

malt syrup*

maltitol

maltodextrin

maltose

manita

manna sugar

mannite

mannitol

masa harina (ground
    corn)

methyl glucoside

modified corn starch

modified food starch

mondamin (cornstarch)

monitans*

monoglyceride

MSG (monosodium
    glutamate)

natural flavors*

partially hydrolized corn
    oil

pectin*

polenta

polydextrose

polysorbate*

popcorn

potassium citrate*

powdered sugar*

pregelatinized starch*

propionic acid*

protachem

Puretose

Resulax

salt (containing dextrose)

salt (iodized)

sodium anhydrous*

sodium citrate*

sodium dihydrate*

sodium starch glycolate

sorbester

sorbilanide

sorbilax

sorbit

sorbitan esters

sorbite

sorbitol*

sorbitur

sorbo\sorbol

sorbostyl

sorlates*

span

starch

starch gum

starch syrup

stearic acid*

succotash

Sweetose

syrup*

tocopherol*

Treacle (golden syrup)

triethyl citrate*

trisodium citrate

tryptophan*

Tweens*

vanilla extract*

vanillin

vegetable "anything"*

vegetable broth*

vegetable flavoring*

vegetable gum*

vegetable oil*

vegetable protein*

vegetable starch*

vinegar (distilled white)*

vinyl acetate

vitamin C (ascorbic acid)*

vitamin E*

vitamins*

wine

Xanthan gum

Xylitol

yeast*

yellow arepa flour

zea mays

zein (corn protein)